ALLIANCE POLITICS
AND ECONOMICS

ALLIANCE POLITICS AND ECONOMICS

Multinational Joint Ventures in Commercial Aircraft

DAVID C. MOWERY

American Enterprise Institute/Ballinger Publication

*COMPETING IN A
CHANGING WORLD ECONOMY
PROJECT*

BALLINGER PUBLISHING COMPANY
Cambridge, Massachusetts
A Subsidiary of Harper & Row, Publishers, Inc.

The publication of this volume was supported by a grant from the U.S. Department of Commerce.

International Standard Book Number: 0-88730-213-0

Library of Congress Catalog Card Number: 86-32178

Printed in the United States of America

Library of Congress Cataloging-in-Publication Data

Mowery, David C.
JR Alliance politics and economics.

  "A joint publication of American Enterprise Institute/Ballinger."
  Bibliography: p.
  Includes index.
  1. Aircraft industry—International cooperation. 2. Aircraft industry—United States. 3. Joint ventures. 4. Technology transfer. 5. Competition, International. 6. International economic relations. I. American Enterprise Institute for Public Policy Research. II. Title.
  HD9711.A2M68 1987   338.8'87   86-32178
  ISBN 0-88730-213-0

To my parents,
a successful joint venture.

CONTENTS

List of Figures   x

Acknowledgments   xi

Chapter 1
Introduction   1

Definition and Significance of Joint Ventures   3
Alternative Channels for the Transfer and Exploitation
   of Technology   6
General Causes of Increasing Reliance on Joint Ventures   14
Why Are Joint Ventures a Major Force in Commercial Aircraft?   19
Implications for Public Policy and Private Management   20

Chapter 2
Market Structure and Technology in the
U.S. Commercial Aircraft Industry   31

The Economic and Technological Significance of the U.S.
   Commercial Aircraft Industry   31
Industry Structure   36

Sources of Technical Change   40
Federal Support for Civilian Aircraft Research   43
Military-Sponsored Research   44
The Demand for Innovation: The Influence of Government   45
The 1970s and 1980s Changes in the Domestic Policy and
   Technological Environment   47
The Rise of a Global Market   50
Military Coproduction Agreements: Technology Transfer
   and Other Effects of U.S.-Foreign Cooperation in
   Military Aircraft Production   52
Conclusion   55

Chapter 3
Case Studies   67

Boeing-JCAC   67
McDonnell Douglas: The Mercure 200 and the MDF100   74
General Electric-SNECMA   80
The Saab-Fairchild 340   85
The International Aero Engines V2500   90
Conclusion   96

Chapter 4
Country Strategies   107

The Japanese Aircraft Industry   108
Brazil: Development with a Large Domestic Market   114
Sweden: "Keep-up" Policy with a Small Domestic Market   121
Airbus Industrie: A Joint Venture of "National Champions"   128
Conclusion   139

Chapter 5
Conclusions and Policy Implications   149

Are International Joint Ventures a Threat to U.S. Competitive-
   ness in Commercial Aircraft?   149
Organization and Management of Joint Ventures   152
Policy Implications   157

Bibliography   171

Index   185

About the Author   195

LIST OF FIGURES

2-1   Annual R&D Investment in Aircraft, 1945–1982   41
2-2   NACA/NASA Aeronautics Manpower History,
      1920–1980   50

ACKNOWLEDGMENTS

This research was funded by the American Enterprise Institute's Competing in a Changing World Economy project, Stanford University's Center for Economic Policy Research, and the National Science Foundation (PRA83-10664). I am grateful to Claude E. Barfield, coordinator of the AEI project, as well as executives at Boeing, McDonnell Douglas, Saab-Scania, Volvo Flygmotor, General Electric, officials of the Office of the U.S. Trade Representative and the Commerce Department, members of the Council on Foreign Relations Study Group on International Corporate Alliances, Peter Cowhey, Steven Klepper, Richard Rosenbloom, W. Edward Steinmueller, David Teece, Lacy Glenn Thomas, Murray Weidenbaum, and Raymond Vernon for useful comments and suggestions. None of these individuals or organizations is responsible for the conclusions and errors that remain. I am also grateful to Pamela Reyner for secretarial assistance.

1 INTRODUCTION

The international commercial aircraft industry has undergone a structural transformation during the past three decades. In the mid-1950s, at least ten British, French, and U.S. firms produced airframes for large commercial aircraft (those carrying more than fifty passengers), while nine firms manufactured engines for such aircraft.[1] The world aircraft industry now includes three major airframe producers and three engine firms. The industry has been transformed in another way, however, as the development of new aircraft and engines now is undertaken largely by multifirm consortia. During the past fifteen years, a complex system of interfirm alliances and other cooperative ventures has developed within the commercial aircraft industry, involving links among the major "prime-contractor" firms and an extensive set of cooperative relationships between these firms and other supplier and subcontractor firms. This situation contrasts with the structure of the innovation process in this industry prior to 1970, when both airframe and engine producers largely developed and manufactured their products independently of other firms.

Many of these interfirm alliances span national boundaries and involve significant exchanges of managerial expertise and technology. Official U.S. assessments have expressed concern over the implications of such interfirm cooperation for the future competitiveness of the U.S. aircraft industry:

World aerospace manufacturers are sharing production with foreign companies in larger and more comprehensive programs. Through these programs,
foreign companies are gaining technology and production knowhow that will
enable them to become more competitive and to acquire larger market shares.
As one result, the U.S. aerospace industry faces increased foreign competition
at home and in third country markets. Japan, already a competitor in small
turbine aircraft, has targeted large transport aircraft as its next major aerospace manufacturing venture. Experience gained in shared high technology
programs will facilitate rapid development of an independent production
capability for large transports in Japan. (U.S. Department of Commerce,
1982, p. 259.)

This monograph analyzes the causes and consequences of international joint ventures in the commercial aircraft industry, focusing
on ventures involving U.S. aircraft and engine producers and foreign
enterprises. I discuss the motives for participation by U.S. firms in
such ventures, managerial and organizational factors that affect the
success or failure of projects, and the consequences of such multinational "teaming" for the structure and competitiveness of the U.S.
aircraft industry.

Although the discussion focuses on joint ventures in commercial
aircraft, the significance of joint ventures extends well beyond this
industry. Multinational joint ventures in research and development or
manufacturing have become an important phenomenon in many U.S.
manufacturing industries.[2] International joint ventures have been a
significant force in the aircraft industry for a longer period than in
many other manufacturing industries, however, as most of the aircraft and engines introduced during the past decade have been
developed by multinational consortia. The aircraft industry therefore is well suited to an analysis of different cases and types of
interfirm cooperation and may yield insights into the consequences
of cooperation.

This chapter discusses the general characteristics of international
joint ventures and considers some implications of interfirm cooperation. Chapter 2 surveys recent developments in the competitive and
technological environment of the U.S. aircraft industry, focusing on
the effect of these developments on the incentives of U.S. firms to
participate in joint ventures with foreign firms. I examine several
joint ventures, including the Boeing 767 and 7J7, the General Electric–SNECMA[3] CFM56 engine, the V2500 engine, the McDonnell
Douglas–Fokker MDF100, the McDonnell Douglas Mercure 200

project with Dassault–Breguet and Aerospatiale, and the Saab–
Fairchild 340 commuter aircraft, in greater detail in chapter 3. Chapter 4 discusses the approach of foreign firms and governments to
joint ventures, focusing on the technological and competitive strategies of Airbus Industrie, Saab–Scania Aircraft and Volvo Flygmotor
of Sweden, Embraer of Brazil, the Japan Commercial Aircraft Corporation, and Japan Aero Engines. Chapter 5 considers the implications of multinational joint ventures for U.S. policy makers and corporate managers.

DEFINITION AND SIGNIFICANCE OF JOINT VENTURES

The term *joint venture* is employed loosely in this monograph. Some
cooperative arrangements in the aircraft industry fit the definition of
a classical joint venture as an incorporated, separate entity in which
equity holdings are divided among the partners, but others do not.
Indeed, some of the cases discussed in chapter 3 are essentially ex-
tensions of prior subcontracting relationships. For present purposes,
however, a joint venture is defined as *product development and
manufacture of commercial aircraft and engines involving more than
one firm and significant levels of interfirm cooperation in research,
design, production, and marketing, as well as significant contributions by all partners of development funds or risk capital.* This definition is intended to exclude coproduction and licensing agreements
for military aircraft (discussed briefly in chapter 2), direct foreign
investment (which denotes complete interfirm control of production
and product development activities), and the sale of technology
through licensing, which is rare in the commercial aircraft industry.
The discussion below also excludes joint ventures whose activities
are restricted to research.

Joint ventures have long been common in extractive industries,
such as mining and petroleum production, and account for a significant share of total foreign investment activity by U.S. manufacturing
firms during the postwar period.[4] Using data from the Harvard Multinational Enterprise Project, Karen Hladik found that joint ventures
accounted for 39 percent of the number of foreign subsidiaries
founded by U.S. manufacturing firms during 1951–1975.[5] Additional, fragmentary evidence suggests that the foreign manufacturing

subsidiaries of multinational firms from the U.S. and Europe increasingly are jointly owned. John Dunning concluded from an analysis of data on foreign investment by multinational firms from the industrialized nations that " . . . the proportion of foreign affiliates established in developed countries between 1961 and 1975 with a 100 percent ownership was 25.3 percent compared with 41.1 percent of those set up before 1960."[6] Joint ventures also have long been important in the foreign investment activities of multinational firms from nations with small domestic markets, such as Sweden.

Although joint ventures have been an important element in the foreign investment activities of U.S. and foreign manufacturing firms throughout the postwar period, several features of recent joint ventures are new. The number of joint ventures among U.S. firms and between U.S. and foreign enterprises has increased dramatically in recent years. Kathryn Harrigan's data suggest that domestic joint ventures among U.S. manufacturing firms have increased in number during the past decade and now appear in a much wider range of industries, while Hladik finds a significant increase during the past decade in the number of international joint ventures involving U.S. firms.[7]

The joint ventures discussed below involve both product development and manufacture, but there also has occurred an upsurge in the reliance by U.S. firms on external sources of R&D expertise, through such multifirm research consortia as the Semiconductor Research Corporation and the Microelectronics and Computer Technology Corporation as well as university-industry research institutes.[8] A full treatment of the factors underpinning this growth in firms' external reliance on sources of R&D is beyond the scope of this monograph, but it seems clear that some of the forces supporting growth in product development joint ventures have also contributed to the rise of domestic interfirm cooperation in research.

The structure and activities of the international joint ventures in which U.S. firms have participated during the past decade also differ significantly from those of the 1950–1975 period. The share of joint ventures in which U.S. firms hold a minority stake has increased consistent with Dunning's data. (Once again, the absence of data on the size of such ventures means that the significance of joint ventures in which U.S. firms have a minority share cannot be precisely determined.) According to Hladik, an average of 80 percent of the joint ventures formed each year during 1974–1982 were "nonmajority" joint ventures, denoting joint ventures in which U.S. firms have an ownership share of 50 percent or less.[9] Moreover, Hladik found that an increasing share of recent U.S.–foreign joint ventures involved production for export, joint conduct of R&D, or both. These features of recent joint ventures differentiate them from those of the earlier postwar period, during which many joint ventures between U.S. and foreign firms were engaged primarily in production for the market of the nation in which the foreign firm was located or in the exploitation of mineral or oil deposits in the foreign nation.

Recent joint ventures between U.S. and foreign firms have also developed in industries and firms that historically have not been characterized by high levels of direct foreign investment or multinational corporate organization. Indeed, commercial aircraft was cited by Seev Hirsch as an industry in which direct foreign investment is rare.[10] International joint ventures have assumed considerable importance in the United States in recent years in both technologically "mature" industries (for example, steel and automobiles) and "young" industries (robotics and microelectronics). Virtually all of these ventures involve significant collaboration in R&D and product development as well as technology transfer. In some cases (for example, aircraft and semiconductors) a preponderance (but by no means all) of the technology transfer operating through joint ventures consists of exports of technology or know-how from the United States. In other industries, however, such as steel or autos, joint ventures involve significant U.S. imports of technology.

Joint ventures between U.S. and foreign firms now incorporate a new range of activities and may represent a significant shift in the characteristic pattern of new product development by U.S. firms. Development and design of new products historically were carried out independently by manufacturing firms rather than cooperatively by several firms. International marketing and manufacture of products occurred through export or direct foreign investment, while international licensing was occasionally employed for the exploitation by a firm of its product or process technology and know-how. Recent joint ventures differ from all three of these mechanisms for the sale of products or technology. Rather than selling products or technology at arm's-length by contract, as in the case of product export or technology licensing, a joint venture establishes a partnership wherein all participants may contribute managerial and technological expertise, as well as capital. Although joint ventures do not involve the sale of products or technology, in contrast to direct foreign investment, more than one firm controls productive or technological assets. The transfer of technology and other assets means that the dynamic consequences of joint ventures may be very different from those of direct foreign invesment.

Joint ventures are based on an exchange relationship, but the assets or commodities exchanged by firms differ from those exchanged via licensing or export. Some international joint ventures allow U.S. and foreign firms to pool their technological assets in a single product line, without merging all of their activities into a single corporate entity. Other joint ventures may support the combination of one firm's technological capabilities with the marketing or distribution assets of another. Why are joint ventures, rather than alternative mechanisms (such as licensing), employed for this exchange? The following section addresses this question.

ALTERNATIVE CHANNELS FOR THE TRANSFER AND EXPLOITATION OF TECHNOLOGY

Many scholars have considered the reasons for a firm's choice among export, licensing, and direct foreign investment as channels for the sale of its products or the exploitation of other assets. A fundamental insight into this issue was proposed by Steven Hymer and extended and enriched by a number of scholars.[11] Hymer argued that the key determinant of a firm's decision to undertake direct foreign investment, rather than serving foreign markets solely through the export of goods, was the possession by the investing firm of some advantage over firms based in the foreign country.[12]

Exploitation by the firm of such an advantage through the export and sale of products in foreign markets was less effective than direct investment, which enabled the firm to realize in foreign markets the returns to its combined strengths in marketing, production, and innovation. In this view, firms invest directly abroad, rather than exporting their products, for the same reasons that many U.S. manufacturing firms in the late nineteenth century expanded their product lines and absorbed a number of functions (for example, distribution and marketing) that extended well beyond production alone.[13] The returns in both foreign and domestic markets to the combined performance of these functions by a single firm are greater than those accruing to firms specializing only in the production of a product for sale in domestic or foreign markets.

Hymer did not discuss at length the nature or causes of the firm's advantage, but the empirical and theoretical investigations of other scholars suggest that firms undertake direct foreign investment as a result of the accumulation of intangible assets that are highly firm-specific.[14] Exploiting such assets through export is in many cases extremely difficult. Direct foreign investment is, however, only one of several methods for realizing a return to these assets. Alternative means for their exploitation include licensing and joint ventures. Each method has advantages and disadvantages that are closely related to the characteristics of the asset in question. A discussion of the key differences among these three channels will illuminate the causes of increased international joint venture activity and the basis for interindustry differences in the importance of foreign investment, licensing, and joint ventures. The next section focuses on the intrinsic characteristics of technology-based intangible assets and channels for their transfer; the role of the "policy environment" within which U.S. firms operate, which is also of great importance in international joint ventures, is considered later in this chapter.

In many cases, intangible corporate assets are based on a firm's technological capabilities.[15] The exploitation of technology-based intangible assets through market channels—licensing, for example—often is very difficult, for several reasons. Research and innovation within the firm typically yield cumulative, firm-specific knowledge, reflecting the close link between the design, production, and marketing of goods and the acquisition of knowledge concerning product and process technologies. As a result, markets for the licensing of advanced technologies that exploit such firm-specific knowledge are thin, with few buyers or sellers. Rather than a competitive market for technology licenses, licensing transactions may more nearly resemble a bilateral monopoly (no more than one buyer or seller) in which opportunistic behavior—that is, the strategic misrepresentation of preferences or the concealment of information—is supported by the absence of alternative outlets for sellers or alternative sources for buyers.[16]

The joint activities of production and the accumulation of technological knowledge by the firm affect the feasibility and attractiveness of licensing in another way. In many cases, the knowledge necessary to bring about an innovation resides in many different areas within the firm—successful innovation requires the combination of a wide range of its capabilities.[17] Packaging the knowledge and individuals needed to exploit an innovation, which is necessary for licensing, without splitting or dismembering the licensor firm may be impossible.[18] Moreover, much technological knowledge is "tacit."[19] Know-how, in addition to blueprints, is critical to understanding, and therefore to transferring, technology. This unwritten character of much of the firm-specific knowledge that is critical to technology transfer undercuts the feasibility of licensing complex technological assets, which typically embody a substantial tacit component.

A further difficulty in licensing technological assets was noted by Kenneth J. Arrow. To justify the price of any asset to a potential buyer, the seller must reveal considerable information concerning the nature and capabilities of the technology in question. If one assumes that the potential buyer can easily absorb and exploit this revealed information, the buyer has little incentive to complete the licensing transaction.[20]

Uncertainty about the behavior of licensor and licensee severely reduces the efficiency of markets for technology licenses. A firm licensing a technology risks the possibility that its monopoly with respect to this technological asset will be undercut as licensees acquire expertise and "reverse engineer" or invent around the license or patent. Many licensing agreements require that licensees provide any improvements to the licensor, but these provisions are difficult to enforce. Licensing also may transfer technology in a more comprehensive or uncontrolled fashion than the licensor firm deems to be in its best interests.

The strength of patent protection also affects the attractiveness of exploiting technologies through licensing. Where patents are comprehensive, well enforced, and difficult to circumvent, licensing a patented innovation poses fewer dangers of reverse engineering. In addition, the comprehensive disclosure of characteristics that is necessary for a patent application facilitates the valuation of the technology by a licensor and the agreement on its value in a contract. Even relatively immature technological assets of this type may be exploited through licensing.

The nature of the innovation processes associated with different technologies also affects the choice between licensing and other mechanisms for their exploitation. Complex capital goods with long production histories, a group that includes commercial aircraft, telecommunications equipment, and robotics equipment, often require extensive after-sales product support and servicing. Separating the responsibilities for manufacture from those of product support establishes a situation ripe for opportunistic behavior.

Even where product support and manufacture both can be carried out by a licensor, however, the role of product support and marketing in providing data for initial product design and subsequent incremental modifications means that the channels of feedback and information ideally should be controlled by the organization responsible for product design and manufacture. Technologies characterized by "user-active" innovation, in Eric von Hippel's phrase,[21] are technologies in which user-supplied operating experience and demands must be relayed to research and design groups. Licensing may deprive a producer of this important channel of information for product modification and improvement; at a minimum, the information must be relayed across organizational boundaries, reducing its quality and quantity. Chapter 3 discusses several joint ventures in which dispersed control of marketing, product support, and design functions among the partner firms created severe problems. Technologies in which product support and user-active innovation are less central may admit more easily of exploitation through licensing.

Empirical evidence on the limitations of international licensing for the transfer of complex technological assets propositions is sketchy but generally supportive. Edwin Mansfield and other scholars have argued that licensing is most common for relatively mature technological assets.[22] The maturity of a technological asset has several direct implications for its exploitation in the international market. Firms are less likely to possess substantial monopoly power over a mature technology, reducing the problems of small numbers and opportunism within the licensing transaction. In two respects an older technology is also more thoroughly codified. The tacit component of the knowledge necessary to exploit the technology will be less significant, and the performance and other characteristics of the technology better understood, making its valuation and packaging in a license contract far easier.

Other studies of licensing also emphasize the thin and imperfect nature of the international market for technology licenses. The analysis by Caves, Crookell, and Killing of a small sample of technology licensing contracts concluded that severe uncertainties about both the quality of technological assets and licensee and licensor behavior prevent licensors from extracting the full potential profits from the assets sold through licenses and preclude the achievement of maximum total benefits.[23]

Imperfections in the international market for technology licenses thus limit the range of technological assets that can be exploited through this mechanism. How does this characteristic of licensing affect its importance within different industries and technologies? Licensing is likely to be preferred to either direct foreign investment or joint ventures in technologies that are not complex, do not have strong, well-enforced patents, are relatively mature, and do not rely on user-active innovation, with its attendant requirements for post-sales product support.

Despite the limited ability of licensing to support the exploitation of technological assets, international licensing is widely employed in a number of technologies and industries. Technologies and industries with short product cycles often are the locus of extensive domestic and international licensing. If the market for a product is expected to be short-lived, a firm may choose to forgo the substantial fixed investment in production capacity necessary to serve this market, instead reaping part of the profits from the production and part from the licensing of the innovation.

A somewhat different motive for licensing arises in industries manufacturing products for which standards are very important, such as those producing semiconductor components or telecommunications equipment. In such industries, the establishment of de facto standards around a particular design may be facilitated through rapid expansion of its production. Such rapid expansion, as well as the establishment of supply reliability, can in some industries (semiconductors, for example) be achieved through licensing other producers, supporting capacity expansion that is both rapid and (from the viewpoint of the licensor) less costly. The establishment of multiple sources of supply through widespread licensing also enhances the supply reliability of a product. Industries in which patents held by competitors overlap also exhibit considerable cross-licensing of innovations as a means of reducing litigation over patent rights.

International licensing of technological assets thus covers a limited subset of technologies and industries, because of market and contract imperfections and uncertainties. Direct foreign investment, which supports the exploitation of firm-specific technological capabilities, also carries substantial risks and costs. Firms operating in industries in which production technologies exhibit a minimum efficient scale that is large relative to the size of the world market, as well as strong plant-specific learning and cost reduction effects, may incur prohibitive cost penalties in establishing multiple production facilities. Foreign direct investment in such industries as commercial aircraft and steel, is unlikely, ceteris paribus, for this reason. The high fixed costs of establishing an offshore production, distribution, and marketing network present a barrier to direct foreign investment—in a world of imperfect capital markets, only the largest firms can undertake such strategies. The uncertainties concerning economic and political conditions in many foreign markets also make direct foreign investment too risky for many firms. Licensing and direct foreign investment, as well as export, also force the innovating firm to bear all of the costs and risks of product or process research and development.

What advantages do international joint ventures have over licensing or direct foreign investment, and how are such advantages likely to affect the importance of joint ventures in different industries? By comparison with direct foreign investment, licensing, and export, joint ventures spread the financial risks of innovation considerably. Joint ventures are also less financially risky than direct foreign investment. Moreover, because the ownership structure within a joint venture need not necessarily match the structure of managerial control or the location of production, multiple production plants are not a central component of many recent joint ventures between U.S. and foreign firms. Many joint ventures, therefore, do not incur the cost penalties associated with direct foreign investment in offshore production capacity.

Joint ventures also have a number of advantages over licensing. Many of the contractual limitations of licensing that historically led U.S. firms to prefer direct foreign investment can be avoided within a joint venture. The noncodified, "inseparable" character of firm-specific assets that makes their exploitation through licensing so difficult need not prevent the pooling or exchange of such assets by several firms within a joint venture.

Joint ventures provide a means for avoiding many of the problems of uncertainty and opportunism of international technology licensing transactions. While the valuation of partners' contributions can be a central issue in these undertakings, such as the 767 and 7J7 aircraft development projects between Boeing and the Japan Commercial

Aircraft Corporation, joint ventures often render more feasible the exchange among firms of assets (technological capabilities, for example) that are not easily assigned a price, while also reducing the severity of the Arrow "revelation" problem. Indeed, Joseph Brodley and others have noted that joint ventures reduce the need for complex negotiations over the value of the technological and managerial assets supplied by each partner and also lower the risks and feasibility of opportunistic behavior by erstwhile partners.[24] If a central reason for the existence of firms is the greater ease with which employee behavior (as compared with that of contractors or licensees) can be monitored, as Armen Alchian and Harold Demsetz and Oliver Williamson suggest, the formation of a joint venture allows for better monitoring by each partner of the behavior of the other(s), while reducing the incentives for opportunistic behavior.[25]

Technology transfer also may be controlled or regulated more effectively through joint ventures than through licensing. Whereas licensing transactions necessitate the sale of a complete package of technological capabilities in many instances, joint ventures enable partner firms to "unbundle" their portfolios of technological assets and selectively transfer individual components of this portfolio, which in isolation may be worthless to a partner.[26] The transfer of technology through a joint venture from a technologically advanced firm to a less advanced enterprise, for example, allows the technologically senior firm to reap some financial returns to mature portions of its portfolio of technological capabilities. In many cases, such returns cannot be attained through licensing, because of the difficulties of unbundling the firm's technological portfolio through licensing. This source of financial reward provides a strong cohesive force in joint ventures involving firms of disparate technological capabilities. Moreover, because monitoring the behavior of the recipient of any such assets is more feasible within a joint venture the transferor is more likely to benefit from improvements in transferred technologies made by the recipient.

Finally, many joint ventures offer a lower-cost alternative to the complete merger of firms as a means of pooling assets. Joint venture partnerships typically cover only a limited range of functions or products, falling well short of a complete merger of firms. Indeed, partner firms may well be competitors in other product areas. Joint ventures thus offer a potentially more flexible mechanism for the pooling or combining of a subset of the total capabilities of partner firms, reducing some of the difficulties of combining large, multi-product enterprises through mergers. In view of the disappointing performance of many of the large mergers of the 1960s and 1970s, this feature of both domestic and international joint ventures may account for some of their recent popularity among U.S. firms. Joint ventures also allow established firms to gain access to nonlicensable new technologies more rapidly than is possible through internal development. The costs and risks of a joint venture are lower than those of acquisition of the technology through the purchase of a firm.

The potential difficulties of joint ventures should not be minimized. Management of such undertakings has proved to be extremely difficult. Joint ventures may reduce problems of opportunism and conflicting incentives, but cannot eliminate these difficulties completely. In addition, the amount of technology transferred within many joint ventures is often a contentious issue, especially in ventures that involve firms with different technological capabilities. The interests of the partners in such ventures are directly opposed, as the senior firm wishes to minimize, and the junior firm to maximize, the amount of technology transfer. These conflicting interests can prevent the formation or contribute to the collapse of a joint venture. Joint ventures between erstwhile competitors that cover only one product line among the many produced by partner firms are also frequently unstable. Technological change may cause independently manufactured products to become competitors with those being jointly developed within the partnership, leading to its dissolution. Finally, the feasibility of joint ventures is limited by the availability of partners. All partners must bring something to the joint venture, be it technology, capital, or access to a foreign market. In many cases, the formation of a joint venture between a technologically junior and senior partner requires that the junior partner first achieve some minimum level of technological expertise in order to absorb the technology being transferred through the joint venture.

The relative attractiveness of these various mechanisms for the exploitation of firm-specific technological and other assets, however, does not explain the recent upsurge in joint ventures in the commercial aircraft and other industries. The primary channel for the exploitation by U.S. firms of their technological assets throughout much of this century, after all, has been direct foreign investment.[27] Previous international joint ventures complemented direct foreign investment, allowing U.S. firms to establish production capacity to serve domestic demand in new foreign markets. These joint ventures generally were restricted to joint ownership of such production capacity. Interfirm cooperation in R&D, whether domestic or international, was rare. Why have international joint ventures recently assumed such importance in commercial aircraft and other industries, and why do these new joint ventures encompass a wider range of activities? At the most fundamental level, the answer is simple— changes in the technological and policy environment of U.S. firms in the aircraft and other industries have rendered the potential contributions of foreign firms to joint ventures much more attractive to U.S. firms. These changes are considered in the following section.

GENERAL CAUSES OF INCREASING RELIANCE ON JOINT VENTURES

The forces underlying the growth in multinational joint ventures affect the nature of product demand, the technological and competitive environment faced by U.S. firms, and the structure of trade policy within the industrialized nations. The effect of these factors on the incidence of joint ventures has varied across industries.

In discussing the factors motivating increased cooperation between U.S. and foreign firms, it is useful to consider Raymond Vernon's model of direct foreign investment.[28] Vernon's "product cycle" model explained U.S. direct foreign investment as a mechanism for the exploitation of firm-specific technological assets. Changes in the variables identified by Vernon as important causes of direct foreign investment by U.S. firms have motivated the development of new channels for international flows of goods, technology, and capital; one such new channel is the joint venture in product development and manufacture. Vernon's model hypothesized that differences in the consumer demand profile of various national markets supported the development of unique capabilities and other assets in the domestic firms serving these national markets. As demand conditions developed in foreign markets that resembled those of the home market, these domestic firms used direct foreign investment as the most effective means of exploiting firm-specific assets. Within the product cycle model, firms were essentially passive channels for the expression of differences between the national markets of the world economy.

Recent international joint ventures in the commercial aircraft and other industries fail to conform in important dimensions with the predictions of the product cycle model. International flows of capital per se are less significant in these ventures, while the establishment of wholly owned foreign production facilities also is rare. International flows of technological information and data, design and marketing capabilities, and managerial expertise, rather than capital, are of primary importance in joint ventures. Furthermore, the characteristics of the domestic markets of the various participant firms frequently have little to do with the character of the firm-specific assets exploited through such agreements; the attributes of the corporate participants now may be less "country-bound."[29]

The decline in the importance of direct foreign investment and of firm-specific attributes based solely on national markets reflects changes in the international economic environment that have increased U.S. firms' demand for foreign partners in joint ventures. Both the supply of inputs and the nature of product demand have changed.[30] On the supply side, the real costs of physical capital and skilled or technical workers across different industrialized economies are increasingly similar.[31] These similarities are reflected in the greatly enhanced technological capabilities of many foreign firms. These enhanced capabilities operate in two ways to make foreign firms more attractive potential partners with U.S. firms. Foreign firms increasingly are able to absorb and exploit advanced technologies from U.S. firms in industries in which there remains a substantial technology gap between U.S. and foreign firms. In other industries, however, foreign firms either are the technological equals of U.S. firms or are more advanced and therefore can make significant contributions of managerial or technological expertise to joint ventures. In this case, U.S. firms form joint ventures with foreign firms as a means of exploiting their technological capabilities.

International Demand

Simultaneously, the profile of product demand in the world market for many goods has become more homogeneous and less dominated by any single market. The U.S. share of world demand for many high-technology products has declined (for example, the U.S. share of world demand for commercial transports has declined in recent years, a trend discussed in chapter 2). This shift in the profile of world demand has rendered penetration of foreign markets by U.S. firms in a wide range of industries essential to commercial success. Joint ventures offer a lower-risk and -cost alternative to direct foreign investment and are more effective in many cases than export in supporting access to foreign markets.

Despite the decline in its share of world demand for many high-technology industries, the United States remains by far the largest single market for the products of most manufacturing industries. Although the European market is potentially as large or larger, incomplete economic integration has failed to end the fragmentation of European markets for high-technology goods. Many joint ventures between U.S. and European or Japanese firms are motivated by the desire of foreign firms to penetrate the U.S. market through such vehicles, drawing (in some industries) on newly achieved technological parity with or superiority to U.S. firms.

U.S. and Foreign Trade Policies

Government trade and industrial policies have greatly influenced global product demand; they have further increased the incentives of U.S. firms to seek foreign partners in product development and manufacture and have motivated foreign firms to seek out U.S. partners to penetrate the U.S. market. In both industrialized and industrializing nations, the development and stabilization of high value-added industries and skilled manufacturing employment are central goals of industrial policies. Purchase decisions of foreign governments play a major role in the export markets for commercial aircraft and frequently are influenced by the availability of offsets, which refer to the production and, increasingly, the design or development of a portion of the components for the purchased product by domestic firms in the purchaser nation. (Offsets occasionally resemble countertrade or barter, in that unrelated products are provided by the purchasing nation in partial payment.) Government demands for offsets create strong incentives for U.S. producers to involve foreign firms as major subcontractors (frequently sharing some financial risk) or as equal partners in product development and manufacture. The application of such official pressure to the parties to a procurement transaction (known as directed procurement) violates provisions of the General Agreement on Trade and Tariffs, as well as the Agreement on Trade in Civil Aircraft (see chapter 2), a fact that is unlikely to deter such pressure in the future.[32] Foreign governments also frequently provide development funding and risk capital to their domestic firms. Combined with high and rapidly increasing product development costs in the commercial aircraft industry, the availability of capital from public sources for foreign firms has considerably enhanced their attractiveness as joint venture partners for U.S. firms.

In addition to government demands for offsets, of course, bilateral "orderly marketing" and other trade agreements that restrict foreign access to the U.S. market are a major factor in a number of industries. Such bilateral, protectionist agreements create an incentive for foreign firms to circumvent restrictions on their exports to the United States by establishing manufacturing operations within the United States. In several instances (the Toyota–General Motors agreement or that between Nippon Kokan Steel and National Steel), joint ventures have been used to establish U.S. manufacturing activities.

Paradoxically, the pursuit by industrialized nations of essentially nationalistic policies of support for "infant industries" has encouraged the development of consortia spanning national boundaries. The earlier growth of multinational firms and direct foreign investment raised the prospect of "global firms" to whom national boundaries mean little or nothing and which are capable of avoiding the constraints of policies developed by governments in industrialized and developing nations. Much of the current wave of joint venture activity, however, reflects an opposite trend.[33] Global firms in the aircraft and other industries increasingly must be cognizant of and responsive to the policy environment of the nations in which they are producing or marketing goods and services.

U.S. Antitrust Policy

The role of U.S. antitrust policy has been a recurrent issue in the recent public debate over the competitiveness of U.S. industry. Have U.S. antitrust statutes prevented the nation's firms from combining their research talents to fend off foreign competition?[34] Historically, of course, Justice Department opposition to domestic joint ventures that conduct only basic or fundamental research has been modest,[35] and will probably decline further in the wake of the National Cooperative Research Act of 1984. Antitrust policy has been cited, however, as a factor contributing to the decision by U.S. firms in a number of industries to seek foreign rather than domestic partners in new product development ventures.[36] The effect of U.S. antitrust policy on joint ventures in commercial aircraft is discussed in chapters 2, 3, and 5.

Innovation in Management and Technology

U.S. involvement in joint ventures, with domestic or with foreign firms, also is closely related to the causes of the development of large multinational U.S. firms. The growth of such firms was in part a response to technological changes that reduced the costs and enhanced the reliability of information transmission, storage, and processing.[37] Combined with other technological and organizational changes, reductions in information costs created considerable economies of scale and scope within the firm. Recent innovations in the technologies of information transmission, storage, and analysis have further reduced information costs and play an important role in interfirm cooperation in the development and manufacture of airframes and engines. The exchange of technical, testing, and other data between development teams and the use of computer-aided design and manufacturing technologies in both development and production have facilitated the "spinning off" to other foreign or domestic firms of numerous tasks in the design and manufacture of aircraft and could prefigure the erosion of the competitive advantages of large firm size.[38]

The dramatic fall in the costs of information transmission, storage, and analysis induced by new information technologies has reduced some of the scale and scope economies that previously supported the intrafirm performance of many tasks. It remains to be seen how far this tendency toward increased subcontracting and spinoff can be carried; marketing, which is critical to both sales and innovation in aircraft, seemingly is still characterized by substantial intrafirm scale economies. Technological changes could, however, alter the firm-specific character of even this asset.

WHY ARE JOINT VENTURES A MAJOR FORCE IN COMMERCIAL AIRCRAFT?

Many of the general factors discussed above, such as changes in global market demand, foreign technological capabilities, and foreign government trade policies, have affected all U.S. export industries. While joint ventures have increased in importance in most U.S. manufacturing industries, however, in no other industry are international joint ventures as important as in commercial aircraft and engines, where virtually every product development program undertaken by U.S. firms in the past decade has involved major foreign participation. What characteristics of commercial aircraft markets and technology contribute to the importance of joint ventures in this industry?

These characteristics (discussed in greater detail in chapter 2) include the sheer scale of commercial risk and development costs within the industry (particularly by comparison with the equity of most firms in the industry). These costs and risks have risen steeply in recent years. Moreover, declining military-civilian technological spillovers within this industry mean that private firms must bear a larger share of the development costs for an airframe or engine. Deregulation of domestic air transportation in the United States also has reduced somewhat the stability and certainty of demand for aircraft, further heightening the financial risk borne by aircraft producers. In addition, the declining share of U.S. demand in the world aircraft market has increased the importance of exports. The growing role of governments in many export markets makes foreign involvement in production or development a prerequisite for market access by U.S. firms and provides a source of low-cost capital to these firms.

An alternative to joint ventures, the international licensing of civil aircraft designs by U.S. aircraft firms, is rare. Examples of licensing include the licensing by Piper Aircraft of Brazilian production of general aviation aircraft in 1974, as well as the 1985 agreement between the People's Republic of China and the McDonnell Douglas Corporation. In both cases, licensed production of the aircraft primarily serves a large domestic rather than a world market, thereby reducing the requirements for the licensor to establish a global distribution and service network. Both licensing agreements also cover the production of technologically mature aircraft designs, which may admit of easier codification and contractual negotiation than would a new, advanced design.

Aircraft and engine design by their very nature are tasks that require the integration of numerous complex subsystems and incorporate a great deal of tacit or firm-specific know-how. As a result, the arm's-length transfer of technology through licensing typically is impractical for advanced aircraft or engine designs. Production experience, which supports cost reductions in component production and assembly, also is critical to the commercial feasibility of a given aircraft, despite the fact that the total production of a specific design rarely exceeds 600 units. The importance of these learning effects means that the establishment of offshore assembly operations—for example, through direct foreign investment—in most cases results in severe financial penalties. Finally, marketing and post-sales service organizations play important roles in collecting and relaying performance information to design and development personnel, who often make significant design modifications. Mechanisms for the exploitation of technological assets in the commercial aricraft industry must preserve the links between marketing, product support, and design, which undercuts the attractiveness of licensing.

The combined effect of these factors has motivated U.S. producers of aircraft and engines to seek greater foreign involvement in the financing, development, and production of new aircraft, while largely restricting the form of this foreign involvement to joint ventures. Much of the technological expertise in commercial aircraft design and manufacture is organizationally based; it is not easily decomposed or separated from the parent firm. Joint ventures therefore are attractive mechanisms for obtaining risk capital and achieving market access.

IMPLICATIONS FOR PUBLIC POLICY
AND PRIVATE MANAGEMENT

The fact that technology exchange or transfer is at the center of most of the joint ventures examined here raises novel issues for government policy and private management, which are considered at greater length in chapter 5. Clearly, the dynamic consequences of technology transfer to foreign firms raise the possibility that foreign competitors may be created or strengthened through joint ventures.[39] The extent of technology transfer that occurs within these ventures and the effect of such transfers on the capabilities of foreign firms therefore are discussed in some detail. The technological and competitive effect of military coproduction agreements between U.S. and foreign firms and governments, many of which have been in operation for nearly thirty years, provides some useful information on this issue. Obviously, to the extent that joint ventures encourage technology transfer that is detrimental to the longer-term prospects for the U.S. aircraft industry, intensive scrutiny of the role of foreign development funds, "directed procurement" policies of foreign governments, and U.S. antitrust regulations in supporting technology transfer through joint ventures is warranted.

A closely related policy issue is the effect on the "second tier" of suppliers and vendors within the U.S. aircraft industry of joint ventures undertaken by the major prime contractor firms (that is, those firms, such as Boeing, McDonnell Douglas, United Technologies, and General Electric, that have the financial and technological wherewithal to undertake overall design and production of new aircraft and engines). The most substantial impact of many joint ventures, especially those involving foreign risk-sharing subcontractors, has been felt by supplier firms in the U.S. aircraft industry. Much of the technology that has been transferred through military coproduction programs or recent joint ventures has affected this sector of the industry, as the role of foreign firms in the production of subassemblies and components has grown. Because a great many U.S. supplier firms provide components for both military and civilian aircraft, this segment of the industry is an important component of the U.S. defense industrial base. To the extent that the supplier sector of the aircraft industry is being eroded by joint venture activities, policies to either restrict joint ventures or directly assist components producers may merit consideration. Nonetheless, while supplier firms in the United States face increasing foreign competition as a result of joint ventures, the internationalization of the aircraft industry has also been a source of major benefits to these firms, as U.S. components are employed extensively in most foreign commercial aircraft.

In addition to their complex implications for policy, of course, multinational joint ventures raise challenging management issues. Because technology is the focus of many such ventures the management of both the firm's portfolio of technological capabilities and the process of transfer to a given partner of some portion of those capabilities become very important. The recent performance of many U.S. firms in managing intrafirm technological development, to say nothing of technology transfer in an international context, suggests that scholarly and managerial knowledge is still limited in this area. Both U.S. managers and the management of prospective foreign partners also must recognize the potential clash in incentives between technological leaders, who are reluctant to allow the transfer of key technological capabilities, and technological followers, whose participation may hinge on the amount of technology transfer within joint ventures.

The managerial feasibility of a joint venture also may be undercut by the attempts of junior partners, motivated by their desire to achieve the greatest possible technology transfer and learning, to participate in all aspects of the project. A tension exists between specialized participation in joint ventures, which enhances the prospects for commercial and technical success, and more generalized participation, which may undercut the commercial or managerial feasibility of a given project while simultaneously increasing the amount of technology transfer and learning within the venture. In most of the successful ventures discussed in chapters 3 and 4, specialization has won out. The complexities of managing joint ventures also mean that projects pushing the technological state of the art may prove less feasible within a joint venture than less technologically demanding undertakings. Production technology and management practices may also require considerable adjustment by the various partners in order to meet specific cost or output targets. Such harmonization may be quite difficult.

Finally, the management structure of joint ventures raises additional challenges. How are decisions among equals to be made? How is feedback from prospective purchasers to be integrated into the design process? How are product support responsibilities to be handled, and how is this source of operating experience to be incorporated into design modifications? Under some circumstances, an autonomous management structure, charged with responsibility and the power for a wide range of design, marketing, production, and product support issues, may be preferable. Such a management structure is also costly, however, inasmuch as it may require the duplication of many senior engineering and design functions. There is no single optimal management structure for a joint venture; the appropriate design depends, among other things, on the financial and technological contributions and capabilities of participant firms.

NOTES

1. Producers of commercial airframes in 1955 included the Convair division of General Dynamics, Boeing, Douglas, and Lockheed in the United States; Vickers, Bristol, Saunders Roe, and de Havilland in Great Britain; and Breguet and Sud-Est Aviation in France; the engine producers were Bristol, Siddeley, de Havilland, and Rolls Royce in Great Britain; Westinghouse, Allison, General Electric, and Pratt & Whitney in the United States; and Dassault and SNECMA in France.
2. International joint ventures between U.S. and foreign firms are now widespread in steel, automobiles, telecommunications equipment, microelectronics, and robotics, among other industries.
3. Société National d'Etudes et de Construction de Moteurs d'Aviation.
4. John S. Stuckey, *Vertical Integration and Joint Ventures in the Aluminum Industry* (Cambridge, Mass.: Harvard University Press, 1983).
5. Karen J. Hladik, *International Joint Ventures* (Lexington, Mass.: D.C. Heath, 1985). Hladik's data do not control for the size of the subsidiaries created by U.S. manufacturing firms during this period and therefore almost certainly overstate the importance of these joint ventures within the total foreign investments of U.S. manufacturing firms.
6. John H. Dunning, *International Production and Multinational Enterprise* (London: George Allen and Unwin, 1981), p. 76. Dunning's data are drawn from a study by the United Nations Center on Transnational Corporations, which examined a limited sample of the foreign investment activities of U.S. and European firms. Dunning also noted that "Affiliates of MNEs (multinational enterprises) from those countries which are expanding their activities the fastest, viz. Japan and the industrializing countries, tend to be increasingly minority owned compared with those of U.S. origin."
7. During the 1960s joint ventures were concentrated in the chemicals; primary metals; paper; and stone, clay, and glass industries but now extend well beyond these sectors, according to Harrigan. See Kathryn R. Harrigan, "Joint Ventures and Competitive Strategy" (Working paper, Columbia University Graduate School of Business, 1984). Hladik's data indicate a considerable increase in the number of joint ventures between U.S. and foreign firms during 1975–1982, a growth trend that almost certainly has continued.

8.   See National Science Board, *University-Industry Research Relationships* (Washington, D.C.: National Science Foundation, 1982) and Dorothy Nelkin and Richard R. Nelson, "University-Industry Alliances" (Paper presented at the Conference on New Alliances and Partnerships in American Science and Engineering, National Academy of Sciences, Washington, D.C. December 5, 1985).

Precise data on the increasing reliance by U.S. firms on R&D consortia and other external sources of R&D are not yet available. Data from the National Science Board indicate, however, that industry support of university research increased from less than 3 percent of total funding in 1979 to more than 5 percent in 1984, growing at an annual rate of 10–15 percent. See National Science Board, *Science Indicators—1985* (Washington, D.C.: National Science Foundation, 1985).

9.   Hladik, *International Joint Ventures*, p. 51.

10. Seev Hirsch, "An International Trade and Investment Theory of the Firm," *Oxford Economic Papers* 28 (1976), pp. 258–69.

11. Steven H. Hymer, *The International Operations of National Firms: A Study of Direct Foreign Investment* (Cambridge, Mass.: M.I.T. Press, 1969). See also, Raymond S. Vernon, "International Investment and International Trade in the Product Cycle," *Quarterly Journal of Economics* 80 (1966), pp. 190–207; Dunning, *International Production*; David J. Teece, "Towards an Economic Theory of the Multiproduct Firm," *Journal of Economic Behavior and Organization* 3 (1982), pp. 39–63; and Alan M. Rugman, *Inside the Multinationals: The Economics of Internal Markets* (New York: Columbia University Press, 1981).

12. Steven Hymer says "Firms are by no means equal in their ability to operate in an industry. Certain firms have considerable advantages in particular activities. The possession of these advantages may cause them to have extensive international operations of one kind or another." Hymer, *International Operations*, p. 41. Hymer's argument is most relevant to foreign investment in the absence of barriers to trade. An alternative motive for direct foreign investment, of course, is the penetration of tariff barriers through the establishment of production facilities within the protected market. This factor has also been an important motivation for joint ventures between U.S. and Japanese firms in the automobile and steel industries.

13. Alfred D. Chandler, Jr., *The Visible Hand* (Cambridge, Mass.: Harvard University Press, 1977).

14. Richard E. Caves, *Multinational Enterprise and Economic Analysis* (Cambridge, England: Cambridge University Press, 1982).

15. Caves notes that " . . . as indicators of these (firm-specific) assets, economists have seized on the outlays for advertising and research and development (R&D) undertaken by firms classified to an industry. That the share

of foreign subsidiary assets in the total assets of U.S. corporations increases significantly with the importance of advertising and R&D outlays in the industry has been confirmed in many studies. . . ." Ibid., p. 9.

16.   In Oliver Williamson's terminology, a "small numbers condition" characterizes such markets: "The transactional dilemma that is posed is this: it is in the interest of each party to seek terms most favorable to him, which encourages opportunistic representations and haggling. The interests of the *system*, by contrast, are promoted if the parties can be joined in such a way as to avoid both the bargaining costs and the indirect costs (mainly maladaptation costs) which are generated in the process [emphasis in original]." Oliver E. Williamson, *Markets and Hierarchies* (New York: Free Press, 1975), p. 27.

17.   Some idea of the different corporate functions that must be brought together in the innovation process is conveyed by the estimates of the Commerce Department Panel on Invention and Innovation of the typical distribution of costs in successful product innovations. Research, advanced development, and basic invention accounted for only 7.5 percent of total costs, while engineering and product design accounted for 15 percent. Tooling and manufacturing engineering accounted for fully 50 percent, manufacturing start-up expenses accounted for 10 percent, and marketing start-up expenses comprised 17.5 percent of total costs. U.S. Department of Commerce, Panel on Invention and Innovation, *Technological Innovation: Its Environment and Management* (Washington, D.C.: U.S. Government Printing Office, 1967), p. 9.

18.   David Teece argues that "The transfer of key individuals may suffice when the knowledge to be transferred relates to the particulars of a separable routine. The individual in such cases becomes a consultant or a teacher with respect to that routine. However, only a limited range of capabilities can be transferred if a transfer activity is focused in this fashion. More often than not, the transfer of productive expertise requires the transfer of organizational as well as individual knowledge. In such cases, external transfer beyond an organization's boundary may be difficult if not impossible, since taken out of context, an individual's knowledge of a routine may be quite useless." Teece, *Towards an Economic Theory*, p. 45.

19.   See Richard R. Nelson and Sidney G. Winter, *A Behavioral Theory of Economic Change* (Cambridge, Mass.: Harvard University Press, 1982), especially chaps. 4 and 5.

20.   This form of market failure is dependent on the assumption that the transfer and absorption of technological knowledge is virtually costless, an assumption made by Kenneth Arrow in arguing that knowledge displays many of the characteristics of a classic "public good"; its use by multiple parties does not degrade its quality or efficacy. Clearly, the assumption that transfer is costless is called into question by much of the above dis-

cussion. Nonetheless, the partial revelation of a technology in the course of establishing its value within a licensing negotiation is a serious one, as the analysis of Richard Caves, Harold Crookell, and J. Peter Killing, which is discussed later, suggests. See, Kenneth J. Arrow, "Economic Welfare and the Allocation of Resources for Invention" in *The Rate and Direction of Inventive Activity* (Princeton, N.J.: Princeton University Press for the National Bureau of Economic Research, 1962); David C. Mowery, "Economic Theory and Government Technology Policy," *Policy Sciences* 16 (1983), pp. 27–43; and Richard E. Caves, Harold Crookell, and J. Peter Killing, "The Imperfect Market for Technology Licenses," *Oxford Bulletin of Economics and Statistics* 45 (1983), pp. 249–68.

21.   Eric von Hippel, "The Dominant Role of Users in the Scientific Instrument Innovation Process," *Research Policy* 5 (1976), pp. 212–39.

22.   Edwin Mansfield states that " . . . the relative importance of direct investment as a means of transferring technology seems to depend on the stage of the new product's life cycle . . . when various important petrochemicals were relatively new, direct investment was the dominant form of technology transfer, but . . . as they became mature, licensing became dominant. One reason for this sort of pattern lies in the changes over time in the relative bargaining positions of the innovating firm and the country wanting the technology. When the technology is quite new, it is quite closely held, and countries wanting the technology are under pressure to accept the firm's conditions, which often are a wholly-owned subsidiary. But as time goes on, the technology becomes more widely known, and the host country can take advantage of competition among technologically capable firms to obtain joint ventures or sometimes licenses. Eventually, the technology may become available in plants that can be acquired by the host country on a turn-key basis from independent engineering firms." Edwin Mansfield, "Technology and Technological Change," in John H. Dunning, ed., *Economic Analysis and the Multinational Enterprise* (London: Allen & Unwin, 1974), p. 164. See also, Robert B. Stobaugh, "The Neotechnology Account of International Trade: The Case of Petrochemicals," in Louis T. Wells, ed., *The Product Life Cycle and International Trade* (Boston, Mass.: Harvard Business School, 1972); Edwin Mansfield, Anthony Romeo, and Samuel Wagner, "Foreign Trade and U.S. Research and Development," *Review of Economics and Statistics* 61 (1979), pp. 49–57; and Edwin Mansfield and Anthony Romeo, "Technology Transfer to Overseas Subsidiaries of U.S.-Based Firms," *Quarterly Journal of Economics* 95 (1980), pp. 737–50.

23.   " . . . the uncertain outcomes of licensing transactions interact with the costs of writing 'complete' contracts to impel the frequent inclusion of inefficient terms in the agreements. The terms are inefficient in the sense of causing the licensing agreement to yield a smaller total cash flow to the

two parties than would an idealized contract in which the licensor and licensee select policies to maximize the cash flow from the shared technology and then divide the spoils between them. . . . The surveys of licensors and licensees reveal a high incidence of protective terms that potentially reduce cash flows while protecting the rents expected by one or the other party." Caves et al., "The Imperfect Market," p. 259.

24.   Joseph Brodley summarizes the advantages of joint ventures, defined as newly created corporate entities in which all partners hold equity shares, over mergers or market transactions as follows: "By providing for shared profits and managerial control, joint ventures tend to protect the participants from opportunism and information imbalance. The problem of valuing the respective contributions of the participants is mitigated, because they can await an actual market judgment. The temptation to exploit a favored bargaining position by threatening to withhold infusions of capital or other contributions is reduced by the need for continuous cooperation if the joint venture is to be effective. Moreover, a firm supplying capital to the joint venture can closely monitor the use of its contributed capital and thereby reduce its risk of loss. Common ownership also provides a means of spreading the costs of producing valuable information that could otherwise be protected from appropriation only by difficult-to-enforce contractual undertakings. Finally, joint ventures can effect economies of scale in research not achievable through single-firm action. Because of these advantages, joint ventures are especially likely to provide an optimal enterprise form in undertakings involving high risks, technological innovations, or high information costs." Joseph F. Brodley, "Joint Ventures and Antitrust Policy," *Harvard Law Review* 95 (1982), pp. 1528–29.

25.   See Armen A. Alchian and Harold Demsetz, "Production, Information Costs, and Economic Organization," *American Economic Review* 62 (1972), pp. 777–95; and Williamson, *Markets and Hierarchies.*

26.   There exists a close analogy, as Paul David of Stanford University has noted, between firms' incentives to form joint ventures and the economics of marriage, as analyzed by Becker. According to Becker, marriages are motivated in part by the fact that the contributions of marriage partners to household production of income and other amenities are worth more jointly than separately, reflecting differences in the market wage rates for the partners. The existence of such a wage gap provides an incentive for one partner to specialize in the production of nonmarket household amenities, while the other partner pursues wage income. The pooling of the partners' productive assets within the marriage relationship effectively allows each partner to realize a larger "income stream" of pecuniary and nonpecuniary benefits, just as the pooling of firm-specific assets within a joint venture facilitates the ability of each partner firm to reap returns to assets that would otherwise command a lower or nonexistent market

price. Gary Becker, "A Theory of Marriage," in Theodore W. Schultz, ed., *Economics of the Family* (Chicago: University of Chicago Press for the National Bureau of Economic Research, 1974), pp. 299–344.

27. Mira Wilkins, *The Emergence of Multinational Enterprise: American Business Abroad from the Colonial Era to 1914* (Cambridge, Mass.: Harvard University Press, 1970) and Wilkins, *The Maturing of Multinational Enterprise: American Business Abroad from 1914 to 1970* (Cambridge, Mass.: Harvard University Press, 1974).

28. Raymond S. Vernon, *Sovereignty at Bay* (New York: Basic Books, 1971).

29. John Dunning and John Cantwell make a similar point in arguing that multinational firms increasingly rely on their ability to coordinate productive activities and transfer technology among widely separated areas rather than on their ownership of a specific asset as a source of competitive advantage. See John H. Dunning and John A. Cantwell, "The Changing Role of Multinational Enterprises in the International Creation, Transfer and Diffusion of Technology" (Paper presented at the International Conference on the Diffusion of Innovations, Venice, Italy, March 1986).

30. Raymond Vernon presents similar arguments on the changing international economic environment. See Raymond Vernon, "The Product Cycle Hypothesis in a New International Environment," *Oxford Bulletin of Economics and Statistics* 41 (1979), pp. 255–67.

31. Kent Jones notes the convergence among the industrialized nations in the share of GNP devoted to R&D, as well as a less dramatic convergence in the proportion of R&D personnel in these countries' labor forces. Harry Bowen also discusses the convergence in the ratio of capital to skilled labor during 1963–1975. K. Jones, "The Economic Implications of Restricting Trade in High-Technology Goods" (Presented at the National Science Foundation workshop, Economic Implications of Restrictions to Trade in High-Technology Goods, October 3, 1984), and Harry Bowen, "Changes in the International Distribution of Resources and Their Impact on U.S. Comparative Advantage," *Review of Economics and Statistics* 65 (1983), pp. 402–14.

32. Recent efforts by a number of European governments to sell off publicly owned enterprises, such as the British government's divestiture of a portion of British Aerospace and British Telecom, as well as recent moves by the Japanese, Italian, Dutch, and German governments to sell their state-owned airlines, may prefigure a significant change in the character of some major foreign markets. This trend is a very modest ripple at present, however, and will not dissolve the informal ties and sources of financial support and pressure through which governments can exert considerable influence on the purchase decisions of "privatized" corporations.

33. Raymond Vernon and Charles P. Kindleberger suggest that the bargaining power of national governments vis-à-vis multinational firms has in fact

been strengthened over time, largely because technological diffusion has undercut the market power exercised by multinational firms with respect to their technological assets; governments increasingly are able to exploit competition among multinational firms for access to their markets, enhancing these governments' bargaining power. See Raymond Vernon, *Sovereignty at Bay*; and Charles P. Kindleberger, *American Business Abroad: Six Lectures on Direct Investment* (New Haven, Conn.: Yale University Press, 1969).

Joseph Grieco provides an interesting case study of bargaining over such assets in his analysis of the Indian computer industry and IBM. See Joseph M. Grieco, *Between Dependency and Autonomy: India's Experience with the International Computer Industry* (Berkeley: University of California Press, 1984).

34. Douglas J. Ginsburg, *Antitrust, Uncertainty, and Innovation* (Washington, D.C.: National Research Council, 1980); and National Research Council, *International Competition in Advanced Technology: Decisions for America* (Washington, D.C.: National Research Council, 1983).

35. Daniel M. Crane, "Joint Research and Development Ventures and the Antitrust Laws," *Harvard Journal on Legislation* 21 (1984), pp. 405–58.

36. Richard R. Nelson, *High-Technology Policies: A Five-Nation Comparison* (Washington, D.C.: American Enterprise Institute, 1984), p. 84.

37. See Chandler, *The Visible Hand.*

38. Michael Piore and Charles Sabel provide a detailed discussion of some implications of this trend. See M.J. Piore and C.F. Sabel, *The Second Industrial Divide* (New York: Basic Books, 1984).

39. Robert Reich and Eric Mankin provide an extreme statement of the potential dangers to U.S. industrial competitiveness created by joint ventures with Japanese firms. R.B. Reich and E.D. Mankin, "Joint Ventures with Japan Give Away Our Future," *Harvard Business Review*, March/April 1986.

2 MARKET STRUCTURE AND TECHNOLOGY IN THE U.S. COMMERCIAL AIRCRAFT INDUSTRY

THE ECONOMIC AND TECHNOLOGICAL SIGNIFICANCE OF THE U.S. COMMERCIAL AIRCRAFT INDUSTRY

The U.S. commercial aircraft industry has been both innovative and internationally competitive throughout the postwar period.[1] Productivity growth in U.S. commercial air transportation, the primary industrial beneficiary of innovation in commercial aircraft and engines, has been equaled or surpassed only by that of telecommunications services.[2] In 1983 total sales of the aerospace industry (including missiles and spacecraft in addition to aircraft) amounted to nearly $76 billion ($28 billion in 1972 dollars), more than 2 percent of the gross national product. Within this total, sales of military and civilian aircraft, engines, and parts were valued at $41.2 billion ($15.2 billion in 1972 dollars).[3] The contribution of aircraft to U.S. foreign trade in 1982 was also important: exports of aircraft, engines, and parts equaled $15.1 billion ($7 billion in 1972 dollars), the largest single category of manufactured exports.

Research and Development

The aircraft industry is a major investor in research and development. R&D expenditures for commercial and military aircraft (nearly 74 percent of which were financed by federal funds in 1983) amounted

31

to 14 percent of the value of 1983 shipments, a level exceeded only by the electronics industry. The aircraft industry also has important links, through its demand for components and parts, with other high-technology sectors.[4] The link between aircraft and electronics is the most obvious (for example, avionics and computer-aided design and manufacturing), but the aircraft industry also contributes to the support of sophisticated materials development and fabrication industries. Indeed, a primary reason for the rapid technological progress in this industry is its ability to draw on and benefit from innovations in other high-technology industries.

An airframe or engine design integrates a number of technologies and complex subsystems, including electronic, hydraulic, and materials technologies. The interaction of these individually complex systems or components is crucial to performance yet extremely difficult to predict, even with the assistance of computer-aided design and simulation technologies. Considerable uncertainty pervades the development of a new airframe or engine design, rendering the systems integration and design phases critical to the introduction of a successful new product. Product development in aircraft and engines is a design-intensive process; design activities consume a large share of the total costs and time in a development project.[5] Continuous changes in the market and technology also contribute to the lengthy duration of the design phase of aircraft development projects. Firms produce dozens of "paper airplanes" before deciding to launch the development of a specific design, in an effort to accommodate the heterogeneous requirements of airline customers. John Steiner notes

> . . . the excruciating pain of trying to achieve a common denominator among varying airline requirements. All commercial programs go through a similar process and the engineers must work with a great many airlines, not just the few who are most likely to become launch customers.[6]

In the development of the Boeing 727, this process consumed two and one-half years and produced at least nine complete aircraft designs. More recently, the "design definition" phase of the development of the Boeing 767 lasted nearly six years.[7] The design phase of new product development is an area in which U.S. aircraft and engine firms currently possess considerable advantages over all but a few foreign competitors, such as British Aerospace and Aerospatiale of France. Although the design phase may be lengthy, once the decision is made to introduce an airframe or engine, it must be brought to market rapidly. U.S. producers historically have been able to move from design commitment to production more rapidly than European firms.[8] Design and design management capabilities, as well as the ability to manage the transition from design to production, are among the most important factors in commercial success and failure in this industry.

A specific aircraft design typically is produced for a long time. The Boeing 727 was produced for twenty years. The manufacture of the DC–8 began in 1957 and ended only in 1972, a termination date that was premature in the view of many industry observers. The typical aircraft design often undergoes major modifications, however—the fuselage may be stretched, for example, to accommodate additional passengers. The design of an aircraft with a high potential for stretching requires, among other things, the development of wing designs that can accommodate significant increases in aircraft payload or new engines without major modifications or redesign. This feat may involve the substitution of new materials, such as composites or aluminum-lithium alloys, into an existing wing design. Production facilities also must be designed to accommodate variations in aircraft fuselage length.

The economic significance of stretching an airframe design is difficult to overstate. Stretching amortizes the high fixed costs of design and development over additional sales in a new market segment (the incremental costs of stretching an airframe rarely exceed 25 percent of the development costs) and allows the significant cost reductions from movement down the production learning curve to be applied to an essentially new aircraft. Design decisions thus have major ramifications for the success of the initial model of an aircraft and affect the ease with which the design can be modified through stretching.[9]

Incremental modifications that do not involve stretching the fuselage or retrofitting an airframe with new engines also are made throughout the life of an aircraft or engine design, relying heavily on information gained from close monitoring of operating experience after the introduction of a product. The importance of this monitoring function, as well as worldwide spare parts supplies and field service, means that a global marketing and product support organization is critical to the commercial success of a new aircraft design. Product support networks are important corporate assets, in which U.S. firms in the commercial aircraft industry typically lead prospective entrants (again, exceptions are Airbus Industrie, which has invested heavily in the development of its product support network, and the established British producers of engines and aircraft).

The requirement for product support and marketing networks is a major barrier to entry into the aircraft industry. Moreover, the high fixed costs of supporting such a network are a strong incentive for producers to market a number of different aircraft or engine models. The ability to supply a "full line," covering all segments of the aircraft or engine market for a given customer class (for example, commercial airlines) enables producers to utilize their marketing network fully. Production of a full line may also improve the market prospects for any single product within the product family. Standardization by an airline around the products of a single producer of airframes or engines can lower maintenance and training costs as well as reduce spare parts inventories.[10] The ability of an aircraft or engine producer to provide a wide range of products thus assumes considerable commercial importance.[11]

Another source of entry barriers is the high cost of new product development within the aircraft industry. Development costs have risen dramatically, increasing (in constant dollars) at an average annual rate of nearly 20 percent from 1930 to 1970, well ahead of the annual rate of growth in aircraft weight of 8.5 percent. Development of the Douglas DC–3 in the 1930s cost roughly $3 million.[12] The DC–8, introduced in 1958, cost nearly $112 million. The Boeing 747, production of which began in the early 1970s, cost $1 billion. More recently, development of the Boeing 767 is estimated to have cost nearly $1.5 billion, and estimates of the development costs for a 150-seat transport range up to and beyond $2.5 billion.[13] The V2500, a high-bypass engine intended for the 150-seat aircraft that is discussed in greater detail later, is expected to require $1.5 billion for development. The growth of development costs means that an increasing proportion of the costs of introducing a new aircraft are incurred during the phase of greatest uncertainty concerning market prospects and technical feasibility.

Partly in response to these dramatic increases in development costs, subcontracting of aircraft production has grown substantially in recent years. According to John Rae, subcontracting in the 1930s "constituted less than 10 percent of the industry's operations."[14] By the mid-1950s, however, 30 to 40 percent of the assembly work for the turboprop Lockheed Electra was subcontracted. With the introduction of the Boeing 747, six major subcontractors accounted for 70 percent of the assembly of the aircraft, according to Hochmuth. Subcontracting fills an important risk-sharing role in the aircraft industry, as in the Boeing 767 and 747 projects, where subcontractors bore a substantial portion of the commercial risk (see chapter 3). Many of the current multinational joint ventures in this industry are motivated by the desire of U.S. firms to reduce the financial risks of new product development.

The sheer magnitude of fixed costs is best appreciated by comparison with total stockholders' equity in a firm such as Boeing which in 1984, were roughly $2.7 billion. These high fixed costs result in a falling short-run average cost curve. Two other factors govern costs in this industry. The first is the small production volume of most aircraft. Since the introduction of the commercial jet transport in the early 1950s, only *four aircraft designs* (the DC-9/MD-80, Boeing 707, 727, and 737) *out of twenty-three produced have sold more than 600 units.* Since the total production history for a specific aircraft design may extend over ten to twenty years, the aircraft industry obviously has low "throughput" (the volume of production in a given period). While average annual production rates typically are low, they are also subject to wide fluctuations—the peak production rate may be as much as eight times that of the trough output rate.

Cost reduction as a function of cumulative output is another important aspect of cost behavior in this industry—the well-known learning curve, first documented in the production of airframes in World War II.[15] Cost reduction over the course of a given aircraft's production history is dramatic—most estimates suggest that a doubling of output reduces unit costs by as much as 20 percent. Rachel McCulloch has noted that the combination of dynamic cost reductions and high fixed costs creates considerable incentives for firms to price below average unit costs in the early production history of an aircraft or engine, since large sales and production volume reduce costs. In addition to such "predatory pricing," of course, these important learning effects mean that government support for or protection of a domestic market can aid the international competitiveness of domestic firms serving that market, allowing them to move down their learning curves more rapidly. By protecting domestic markets, thereby allowing local firms to reduce their costs significantly through production learning effects, government policies supporting domestic demand eventually may stimulate exports, as Paul Krugman has argued.[16]

INDUSTRY STRUCTURE

The commercial aircraft industry is in fact two industries, airframes and engines. Virtually without exception, firms active in one industry are not active in the other. While it is impossible to design airframes without a sophisticated understanding of propulsion technology, and vice versa, the producer structure and technology characteristic of these two sectors of the commercial aircraft industry display some interesting similarities and contrasts.

Both the airframe and the jet engine industries during the past two decades have witnessed a gradual reduction in the number of firms in the commercial market. The development of the first high-bypass ratio engines, producing 45–55,000 pounds of thrust for the Boeing 747, the DC-10, and the L-1011 inaugurated a bruising competition among Pratt & Whitney, General Electric, and Rolls Royce that left Rolls Royce bankrupt and nationalized and simultaneously brought Rolls's primary customer for its new engine, Lockheed, to the brink of bankruptcy. Since that period, three segments have developed within the commercial engine market: 20–27,000 pounds of thrust, 30–40,000 pounds, and 50–60,000 pounds, respectively powering the Boeing 737-300 and DC-9/MD-80; the Boeing 757; and the Boeing 767 and 747 and Airbus A300–600 and A310. In all three market segments, new high-bypass ratio engines have been or are being developed.[17]

Following its development for military applications in Great Britain and Germany, the jet engine was developed for the U.S. military by General Electric during and after World War II. General Electric, Westinghouse, and the Allison division of General Motors all had substantial development programs under way in 1945; they were joined by Pratt & Whitney shortly thereafter. By the mid-1960s, however, the only significant U.S. producers of jet engines were General Electric and Pratt & Whitney. The commercial jet engine market was dominated by Pratt & Whitney during the 1960s and early 1970s, based on the firm's production of the JT8 and JT9 series of engines, as well as its close working relationship with Boeing. The firm's position within the engine market has eroded during the past decade, as both General Electric and Rolls Royce have increased their market share. Barry Bluestone *et al.* (1981, p. 62) estimated that Pratt & Whitney's share of large commercial engine orders in 1966 exceeded 90 percent, while General Electric accounted for only 1.7 percent. By 1978, according to these authors, the General Electric share of total orders had climbed to 24.6 percent, while Pratt & Whitney's share had declined to 62.7 percent.[18]

Selective withdrawal during the 1970s by each of the three engine producers from one or more market segments until recently raised the possibility that no one segment of the engine market would have more than two producers. This withdrawal frequently took the form of joint ventures between two of the three firms, as in the V2500 venture between Rolls Royce and the Pratt & Whitney division of United Technologies. Recent agreement between General Electric and Rolls Royce to collaborate on the production of large engines, however, has collapsed. At present, General Electric, Rolls Royce, and Pratt & Whitney are the major producers in the upper end of the engine market (the JT9D and PW4000 for Pratt & Whitney, the RB211-524 for Rolls Royce, and the CF6-80 for General Electric), while Pratt & Whitney and Rolls Royce compete for the middle segment with the PW2037 and the RB211-535. CFM International, the General Electric-SNECMA joint venture, is in the lower end of the engine market, competing against the consortium teaming Pratt & Whitney with Rolls Royce (the V2500, managed by International Aero Engines) and derivatives of Pratt & Whitney's older engine, the JT8D. While the number of firms active in each segment has declined, competition in the engine market has been enhanced by the fact that airframes now are designed to accommodate several different engine types.

Throughout the recent history of the commercial aircraft industry, the development of new aircraft has been paced primarily by the development of new engines. Moreover, a critical element in the timing of airframe and engine development projects is the development of an all-new engine, which typically requires one more year than does airframe development. During the 1970s, repeated forays by airframe producers into new product development discussions were stymied by the lack of a new engine. Conversely, the early years of the CFM56 engine program (see chapter 3) were plagued by the lack of an airframe on which to employ the engines. The desire of airframe manufacturers and airline customers for an entirely new engine for new airframes is, of course, tempered by the knowledge that an all-new engine design (for example, the JT9D, developed concurrently with the 747)[19] may experience a difficult service introduction, during which reliability is low and maintenance expense high.

Engine production technology also differs somewhat from that of airframes by virtue of the fact that production volume typically is much greater for engines. Given that all large commercial transports have multiple engines and most are sold with one extra engine as a spare, this difference in production volume is hardly surprising. Among other things, however, it means that the learning-curve and other cost penalties resulting from the establishment of multiple production lines often are less severe for engines than for airframes. While economies of scale due to reductions in variable production costs may be less central in engine production, however, the fixed costs of testing and design for an engine remain very large and act as a barrier to entry into engine development and production. Another area of contrast between airframes and engines is the fact that the profitability of an engine sale is influenced much more by the spare parts sales that follow the initial transaction. Indeed, most observers estimate that all of the parts in a given engine are replaced after ten to fifteen years. As a result, engine producers operate both as prime contractors, undertaking large-scale development and integration projects, and as vendors of spare parts and assemblies.

Engine design, production, and marketing practices are similar to those for airframes. In both airframes and engines, the upper market segment (for example, the Boeing 747, the CF6-80, the JT9D, and the PW4000) is the most profitable. Airframe manufacturers serving this market segment profit because of the absence of competition, engine producers because of the huge spare parts requirements. Engines also share with airframes a considerable capacity for stretching; stretching, however, may produce reductions in performance quality. Variations in compressor, turbine, and inlet temperatures, achieved through incremental design changes and the application of new materials, may enable a single basic engine design, such as the Rolls Royce RB211, to be employed in thrust classes from 38,000–58,000 pounds. Finally, both airframes and engines require extensive product support networks.

During the postwar period, the jet engine came to dominate the large commercial transport market, causing substantial shifts in the market shares of both airframe and engine firms. The adoption of jet engine and electronics technologies by the commercial aircraft manufacturers also contributed significantly to the rise in development costs for new commercial aircraft.

A number of airframe producers have left the industry. Douglas, Lockheed, Convair (then known as Consolidated Vultee), and Martin dominated the commercial airframe market during the heyday of the four-engine propeller transport. After 1958, however, when Boeing introduced the 707 and Douglas followed with the DC-8, Lockheed, Martin, and Convair (by this time a division of General Dynamics, and the producer of the CV-880 and CV-990) all went into eclipse, out of which only Lockheed emerged briefly in the 1970s as the producer of the L-1011. Boeing has come to dominate the commercial aircraft market during the past twenty years as thoroughly as Douglas dominated the commercial market of the 1930s. By 1983, nearly 55 percent of all commercial jet aircraft produced since 1952 had been manufactured by Boeing. The only other major U.S. producer of large commercial aircraft is McDonnell Douglas, which now manufactures one aircraft design (the MD-80 and its various derivatives), although the launch of the MD-11, a derivative of the DC-10, may be announced soon.

Despite high levels of producer concentration, both the engine and airframe industries have been intensely competitive throughout the postwar period. High fixed costs and the small number of major customers make the market resemble a bilateral oligopoly or even a bilateral monopoly. Competition among airframe producers has been responsible for several near failures of major firms.

In 1966 the Douglas Aircraft Corporation approached bankruptcy as a result of poor financial management and overly energetic sales efforts for the DC-9. Despite an order backlog of $2.3 billion, Douglas was forced to merge with McDonnell Aircraft in 1967, with the acquiescence of the Department of Justice and the aid of a federally guaranteed loan of $75 million. Sales competition between the McDonnell Douglas DC-10 and the Lockheed L-1011, the bankruptcy of Rolls-Royce (sole engine supplier for the L-1011), and the C-5A contract nearly bankrupted the Lockheed Aircraft Corporation. Collapse of Lockheed was averted in 1971 only by a federal loan guarantee of $250 million. The Boeing Company also came close to financial catastrophe during the late 1960s and early 1970s because of its efforts simultaneously to sustain high rates of production of the 707 and 727, to develop the supersonic transport (SST) under a federal contract, and to develop the first wide body passenger jet, the 747. The cancellation of the SST and the introduction of the 747 were followed by massive layoffs.

Bolstered by a somewhat more stable flow of military and spare parts orders, the major U.S. engine producers have not encountered comparable turbulence during the postwar period. Competition for the initial order for the Lockheed L-1011 engines, however, contributed to the eventual collapse of the winner of the order, Rolls Royce. Both the commercial aircraft and engine industries also contain a large population of vendor and subcontractor firms engaged in the production of assemblies and components for the much smaller group of major contractors. This group of supplier firms in the United States includes as many as 15,000 firms, many of which produce components for both military and civilian aircraft. Many of these firms are now exposed to greater competition from foreign producers as a result of international joint ventures in commercial aircraft and foreign coproduction and offset programs in military aircraft.

SOURCES OF TECHNICAL CHANGE

The impressive record of innovation exhibited by the commercial aircraft industry reflects the industry's status as a beneficiary of at least three important external sources of innovation or research support: innovations in other industries, such as metallurgy or electronics; government-supported research in civil aviation; and military procurement and research support.[20] Figure 2–1 displays trends between 1945 and 1982 in research and development investment in both commercial and military aircraft by the U.S. military, federal civil aeronautics research programs (including the Atomic Energy Commission, Federal Aviation Administration, NACA, and NASA), and industry. The R&D data are in 1972 dollars.[21] Industry-financed R&D investment excludes independent R&D (IR&D) overhead allowances on federal procurement contracts.

Total R&D expenditures from all sources (industry and the federal government) rose by more than 224 percent in real terms from 1945 to 1982, from $963 million in 1945 to roughly $3.1 billion in 1982. The vast majority of this increase took place in the decade immediately following World War II, with the onset of cold war tensions and rearmament during the late 1940s and early 1950s. In fact,

Figure 2-1. Annual R&D Investment in Aircraft, 1945–1982 (*in millions of 1972 dollars*).

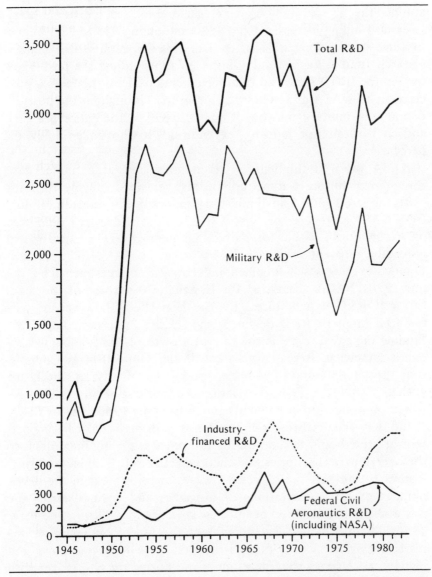

Note: R&D figures for 1945–69 are taken from the study by Booz, Allen and Hamilton Applied Research for the NASA-Department of Transportation study (1971), converted into 1972 dollars. Post-1969 R&D data were taken from *Aerospace Facts and Figures*, as well as the National Science Foundation's product field R&D data, and modified to account for independent R&D.

Source: Mowery, "Federal Funding of R&D in Transportation."

the amount invested in R&D within the U.S. aircraft industry from all sources has been essentially unchanged (ignoring fluctuations around the $3–3.2 billion mark) since the early 1950s. Military research funding increased from $820 million in 1945 to $2.1 billion in 1982—if anything, this latter figure may overstate total military research funding, as a result of the effort to adjust the post–1969 figures for IR&D overhead reimbursements paid by the federal government to NASA and military contractors. Throughout the postwar period, the military portion of annual R&D by the entire (military and civilian) aircraft industry expenditures has not fallen below 65 percent.[22]

NASA research funding for aeronautics grew at a modest rate throughout the postwar period, and has remained roughly constant since the late 1960s. The diminishing importance of research funding from NASA's predecessor, NACA (the National Advisory Committee on Aeronautics), within total aircraft industry R&D investment also is readily apparent in Figure 2-1. Whereas in 1945 NACA research support exceeded self-financed industry R&D investment, by the mid-1950s NACA accounted for less than 20 percent of industry-financed R&D expenditures. By the late 1970s, however, as self-financed industry R&D declined, the relative importance of NASA funding increased, even as the rate of growth of this funding was reduced somewhat. Research programs in the Atomic Energy Commission supported work on nuclear propulsion of aircraft and space vehicles, while the Federal Aviation Administration invested in research on navigation instruments and, during the 1960s, on the SST.

Industry-financed research expenditures display an oscillating pattern of growth and decline during the postwar period, in contrast to the overall pattern of privately financed R&D in U.S. manufacturing. Figure 2-1 reveals the successive waves of investment in the development of three generations of airframes and engines during the postwar period. R&D expenditures grew rapidly during the early 1950s, the period of development of the first commercial jet aircraft; during the late 1960s, as the first wide-body transports and high-bypass engines were developed; and during the late 1970s, with the development of the most recent generation of aircraft equipped with high-bypass engines in a smaller thrust class.

The cumulative R&D investment in aircraft from all sources between 1945 and 1982 amounts to nearly $104 billion in 1972 dollars. Of this total, almost 75 percent, $77 billion, was provided by military sources. Industry-financed R&D during the period amounted to $17.4 billion, roughly 15 percent of the total. Federal nonmilitary funding of research in this industry was a small portion of the total investment of federal funds, totaling some $9 billion. This enormous public investment clearly was not directed solely toward the support of technological innovation in commercial aircraft; national security considerations motivated the majority of these massive expenditures. Nonetheless, federal investments in military aircraft technology have had a significant impact on the course of innovation in commercial aircraft.

FEDERAL SUPPORT FOR CIVILIAN AIRCRAFT RESEARCH

The commercial aircraft industry is unique among U.S. manufacturing industries in that a governmental research organization (first the National Advisory Committee on Aeronautics, NACA, and subsequently the National Aeronautics and Space Administration, NASA), has long existed to carry out and support aeronautics and propulsion research. Indeed, NACA and NASA have been cited as examples of successful federal support for research on generic technologies with the potential for widespread application within a given industry.[23] Prior to World War II, however, NACA carried out little research that could be described as basic. The committee primarily provided research infrastructure, such as extensive experimental design data and testing facilities, for the aircraft industry.[24] The division of labor in aeronautical research changed somewhat in the aftermath of World War II. The major aircraft producers had built up substantial in-house research facilities. NACA's infrastructure was less critical, although the agency's research continued to yield important advances in fundamental design principles. Military support of research and development occupied a more important role than had been true in the pre-1940 period.

Despite their diminished importance after World War II, NACA and NASA played an important strategic role in supporting research within the aircraft industry. NASA-funded research data and results were made widely available within the industry. In addition, NASA projects frequently involved two or more competing firms, encouraging, to a limited extent, the pooling of research efforts and results.[25] NACA also sponsored the development of a liberal system of cross-licensing of patents, disbanded in 1975 because of the objections of the Antitrust Division of the Justice Department. This cross-licensing system aided in the development of a widely shared technology base within the U.S. commercial aircraft industry.[26]

MILITARY-SPONSORED RESEARCH

Another important source of support for commercial aircraft innovation is military-supported research and military procurement. Research supported by the armed services yielded indirect but important technological spillovers to the commercial aircraft industry, most notably in aircraft engines. From the Pratt & Whitney Wasp of 1925 to the high-bypass ratio engines of the 1970s, commercial aircraft engine development has benefited from, and frequently has followed, the demands of military procurement and military support of research. Most recently, military-supported research on power plants for the military C-5A transport led to the development of the high-bypass engines that power the latest generation of commercial transports.

Military-civilian technological spillovers have been most important in aircraft propulsion technologies, but commercial aircraft have also benefited from military-sponsored research and procurement in airframes. The importance of technological spillovers from military to civilian applications in aircraft design and development has fluctuated over time, since different military aircraft types yield different amounts of commercially applicable technology. Military procurement or development programs in military transports or strategic bombers, however, typically have produced some significant military-civilian spillovers. In the aftermath of World War II, the development of jet-powered strategic bombers and tankers allowed airframe makers to apply knowledge gained in military projects to commercial aircraft design, tooling, and production. Both the Boeing 707 and the firm's military tanker (the KC-135), for example, drew on a single prototype design. Although the design of the military and commercial versions of this prototype diverged significantly, a comparison of the development costs for the 707 with those for the

DC-8 suggests that some tooling and development costs were shared by the military and commercial Boeing aircraft:

> Douglas lost $109 million in the two years 1959 and 1960, having written off $298 million for development costs and production losses up to the end of 1960. Boeing did not suffer so badly. They wrote off $165 million on the 707 by then; some of the development cost may have been carried by the tanker program, which also provided a few of the tools on which the airliner was built.[27]

The revenues from military sales and development contracts also sustained major producers of commercial aircraft and engines through lean periods in the commercial market. Military sales have remained important during the postwar period for several commercial airframe producers, providing a source of profits with which to support commercial gambles. In addition, the importance of the major aircraft and engine producers to the U.S. defense industrial base has motivated occasional federal intervention to prevent the financial collapse of these firms.[28]

THE DEMAND FOR INNOVATION:
THE INFLUENCE OF GOVERNMENT

Through the 1960s, much of the technical development in civilian transports consisted of the commercial application of technical knowledge developed at government expense, either through NACA/NASA or military research programs. While government research funding increased the supply of potential innovations, federal policies also affected the demand for innovation by the commercial aircraft industry. Civil Aeronautics Board regulation from 1938 to 1978 supported the rapid adoption of innovations in commercial aircraft. Indeed, U.S. government policy toward the commercial aircraft industry during the postwar period is unique in its impact on both the supply of technical knowledge and the demand for application of this knowledge in innovation within the civilian sector.

Congressional dissatisfaction with passenger safety and regulatory policy led to the establishment of the Civil Aeronautics Board in 1938.[29] From 1938 to 1978 the CAB effectively controlled airline pricing policies, as well as entry into or exit from the U.S. domestic air transportation industry. These powers were used to prevent entry into scheduled trunkline air transportation and to prevent price competition. The CAB regulatory environment gave rise to a high level of service quality competition, which increased the demand by airlines for innovative aircraft designs. Service quality competition supported rapid adoption of new aircraft designs by the major carriers in the belief that rapid introduction of state-of-the-art aircraft was an effective marketing strategy in the absence of price competition. Jordan's study compared California's intrastate air carriers (not regulated by the CAB and subject to price competition as well as to easier entry) with the interstate carriers in the rate of adoption of cabin pressurization and jet aircraft:

> The trunk carriers were consistently the first to introduce each innovation. In fact, they introduced all but two of the over 40 aircraft types operated by all three carrier groups between 1946 and 1965. In addition, they adopted these innovations rapidly and extensively. The local carriers, on the other hand, were slow to introduce the two innovations and their rates of adoption were low.[30]

The drive to be first with a new design meant that major airlines were willing to make early purchase commitments to airframe manufacturers in order to obtain rapid delivery. The importance of an early position in the delivery queue for a new aircraft design also gave considerable leverage to aircraft producers in extracting advance orders from the airlines, effectively defraying a portion of the costs of new aircraft development with advance customer payments. By encouraging a rapid pace of innovation and adoption within the commercial aircraft and air transportation industries, CAB regulation reduced somewhat the financial risks faced by aircraft manufacturers.

This rapid rate of innovation, however, and the associated impressive productivity growth of U.S. domestic air transportation, came at a considerable cost. Consumer welfare was impaired by the lack of variety in service quality and price, as government regulation restricted the range within which consumers were free to trade off price against quality. In 1977 the U.S. General Accounting Office, employing a model based on Keeler (1972), concluded that an efficient, deregulated air transportation system would have cost consumers $1.4–1.8 billion less (in nominal dollars) during each year of the 1969–1974 period.[31] Moreover, in view of the high probability that lower fares would lead to more passenger traffic, the GAO calculation almost certainly understated the total annual costs. In other words, a cost equal to nearly two-thirds of the total annual R&D investment in the commercial and military aircraft industry (in 1970, slightly more than $3 billion in nominal dollars) was borne by the traveling public as a cost for the rapid diffusion of commercial aircraft innovations.[32]

Although this policy structure was not consciously designed to support innovation, the combination of public financial support for innovation and regulatory support for the embodiment of innovation in new aircraft designs had a substantial effect on the U.S. aircraft industry during the postwar period. By supporting U.S. domestic demand for long-haul commercial aircraft, CAB regulation enabled U.S. producers to gain experience in the production and design of aircraft with both foreign and domestic markets. In view of the great importance of learning effects in the design and the production of commercial aircraft, CAB support for domestic market demand supported U.S. aircraft exports, enabling U.S. firms to acquire production experience and lower their costs in the fashion outlined by Krugman.[33] Federal support for research and for the diffusion and adoption of innovations within the domestic commercial aircraft market thus enhanced the international competitiveness of this industry, and expanded its export markets.[34] The importance of this policy structure for international competitiveness of the aircraft industry may be inferred from the fact that commercial aircraft and engines are the largest single class of U.S.-manufactured exports. Although the costs of this policy structure to both taxpayers and air travelers were high, and its effects almost certainly were unintended, federal policy in the commercial aircraft industry during much of the postwar period bears a remarkable resemblance to Japanese industrial policy in such export industries as electronics.

THE 1970s AND 1980s
CHANGES IN THE DOMESTIC POLICY
AND TECHNOLOGICAL ENVIRONMENT

As the beneficiary of a unique federal policy structure, the aircraft industry was severely affected by three changes in the domestic environment during and after the 1960s: the deregulation of domestic air transportation in 1978; a decline in the commonality of military and civilian aircraft technology; and some erosion in the aeronautics research and technology budget within NASA. Combined with steady growth in development costs, these changes made market demand more uncertain and increased the financial risks borne by aircraft and engine producers.

Deregulation of domestic air transport has reduced the importance of service quality competition in the U.S. airline industry. As a result, U.S. airlines are now less eager to adopt new aircraft without significant improvements in seat-mile operating costs. Moreover, as fuel prices have become more stable or declined, significant improvements in the operating costs of new aircraft and engines have become more difficult to obtain.

The effect of deregulation on the structure of the airline industry has also been disruptive. As price competition was unleashed within the industry and entry restrictions were liberalized, established carriers faced severe competition from new entrants with far lower operating costs. The period of "shakeout" appears to have ended, and most U.S. airlines now are operating profitably. Nonetheless, aircraft producers face a market that is no longer supported by regulation, populated by airlines that in some cases are financially weaker and far more reluctant to commit funds to major product development programs. The market for large commercial aircraft is more uncertain, and the ability of producers to share this risk with major customers has been reduced.

Increasing divergence between civilian and military aircraft technologies and the absence of major defense programs in large transports since the late 1960s have reduced the amount and significance of military-civilian technological spillover. These two factors are obviously related—a primary reason for the divergence of military and civilian materials and engine requirements, for example, is that fighter aircraft do not require the same long-term durability or operating efficiency as civilian and military transports. The magnitude of the shift in the relationship between military and civilian technological developments is striking. In many cases, technological spillovers now flow from civilian to military applications. Whereas the Boeing 707 and the military KC-135 tanker were developed from a common prototype, the current military tanker design (the KC-10) is a derivative of the DC-10, originally designed for commercial passenger transportation. Similarly, as the National Academy of Engineering study of the U.S. aircraft industry pointed out, "Commercial engines gain service experience 10 to 15 times faster than military

engines, even military transport engines. . . . some of the improvements in the CF6 turbofan engine (derived from the TF39 used in
DOD's large C5A cargo airplane), developed during commercial service, are being incorporated in later versions of the TF39."[35]

Spillovers from military to civilian applications remain significant
in the areas of propulsion, avionics, and flight control systems, but
they have become less important. In addition, according to the NAE
panel, " . . . for the last 15 years DOD has tended to define its interests more narrowly, to fund less generic research, and to insist on a
specific demonstrable relevance to present or proposed weapons systems for all DOD-sponsored R&D. For all but advanced supersonic
aircraft or highly specialized mission requirements, DOD is largely
prepared to buy off-the-shelf engine technology."[36] Both aircraft
and engine producers now must rely more heavily on self-financed
research and development for technological advances. In view of the
risks of innovation in the aircraft market, the assumption of a greater
share of the financial burden of development considerably increases
the risks of operating within this industry.

While the indirect contribution of military R&D and procurement
to the development of civilian aircraft technology has been reduced
in recent years, limited evidence also suggests that NASA's support
of aeronautics research may have declined during the 1970s and
1980s. Aeronautics research was a much less important component
of NASA's mission by comparison with its predecessor agency. As
Figure 2–2 shows, the transformation of NACA into NASA in 1958
considerably reduced the agency's commitment of engineering and
scientific manpower to aeronautics R&D. A Senate study noted in
1966 that "Space budget demands have probably hampered what
might have been expected to be a normal growth of the level of effort
in aeronautics within the agency . . ."[37] In the aftermath of the
Apollo program, as NASA's operating budget increasingly was hos-
tage to the fortunes of the space shuttle, budgetary pressures on
aeronautics research programs mounted. Appropriations for aeronautics research continued to grow during the 1970s, but at a lower
rate than had been true of the 1960s. Moreover, modest growth in
real spending for NASA aeronautics programs during the 1970s and
1980s masks an apparent decline in the R&D component of NASA's
aeronautics research program.[38] The growth in NASA's overall aeronautics R&D expenditures revealed in Figure 2–1 thus includes increases in the costs of staff, management, and construction, at the

Figure 2-2. NACA/NASA Aeronautics Manpower History, 1920–1980.

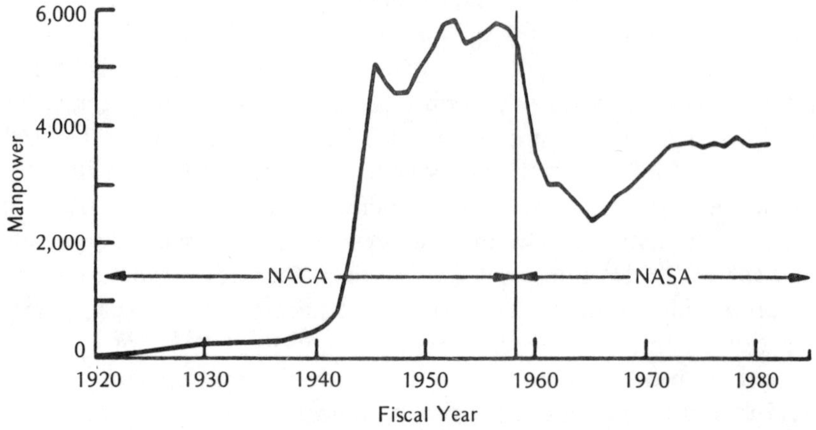

Source: *NASA's Role in Aeronautics: A Workshop*, Volume I Summary (Washington, D.C.: National Academy Press, 1981), p. 41. Reprinted from National Academy of Engineering, "Competitive Status," figure 5-13, p. 135.

expense of research programs. An obvious result of this reduction in research funding and manpower is an increase in the share of the costs of R&D that private firms must assume.

THE RISE OF A GLOBAL MARKET

The U.S. aircraft industry during the 1970s and 1980s was also affected by developments in the world market. One of the most important was the decline in the rate of growth of demand for commercial air travel in the United States, relative to the rest of the world (notably, the industrializing nations of East Asia). Between 1950 and 1970, U.S. airlines purchased 67 percent of the aircraft produced by U.S. firms, and the United States accounted for 57 percent of total world revenue passenger miles flown in 1971. During the 1970s, however, reflecting the operation of demographic factors, as well as slower U.S. economic growth, air travel in the United States grew at an annual rate of 5 percent, well below the average of 9 percent in other regions. Between 1977 and 1982, only 40 percent of all orders for new commercial aircraft were placed by U.S. carriers.

The U.S. market for commercial aircraft is still the largest single market within the world market, but it no longer constitutes an absolute majority of world demand. Moreover, current trends are expected to continue, resulting in a decline in the U.S. share of world air traffic to roughly 36 percent by 1990.[39] Because of the steady increase in development costs, a new commercial aircraft or engine cannot achieve financial success without substantial foreign sales. Penetration of foreign markets, always important to U.S. firms, now is essential. But the sheer size of the U.S. market means that U.S. sales are very important for the commercial success of foreign aircraft as well.

Foreign markets also have become significant for firms in the "second tier" of the U.S. aircraft industry. U.S. exports of components and other parts grew at an average annual rate of 36 percent from 1977 to 1982, from roughly $2 billion to more than $4 billion. Exports of aircraft engines increased from slightly more than $200 million to more than $800 million during the same period.[40] Reflecting this rapid expansion in components trade, U.S. content in many aircraft produced by foreign firms is substantial. Approximately 30 percent of the value of the Airbus A300, for example, is considered to be U.S.-produced components,[41] while estimates of the U.S. content of the Embraer Bandeirante, produced in Brazil, range above 40 percent. Producers of components and other firms in the second tier have a stake in open international markets for aircraft and components that is no less considerable than that of the major U.S. firms.

Growth in the foreign market for aircraft, engines and components, apparent increases in violations of the General Agreement on Tariffs and Trade (GATT) in the aircraft industry, and the desire of foreign producers for the elimination of the tariff on U.S. imports of aircraft, engines, and components, resulted in a unique trade document, the Agreement on Trade in Civil Aircraft, negotiated under GATT auspices and effective as of January 1, 1980. The agreement abolished all customs duties on aircraft and components and contains provisions designed to control directed procurement practices and government subsidization of the development and sale of aircraft.[42] U.S. exports of aircraft parts and components grew rapidly following the signing of the agreement and undoubtedly were facilitated by its abolition of duties. Because many joint ventures also depend on extensive international flows of components and parts, the treaty has supported the rise of interfirm cooperation. Indeed, a major factor behind U.S. support for the agreement was the desire of major U.S. producers to expand their offshore procurement of components. The agreement has also provided a mechanism for monitoring subsidies for the development of commercial aircraft and may have influenced the terms of West German and British financial support for recent aircraft and engine development programs.[43]

MILITARY COPRODUCTION AGREEMENTS: TECHNOLOGY TRANSFER AND OTHER EFFECTS OF U.S.-FOREIGN COOPERATION IN MILITARY AIRCRAFT PRODUCTION

Although joint ventures between U.S. and foreign firms in commercial aircraft have been a significant phenomenon for only the past ten to fifteen years, cooperation between U.S. and foreign firms in the production of military aircraft has a much longer history. From 1947 to 1980, at least forty-four different weapons systems, of which twenty-eight were aircraft, missiles, or rotorcraft, were produced by foreign firms in more than twenty countries under licenses granted by U.S. producers.[44] Coproduction of military aircraft began as a U.S. government policy designed to allow foreign nations to reap economic benefits, in the form of employment and industrial development, from purchases of U.S. weapons systems. In view of the number and long history of these agreements, the effect of coproduction programs on the competitiveness of foreign producers of commercial aircraft provides useful information on the implications for technology transfer and industrial competitiveness of joint ventures in civil aircraft and engines.

Coproduction agreements in military aircraft differ from commercial aircraft joint ventures in a number of significant ways. Before 1978 these agreements were negotiated largely on a government-to-government basis, indicative of the extent to which commercial and security interests were blended in coproduction programs. The amount and type of technology transferred through these programs were affected by the fact that until the late 1970s coproduction did not involve foreign firms in the design or development of any part of the weapons system being produced. In most cases, licensed coproduction began with the assembly by foreign manufacturers of knock-down kits from the United States, followed by gradual expansion in the range of locally produced components incorporated into the aircraft. Production of certain sensitive components (for example, electronic countermeasures equipment for fighter aircraft) remained in the United States—these components were shipped as sealed "black boxes" for assembly into the aircraft in the licensee nation. The available evidence indicates that the design and technical data necessary for these production tasks were readily transferred to licensees by U.S. firms.[45]

In most cases, foreign licensed producers of military aircraft are also producers of civilian aircraft, which is similar to the situation in the United States. The effect of military coproduction programs on the ability of foreign producers to enter the commercial aircraft and engine industry thus has been the subject of several recent expressions of concern by the U.S. government.[46] But coproduction programs appear to have had a modest influence thus far on the ability of foreign firms to enter the industries as prime contractors.

The failure of coproduction agreements to enhance foreign firms' competitiveness in the commercial aircraft industry can be attributed to several factors. Most coproduction agreements have involved foreign production of fighter aircraft or rotorcraft, rather than large military transports. Spillover from military to civilian applications of the aircraft technologies utilized in most coproduction programs therefore has been modest at best and has declined over the past thirty years, reflecting general trends in the evolution of civilian and military aircraft technologies. Of even greater importance, however, is that the knowledge of production technologies acquired from licensors through military coproduction programs is insufficient to support independent entry into the civilian aircraft market—the critical design, development, and marketing capabilities are not transferred through licensing agreements.[47] Inasmuch as most coproduction agreements have not included joint development or design activities, the critical skills for design and systems integration typically have not been transferred to foreign participants.[48]

Although the coproduction programs of the 1950s and 1960s did not substantially enhance the design and engineering capabilities of most foreign producers of commercial aircraft, they did contribute to the expansion of aircraft and components production capacity and employment in many European nations. The expanded capacity, as well as European dissatisfaction with the costs and benefits of coproduction licensing,[49] has led to significant changes in U.S.-European cooperation in weapons systems production and procurement.[50] Rather than concentrating on licensed production of a wide range of components for purely domestic use, European firms are increasingly pursuing specialized development and production of components for sale in a wider market.

Specialized production of components supports a European role in the design and development activities widely thought to yield the greatest spinoff effects, and enables European firms to exploit economies of scale and learning in the production process. This new strategy has taken two forms. European governments increasingly demand a role for their aerospace and other firms in the development or production of components (so-called offsets) for a significant share of the aircraft in exchange for the purchase of U.S. weapons systems (for example, the F-16).[51] An alternative approach involves the formation of trans-European consortia for the design and production of weapons systems, such as the Tornado or Jaguar fighter aircraft. While this second strategy yields considerable learning benefits, thus far it has produced exceedingly expensive military aircraft.[52]

These new forms of transatlantic and trans-European cooperation in military aircraft production have raised several management issues of direct relevance to commercial aircraft joint ventures. European firms have encountered considerable difficulty in adapting to production fluctuations and scaling up rapidly to high production rates because of restrictions on their ability to vary the size of their work force.[53] According to some observers, the requirements for work force stability also contribute to significant differences in production technologies in European and U.S. aircraft firms, as European production techniques rely on higher skill levels in the labor force.[54] Adaptation of component designs to different production environments has created severe difficulties in some U.S.-European cooperative weapons projects, occasionally requiring U.S. producers to absorb the brunt of output fluctuations and to compensate for longer European lead times in tooling and production. Specialized participation by European components producers in such programs as the multinational F-16 project also has created additional European production capacity and competition for U.S. producers of components and assemblies.[55]

The experience of U.S. and foreign firms in military coproduction and offset programs illustrates several important features of technology transfer and management of joint ventures in aircraft. Early coproduction agreements had a modest influence on the design and management capabilities of European and Japanese firms, reflecting the fact that assembly and components fabrication transferred little of the crucial technology and know-how for aircraft design and production. Coproduction programs therefore did not lead to European or Japanese entry into the commercial aircraft industry as designers and systems integrators. The newer forms of transatlantic and trans-European cooperation in weapons design and production have been in place for only a brief time, but the available evidence suggests that participation in these specialized production and design activities by European firms may have enhanced their competitiveness as producers of components or subassemblies, strengthening a potential threat to U.S. supplier firms. It is not likely, however, that these newer participation and technology transfer activities will threaten the major U.S. prime contractors in military or commercial aircraft.[56] Finally, conflicts have arisen between U.S. and European participants in joint military aircraft programs over contrasting labor force and production management practices.

The U.S. government has played an important role throughout the history of coproduction and offset agreements. In supporting these programs, at least some of which have helped to establish offshore sources for components and assemblies, federal policy has had a major influence on the competitiveness of the U.S. aircraft and engine industry. Coproduction and offset agreements not only have affected the growth of European capabilities in components for military aircraft, but also have aided in the growth of potential suppliers of components for civilian aircraft. U.S. coproduction programs have also enhanced the ability of foreign producers to participate in cooperative ventures in commercial aircraft development and production, be these all-European or undertakings in which U.S. firms participate.

CONCLUSION

This chapter has described some of the characteristics of the design, production, and marketing technology of the aircraft and engine industry and the origins of the competitive environment in which

U.S. producers of aircraft and engines currently find themselves. The commercial aircraft industry generally is characterized by high barriers to entry, substantial economies of scale, and intense competition. The technological requirements of aircraft design are such that a substantial research infrastructure is necessary to support the aircraft and engine industry; this infrastructure has been funded with both public and private money in the United States during the postwar period. The research-intensive nature of the processes and products associated with the aircraft and engine industries means that they are important markets for the suppliers of research-intensive electronics and materials.

The most important factors for the competitiveness of individual firms are not easily embodied in a product or license. Moving from paper design through a complex development process to the rollout of a new aircraft on schedule is critical and requires considerable managerial and technological expertise. Management of wide swings in production volume without incurring major cost penalties is also crucial, given the wide fluctuations in demand that typify this industry. Post-sales servicing and performance assessment and the incorporation of information from product support activities into subsequent design modifications are other key competitive assets. None of these characteristics is easily transferred in an arm's-length sale or a licensing agreement, yet all are necessary for independent entry into the production of commercial aircraft or engines. The difficulty of transferring these intangible assets through licensing agreements, as well as the essential contribution that they make to competitiveness, may be inferred from the experiences of Japanese and European licensed coproduction of U.S. military aircraft. Production expertise is necessary to support entry into the commercial aircraft industry, but it is far from sufficient. Although entry into the aircraft industry as a prime contractor requires all of the intangible assets discussed here, specialized entry as a partner in a multinational consortium, or as a producer of a narrow range of components for export, may not.

Throughout much of the postwar period the U.S. aircraft industry was the beneficiary of a unique policy framework. Its overall structure was not the result of a conscious "targeting" strategy, but federal policy in some respects resembled the industrial policies of Japan's Ministry of International Trade and Industry, combining direct and indirect support for both research and the adoption of innovations. Since the early 1970s, many of the components of this policy framework have been dismantled. Commercial aircraft remains a favored industry (there is no equivalent of the NASA aeronautics research program for the steel industry), but the industry now faces far greater market uncertainty and risk. Combined with the declining importance of the U.S. aircraft market and other changes in the global market environment, these changes in the domestic environment have served as powerful incentives for U.S. firms to seek risk-sharing foreign partners in development projects.

The growth of the U.S. commercial aircraft industry has been closely intertwined with evolving public policies toward air transportation, military procurement, and the aircraft industry itself. The vertically disintegrated structure of the airline and aircraft industries, the research investment in military and civilian aircraft technologies, the CAB regulatory regime, the postwar bailout of Lockheed and financial support for the McDonnell Douglas merger, and the transfer of production and some design technology to European and Japanese manufacturers all are direct results of public policy decisions. Although each of these policies has had costs and benefits, each typically has been considered separately in the overall structure of policy toward this industry. Nonetheless, this policy structure and recent alterations in its key components have had a great effect on the U.S. commercial aircraft industry. Policy makers concerned about current actions of industry management (for example, partnerships with foreign firms that involve significant technology transfer) must recognize that such actions are in part a response to the wrenching changes in public policy that have occurred during the past two decades. At the same time, private managers within the industry must acknowledge the substantial financial, technological, and diplomatic support that the U.S. government has provided to aircraft and engine firms thoughout the past fifty years.

NOTES

1. The discussion in this chapter is drawn from David C. Mowery, "Federal Funding of R&D in Transportation: The Case of Aviation" (Presented at the National Academy of Sciences Symposium on the Impact of Federal

R&D Funding, Washington, D.C., November 21–22, 1985); Mowery and Nathan Rosenberg, "The Commercial Aircraft Industry," in Richard R. Nelson, ed. *Government and Technical Progress: A Cross-Industry Analysis* (New York: Pergamon Press, 1982); and Mowery and Rosenberg, "Competition and Cooperation: The U.S. and Japanese Commercial Aircraft Industries," *California Management Review*, 1985.

2. See John W. Kendrick, *Productivity Trends in the United States* (Princeton, N.J.: Princeton University Press, 1961) or John W. Kendrick, *Postwar Productivity Trends in the United States, 1948–69* (New York: Columbia University Press, 1973). See also, Barbara M. Fraumeni and Dale W. Jorgenson, "The Role of Capital in U.S. Economic Growth, 1948–76," in G. M. von Furstenberg, ed., *Capital, Efficiency and Growth* (Cambridge, Mass.: Ballinger Publishing Co., 1980).

    Alternatively, a calculation of the "social savings" resulting from reductions in the operating costs per seat-mile of the U.S. domestic air transportation fleet since 1939 suggests that these savings amount to nearly 75 percent. In other words, employing 1939 equipment to carry 1983 traffic would cost $24 billion (1972 dollars) rather than the current cost of less than $6 billion. See Mowery, "Federal Funding of R&D," for additional discussion.

3. All figures taken from Aerospace Industries Association, *Aerospace Facts and Figures, 1983/84* (New York: McGraw–Hill, 1983).

4. The 1981 study of aeronautics R&D by the Office of Science and Technology Policy concluded that " . . . the aeronautics industry is characterized by high research intensity and a wide technology base. That is, aeronautics depends on R&T (research and technology) performed within the aeronautics industry and on R&T performed by virtually every other high-technology industry," (V-28). Statistical support for this characterization may be found in a recent study by the International Trade Administration of the U.S. Department of Commerce, analyzing "embodied" research intensity in various American industries. Embodied research intensity attempts to account for R&D expenditures that are incorporated in the inputs purchased by a given industry. The aircraft industry ranked third among U.S. manufacturing industries on this index with an embodied research intensity of 15.4 percent of the value of shipments in 1980, exceeded only by missiles and spacecraft and electronic components. See Office of Science and Technology Policy, *Aeronautical Research and Technology Policy*, vol. 2, *Final Report* (Washington, D.C.: Executive Office of the President, 1982), p. V-28, and U.S. Department of Commerce, International Trade Administration, *An Assessment of U.S. Competitiveness in High Technology Industries* (Washington, D.C.: U.S. Government Printing Office, 1983), p. 42.

5. See John E. Steiner, "How Decisions Are Made," AIAA Wright Brothers Lectureship in Aeronautics, Seattle, Washington, 1982.

6. Ibid., p. 14.

7. "When the market is ready, the successful manufacturer may have to *go*. The eventual prize sometimes goes to the company which is fast on its feet . . . ," ibid., p. 31. [Emphasis in original]

8. "Although the time between design and service release of civil and military aircraft increased over the years in the United States as it did in Europe, data for the late 1960s showed the United States well ahead of the United Kingdom and France. The average development time for civil aircraft was 52 months in the United Kingdom and 62 months in France, but it was 43 months in the United States." See M.S. Hochmuth, *Organizing the Transnational: The Experience with Transnational Enterprise in Advanced Technology* (Cambridge, Mass.: Harvard University Press, 1974), p. 149. The history of the British Aircraft Corporation BAC 111 is instructive. The BAC 111 was a three-engine, medium-range passenger aircraft with a design that closely resembled that of the Boeing 727. Despite the fact that development of the BAC 111 began more than one year prior to the launch of the 727, however, the 727 reached the commercial market first and greatly reduced the sales of the BAC 111, which was a commercial failure.

9. According to some observers, the commercial prospects for the Airbus Industrie A300 and A310 have been hampered by the limited stretch potential of these designs. While the A300 and A310 share a great many components and fuselage sections, the two aircraft employ entirely different wings, one of the most expensive and complex airframe components.

10. A recent discussion of Northwest Orient Airlines, which employs Pratt & Whitney engines exclusively on an aircraft fleet made up largely of Boeing aircraft, noted that "Standardization of those engines and airframe types allows Northwest to maintain spare parts and inventory equal to about 9 percent of fleet value, he [Steven G. Rothmeier, Northwest Orient chief executive officer] said, compared with an industry average believed to be about 22 percent. 'That difference alone is worth several million dollars a year just in carrying costs,' he said." Carole A. Schifrin, "Boeing Launches Long-Haul 747-400 with Northwest Order," *Aviation Week and Space Technology*, October 28, 1985, pp. 33-34.

11. As is discussed later, the commercial importance of a product family means that the decision by Airbus Industrie to proceed with the development of a family of designs, including the A300-600, A310, and A320, may be one of this consortium's most important strategic policy decisions. The recent acquisition by Boeing of de Havilland of Canada was similarly motivated by Boeing's desire to expand the range of aircraft types within

its product family, in response to the increased acquisition by large U.S. airlines of commuter airlines, as well as growing resort to operating agreements between trunk and commuter carriers. See Richard G. O'Lone, "Boeing Cools on Cooperative Programs," *Aviation Week and Space Technology*, June 6, 1977, pp. 218–19.

12.   R. Miller and D. Sawers, *The Technical Development of Modern Aviation* (London: Routledge & Kegan Paul, 1968), p. 267.

13.   The recent bid by British Aerospace for 26 percent of the development and production activity and costs of the Airbus Industrie A320, a 150-seat aircraft was estimated to be $900 million, implying an overall cost for the A320 of nearly $3 billion. See Arthur Reed, "Airbus A320 Launched with British Loan to BAe," *Air Transport World*, April 1984, pp. 17–18.

14.   John Rae, *Climb to Greatness* (Cambridge, Mass.: M.I.T. Press, 1968), p. 83.

15.   See Alchian (1963) and Hirsch (1976). The "curve" simply refers to the fall in production costs as a function of cumulative output.

16.   Clearly, the success of this export-oriented infant industry strategy depends on a number of factors, including the size of the domestic market, the slope of the learning curve, and the ability of firms serving the protected market to reduce their costs more rapidly than foreign firms. The importance of the size of the domestic market is discussed in greater detail in Chapter 4. See R. McCulloch, "International Competition in High-Technology Industries: The Consequences of Alternative Trade Regimes for Aircraft" (Presented at the National Science Foundation Workshop on the Economic Implications of Restrictions to Trade in High-Technology Goods, Washington, D.C., October 3, 1984) and Paul W. Krugman, "Import Protection as Export Promotion: International Competition in the Presence of Oligopoly and Economies of Scale," in H. Kierzkowski, ed., *Monopolistic Competition and International Trade* (Oxford: Oxford University Press, 1984).

17.   The "bypass ratio" denotes the relationship between the amount of air forced through the engine that bypasses the central core compressor and the total volume of air forced through the engine. As this ratio increases, due to improvements in the core compressor and engine fan design, greater thrust can be achieved for a fixed amount of fuel, thereby lowering operating costs.

18.   "The initial JT9D experience on the 747 was painful from the standpoint of maintenance cost, thrust deterioration, and engine reliability." (Steiner, "How Decisions Are Made," p. 24). Subsequent models of the JT9D have far better maintenance and reliability records.

19.   Barry Bluestone, Peter Jordan, and Mark Sullivan, *Aircraft Industry Dynamics: An Analysis of Competition, Capital and Labor* (Boston: Auburn House Publishing, 1981).

20. The role of innovation in other industries is discussed in Mowery and Rosenberg, "The Commercial Aircraft Industry."

21. The construction of R&D data is discussed in Mowery, "Federal Funding of R&D."

22. Although the military portion of total R&D investment in the commercial and military aircraft industry has been high, the size of the benefits reaped by commercial aircraft technology remains uncertain. Clearly, much of the basic or fundamental military research generates results that are applicable to commercial uses. Military research, however, typically contains a very large development component (at least 60 percent), the commercial benefits from which have fluctuated during the postwar period. This issue of "spillovers" is discussed in greater detail later in this chapter.

23. Federal financial support for such generic technology development was mandated in the Stevenson–Wydler Act of 1980, which authorized a number of "centers of generic technology" (COGENTs). The seminal document for postwar science policy, written by Vannevar Bush, cited NACA as an example of successful federal support of basic and fundamental research. Nelson (1982) discusses NACA and NASA as models for generic research programs supported by public funds. See V. Bush, *Science—The Endless Frontier* (Washington, D.C.: U.S. Government Printing Office, 1945); and (Nelson '82, see Biblio).

24. Indeed, a recent account of the development of the jet engine characterizes the United States prior to 1940 as a backwater of research-theoretical aerodynamics, attributing the failure of American engineers to originate the concept of the jet to their ignorance of aeronautical design theory. E.W. Constant, *The Origins of the Turbojet Revolution* (Baltimore, Md.: Johns Hopkins University Press, 1980).

25. In operating philosophy and impact on the aircraft industry, the aeronautics research programs supported by NACA and NASA resembled domestic R&D joint ventures among modern Japanese firms in computers and electronics. See David C. Mowery and Nathan Rosenberg, "Competition and Cooperation: The U.S. and Japanese Commercial Aircraft Industries," *California Management Review* 27, no. 4, 1985.

26. Miller and Sawers, "Technical Development," described this licensing system of the Manufacturers' Aircraft Association as a system "under which all aircraft manufacturers agreed to let all their competitors use their patents. No member can have a patent monopoly on any inventions which his staff can make, or even for any invention that he may license from an outside inventory. If he takes an exclusive license, the patent has to be available to the other members of the MAA, but the original licensee can claim that he should be granted compensation by the other licensees. Manufacturers apparently believe that it is a good bargain to give up their right to a

patent monopoly in return for the protection from litigation with other companies in the industry that the right to use their patents brings." (pp. 255–56). Roland discusses the origins of the cross-licensing agreement in Alex Roland, *Model Research: The National Advisory Committee for Aeronautics, 1915–58* (Washington, D.C.: U.S. Government Printing Office, 1985), pp. 37–43.

27. Miller and Sawers, "Technical Development," pp. 193–94.

28. " . . . large government and space involvement, provides the safety net that catches a plummeting airframe company. Large backlogs of government contracts furnish rather steady income during periods when commercial activities make sales and earnings volatile. Government-sponsored research provides the bulk of airframe technology. Finally, the government simply will not allow a major defense contractor to fail completely, whatever its commercial sins." Sidney L. Carroll, "The Market for Commercial Airliners," in Richard E. Caves and M. J. Roberts, eds. *Regulating the Product* (Cambridge, Mass.: Ballinger Publishing Co., 1975), p. 162.

29. The federal government has played a critical role in the evolution of the airline industry's structure since the inception of this industry. Divestiture of airlines by aircraft and engine manufacturers was mandated by law in 1934, following a series of congressional investigations of political influence in the awarding of contracts for mail transportation. The award of these contracts during the 1920s had been employed by then-Postmaster General Brown to build up large transcontinental carriers, which in turn would provide a market for advanced aircraft. For further details, see Mowery and Rosenberg, "The Commercial Aircraft Industry."

30. William A. Jordan, *Airline Regulation in America* (Baltimore, Md.: Johns Hopkins University Press, 1970), p. 53.

31. Despite their high costs to consumers during the era of regulation, airlines on average earned only a normal rate of return on capital. Keeler argued that "with fares set at high, cartel levels, the airlines have competed away profits through excess capacity." See Theodore E. Keeler, "Airline Regulation and Market Performance," *Bell Journal of Economics* 3 (1972), p. 421. Service quality competition caused costs to rise to the level of fares and largely prevented airlines from reaping excess profits, as noted by G.W. Douglas and J.C. Miller in *Economic Regulation of Domestic Air Transport* (Washington, D.C.: Brookings Institution, 1974).

32. In "Federal Funding of R&D," the author employs estimates of the costs of CAB regulation and airline operating cost improvements from 1966 to 1984, finding that if the costs to consumers of CAB regulation are included as a part of the costs of the policy framework supporting innovation, diffusion, and reductions in operating costs within the U.S. domestic air fleet, the rate of return on the total R&D investment becomes negative.

33. Krugman, "Import Protection."

34. The similarities with Japanese industrial policy, which in many industries has worked to develop competitive firms serving domestic markets that are formally or informally protected, followed by these firms' entry into international markets, are striking. This argument is developed further in Mowery and Rosenberg, "Competition and Cooperation."

35. National Academy of Engineering, *The Competitive Status of the U.S. Civil Aircraft Manufacturing Industry* (Washington, D.C.: National Academy Press, 1985), p. 101.

36. Ibid., p. 102.

37. U.S. Senate Committee on Aeronautical and Space Sciences, *Policy Planning for Aeronautical Research and Development: A Staff Report* (Washington, D.C.: U.S. Government Printing Office, 1966), p. 20.

38. A National Research Council study argues that NASA's Aeronautics Research and Technology Program budget has declined in real terms during the past decade. The other components of the NASA aeronautics budget are Construction of Facilities and Research and Program Management.

39. Data on world and U.S. market demand are taken from the study by the National Academy of Engineering, "Competitive Status."

40. See U.S. Commerce Department, International Trade Administration, A Competitive Assessment of the U.S. Civil Aircraft Industry (Washington, D.C.: U.S. Government Printing Office, 1984), p. 31.

41. Airbus Industrie is currently working to reduce the U.S. content in its new aircraft designs: "To ensure that the European partners obtain a bigger share on the A320, the past reliance on U.S. manufacturers will be reduced. There are two other reasons for this trend: with the experience of the A300 and A310 behind it Europe now feels more technically able to produce its own equipment. Secondly, the Europeans believe that they have lost aircraft sales due to the amount of U.S. equipment which the aircraft contained. They cite a potential contract for ten A300s with Libya which was blocked because Libya is on the U.S. embargo list." See Arthur Reed, "Airbus Talks about A320; Future Projects," *Air Transport World*, May 1984, p. 33. Current estimates of the U.S. content of the A320, for example, are as low as 20 percent. See *Aviation Week & Space Technology*, "U.S.-European Trade Talks Focus on Subsidy Issues," March 31, 1986, p. 36.

42. For a more detailed discussion of the agreement, see W. Stephen Piper, "The Agreement on Trade in Civil Aircraft," written statement printed in Subcommittee on International Trade, U.S. Senate Committee on Finance, *Hearings on S. 1376*, 96th Congress, 1st session, 1979; and Piper, "Unique Sectoral Agreement Establishes Free Trade Framework," *Journal of World Trade Law* 12 (1980), 221–53.

43. See the National Academy of Engineering, "Competitive Status," p. 78. Government subsidization of the sale of commercial aircraft and engines remains a very vexed issue, despite efforts to control these export subsidies in the "standstill" and "commonline" agreements between the United States and members of the Organization for Economic Cooperation and Development.

44. An excellent analysis of U.S.-European collaboration in weapons coproduction is Michael Rich, William Stanley, John Birkler, and Michael Hess, *Multinational Coproduction of Military Aerospace Systems* (Santa Monica, Calif.: Rand Corporation, 1981).

45. Hall and Johnson state in their account of the Japanese production of the F-104 that "Access to technical information was not a problem. When discussing data transfers, U.S. aerospace officials were emphatic in saying that their coproduction partners could have access to any document. One U.S. executive flatly stated, 'We were paid to put them in business, and we gave them everything we had.' Nor does the story change when talking to Japanese executives." G.R. Hall and R.E. Johnson, "Transfers of United States Aerospace Technology to Japan," in R. Vernon, ed. *The Technology Factor in International Trade* (New York, Columbia University Press for the National Bureau of Economic Research, 1970).

46. A study of the Japanese F-15 coproduction program concludes that "Almost 30 years of coproduction of U.S. military aircraft has aided the growth of the Japanese industry by transferring technology and building an aircraft production base." U.S. General Accounting Office, *U.S. Military Co-production Agreements Assist Japan in Developing Its Civil Aircraft Industry* (Washington, D.C.: U.S. Government Printing Office, 1982), p. 18.

47. Reich and Mankin in "Joint Ventures with Japan," p. 80, ignore the history of these Japanese coproduction programs in arguing that through joint ventures "the Japanese are gradually taking charge of complex production—the part of the value-added chain that will continue to generate tradable goods in the future and simultaneously raise the overall skill level of the population."

48. In addition to transferring little of the managerial and technological knowledge necessary for entry into the aircraft industry, coproduction programs have resulted in high costs for foreign military procurement programs. The small size of production runs in most coproduction programs means that unit costs are extremely high. The GAO study of Japanese F-15 production, "U.S. Military Co-production Agreements," estimated that the F-15J cost roughly twice as much as would F-15s purchased directly from McDonnell Douglas.

49. According to a recent survey, "'We've seen about the last of the straight sales deals,' one U.S. official said. 'Now there will be more codevelopment,

if there's any cooperation at all,' he said. 'Co-production right now is a dirty word in Europe.'" *Aviation Week and Space Technology*, June 3, 1985, p. 243.

Similar misgivings have been expressed by Japanese industry and government officials:

> [The] Japanese government and its aerospace industry are showing a marked reluctance to continue a variety of licensing programs, largely due to the high cost of imported components and a reluctance by the U.S. Defense Department to release high-technology data to increase the Japanese national rate of participation.
>
> At Ishikawajima-Harima Heavy Industries, it is noted that in the case of the Pratt & Whitney F–100–IHI–100 powering the McDonnell Douglas/Mitsubishi F–15J built under license, more than 40 percent of the components are supplied from the U.S. in completed form."

See *Aviation Week and Space Technology*, "Japan Pushing Industry to Design New Engines," June 28, 1982, p. 208.

50. The negotiation of such agreements between U.S. and NATO firms and governments also has been removed from Pentagon control under the Reagan Administration, which " . . . relies on industry to arrange for efficient means of arms collaboration on each sale. If industry is unable to satisfy any particular government's demands, then government-to-government agreements, which may include offsets, can be considered." U.S. General Accounting Office, *Trade Offsets in Foreign Military Sales* (Washington, D.C.: U.S. Government Printing Office, 1984), p. 1.

51. One of the most complex of these offset agreements was established in 1976 as part of the agreement by Norway, Denmark, the Netherlands, and Belgium to purchase the F–16 fighter aircraft from General Dynamics. European firms were responsible for producing components amounting to 10 percent of the value of the aircraft model sold to the U.S. Air Force, 40 percent of the value of the aircraft sold to these four nations, and 15 percent of the value of the aircraft sold to third countries. None of the components for the aircraft, however, were to be produced solely in Europe.

52. See Mark A. Lorell, *Multinational Development of Large Aircraft: The European Experience* (Santa Monica, Calif.: The Rand Corporation, 1980); and Rich et al., *Multinational Coproduction.*

53. "The desire for long-term workforce stability and the lack of significant flexibility and expansion capability in Europe have important ramifications for programs involving U.S. and European industries. Dealing with differences in these areas is one of the most difficult program planning and execution challenges." Rich et al., *Multinational Coproduction*, pp. 20–22.

54. European reliance on single-shift production also results in a higher capital-output ratio because of higher tooling requirements: " . . . most companies work a single daily shift. As a result, tooling requirements are greater in Europe than they are for an equivalent production volume in the

U.S. because European tooling is used for a shorter period each day."
Aviation Week and Space Technology, "Europeans Ready Production
Tooling," May 2, 1977, p. 99.

55. According to *Aviation Week and Space Technology*, "The F–16 offset
agreements have, to a large extent, established many of the component
manufacturers in Belgium and the Netherlands in the field of aerospace.
. . . Since the aerospace industry in the two countries was so small at the
time, General Dynamics often had to help non–aerospace firms begin producing aerospace products." See *Aviation Week and Space Technology*,
"Small Firms Cooperate for U.S. Market," September 3, 1984, p. 87.

56. An exception to this conclusion may be engine producers, for whom spare
parts sales are essential to the profitability of engine sales. Foreign production of such spare parts may undercut even prime contractors' sales of
these products.

3 CASE STUDIES

This chapter examines the history of a number of joint ventures formed by U.S. aircraft and engine producers during the past fifteen years: the Boeing 767 project, involving Boeing, Aeritalia, and the Japan Commercial Aircraft Company, as well as the proposed Boeing 7J7; the unsuccessful ventures involving McDonnell Douglas and Fokker (the MDF100), and McDonnell Douglas, Dassault, and Aerospatiale (the Mercure 200); the Saab–Fairchild SF340; CFM International, the joint venture of General Electric and SNECMA of France; and the International Aero Engines venture, involving Pratt & Whitney, Rolls Royce, MTU of West Germany, Fiat of Italy, and Japan Aero Engines. The discussion of each venture considers the motives of the participants, the structure of the venture, the nature and impact of any technology transfer within the joint venture, and the overall results of the collaboration. The primary focus is the motives and behavior of the U.S. participants in the joint ventures. Chapter 4 considers the behavior and policies of foreign firms and governments in a discussion of national strategies for industrial development.

BOEING–JCAC

During the past twenty years, the Boeing Company has responded to the higher costs and risks of commercial aircraft development by

67

relying more frequently on subcontractors to assume a significant share of the costs and risks of launching new aircraft. Roughly 70 percent of the value of the early production of the 747 was subcontracted, and a number of subcontractors contributed funds to support nonrecurring costs for the first 200 aircraft produced.[1] The Boeing 767 joint venture with Aeritalia of Italy and the Japan Commercial Aircraft Company differs from the 747 program primarily in its increased reliance on foreign subcontractors, who are sharing a greater portion of the risk.[2] The involvement of the Japanese partners in the 7J7 project will be more extensive, potentially including significant roles in product design and development, marketing, and product support, in addition to manufacturing.

In recent years, the Japanese Ministry of International Trade and Industry (MITI) has supported efforts by several major Japanese industrial corporations, including Mitsubishi Heavy Industries, Kawasaki Heavy Industries, Fuji Heavy Industries, and Ishikawajima-Harima Heavy Industries, to enter the large commercial transport industry.[3] MHI, KHI, and FHI all have prior experience in the production of airframes in military coproduction agreements with the United States, while IHI has produced military engines in such programs. During the 1970s, Boeing utilized several of these firms as producers of components for the 737 and 747. These subcontracting relationships typically involved production by Japanese firms of components from Boeing designs and specifications, rather than significant independent design or development activity.

During the 1970s, Boeing began a lengthy process of design and evaluation of the successor aircraft to the 727 and 707. The impending retirement of these aircraft opened up a market for a transcontinental transport and a shorter-range transport, known respectively through much of the 1970s as the 7X7 (later the 767) and the 7N7 (later the 757). Simultaneous development of aircraft in each of these two market segments was necessary for Boeing to remain a "full-line" producer. The costs of such an ambitious development program, however, estimated to be $1.5-2.5 billion, exceeded Boeing's resources. The participation of risk-sharing partners would provide capital and reduce the firm's financial risk.[4]

Foreign aircraft firms were attractive candidates for some form of partnership with Boeing because the foreign firms' governments were able to provide funds to support development and production start-up costs for these firms. The importance of foreign markets for the commercial success of the 757 and 767 further enhanced the attractiveness of foreign firms as partners. Nonetheless, Boeing approached several U.S. firms about participation as risk-sharing subcontractors in the 757 and 767 projects, without success.[5]

The complex negotiations involving Boeing, U.S. and foreign airlines, and various potential partner firms and governments that culminated in the final design and work-sharing arrangements for the 757 and 767 lasted more than six years. During this period, Boeing held talks with firms in the United States, Great Britain, France, Italy, and Japan. Although Boeing's choice of prospective partners in these projects was influenced heavily both by the willingness of foreign firms to assume a risk-bearing role and by their technological and managerial expertise, market access considerations were also important. Thus, much of the negotiation over partnership arrangements for the 7N7, an aircraft with a potentially large European market, involved British and French firms. Boeing executives held lengthy talks with British Aerospace (BAe) in 1976 and 1978 about the firm's participation as a risk-sharing partner, a role that entailed greater responsibilities than those of a risk-sharing subcontractor. Boeing was willing to consider a major role for BAe, but insisted on retaining overall managerial and design control of the project.[6]

Under the terms of Boeing proposals made in 1976 and 1978, BAe would undertake much of the wing design work, exploiting the talents of the firm's Hawker Siddeley division that had worked with Airbus Industrie on wings for the A300. Boeing also proposed that a second assembly line for the 7N7 be located in Great Britain, an action that could have increased production costs, despite its obvious benefits for the BAe payroll and British industrial employment. BAe ultimately rejected the Boeing offer, however, as one that would relegate the British firm to the status of a subcontractor, weakening its design, management, and systems integration capabilities.[7]

Boeing also discussed development projects with other European firms, such as Aerospatiale of France and the Airbus Industrie consortium. An alternative to the 767, the Airbus A300-B10 (later the A310), elicited Boeing interest, culminating in a loosely structured memorandum of understanding, signed by Boeing and Aerospatiale in 1976. The memorandum of understanding would have committed Boeing to participation in the A300-B10 project, while simultaneously involving Aerospatiale in the 7N7. The agreement foundered on Boeing's insistence on overall control of the A300-B10 development project.[8]

Boeing eventually proceeded with the development of the 757 without foreign or domestic risk-sharing partners. Although more than 50 percent of the aircraft was produced by subcontractors, they did not share the risks. Boeing's ability to undertake the 757 development program on its own was aided by the fact that the final designs for the 757 and the 767 utilized many of the same components and assemblies.[9]

The search for foreign risk-sharing partners on the 767 project was confined largely to Italy and Japan. Negotiations between Boeing and the Japan Commercial Transport Development Corporation (JCTDC) (a consortium made up of Mitsubishi, Kawasaki, and Fuji Heavy Industries) and Aeritalia, an Italian producer, were concluded in 1978 with the signing of a memorandum of understanding. As risk-sharing subcontractors, Aeritalia and the JCTDC each assumed the costs of development and production tooling for 15 percent of the total value of the aircraft, the overall design of which was largely fixed at that point, for the first 500 aircraft.[10] The JCTDC was responsible for several sections of the fuselage and wing and for rudder flaps, a component employing sophisticated composite materials. The Italian participants were responsible for wing flaps. Both the Japanese and Italian groups received government funding for up to 50 percent of the development costs for their components. For the Japanese partners, government funding took the form of loans, repayable out of profits from production of the aircraft, and amounted to at least $73 million. Final assembly of the aircraft, marketing, and product support remained the responsibility of Boeing. Since Boeing retained overall control of design, production, and marketing, the 767 venture was not organized as a separate corporate entity.

Boeing had made the major design decisions on the 767 by the time the consortium was formed in 1978. Much of the remaining development and design work concerned components and was the responsibility of Boeing's Japanese partner firms. In order to facilitate the work, Japanese engineering personnel were transferred to Boeing headquarters for up to a year. Considerable interaction and transfer of component design skills and technology assuredly occurred through this channel, although fundamental design and development skills remained largely with Boeing. Boeing also retained sole responsibility for such key elements of the aircraft as the cockpit, the avionics package, wing design and assembly and final assembly of the airframe. In the development and subsequent production of these and other components, Boeing, its foreign partners, and U.S. subcontractors made extensive use of computer-aided design and manufacturing technologies: design specifications were sent to the Japanese and Italian partners in digital form through direct transmission or magnetic tape.[11]

Since the introduction of the 767 in 1983, unexpectedly slow sales have resulted in low production rates, and profits have fallen well below the levels that the Japanese consortium had expected. One recent account of the Japanese Commercial Aircraft Corporation, formed at the conclusion of the design and development phase to manage the production of the Japanese share of the 767, noted that

> CAC [JCAC] ... had been planning on a production rate for fiscal 1983 of up to 10 aircraft a month. Due to the sales slump, the rate will be only 2–3 a month, cutting CAC's profits and reducing its ability to repay the government. .... The reduced production rate also has left the CAC companies with excess capacity—a particularly heavy burden in Japan, where firms traditionally do not lay off employees, even in hard times.[12]

The contracts between Boeing and both the Italian and the Japanese firms are based on a production run of 500 units and incorporate cost reductions resulting from the movement down the learning curve to this cumulative output level. In other words, the contracts assume that Boeing's risk-sharing subcontractors are substantially further down their learning curves than is in fact the case. Very few established U.S. subcontractors could match the cost performance assumed under the terms of this agreement with Boeing, widely acknowledged to be a very efficient producer of such components.[13]

While the technological and financial benefits for the Japanese firms from participation in the Boeing 767 project have been modest so far, Boeing has gained in a number of ways. By selectively transferring design and production technology to Japanese firms, Boeing has reaped a substantial return on its more mature technological capacities, a return that would be unattainable through licensing.[14] Boeing's access to the Japanese market and, possibly, to rapidly growing Southeast Asian markets may have been enhanced by its partnership with Japanese firms.[15] The access of Japanese firms to limited supplies of government-subsidized risk capital has reduced the size, cost, and risks of Boeing's financial commitment to the development of new commercial aircraft. Boeing also has benefited by supporting the entry of Japanese firms into the components supply sector, thereby increasing competition among component suppliers and subcontractors.[16] Finally, the potentially valuable contributions of capital, production expertise, and market access that the Japanese consortium would offer Airbus Industrie have been preempted by the link between Boeing and the consortium.

In March 1984 Boeing announced the formation of a joint venture involving the Japan Aircraft Development Corporation (JADC, the successor to the JCTDC, is charged with managing new aircraft development projects) in the development of a 150-seat aircraft, then expected to be introduced in 1990. The memorandum of understanding between Boeing and the JADC that was signed in March 1984 committed the Japanese group to an equity share of 25 percent in the "7-7" (now the 7J7). As outlined in the memorandum of understanding, Japanese participation in the 7J7 project differs qualitatively from the 767 venture. Rather than participating as a risk-sharing subcontractor, with responsibilities limited to design and production of components to meet Boeing specifications, the firms in the JADC will participate in all phases of the project, ranging from fundamental design to marketing, finance of aircraft sales, and product support. Boeing remains the senior partner in this joint venture, however, a status reinforced by the U.S. firm's insistence on a higher return on its investment as an acknowledgement of its design, project management, marketing, and product support experience.[17]

Despite the fanfare with which the March 1984 memorandum of understanding was signed, agreement among Boeing, the JADC, and prospective customers on the aircraft's design proved elusive—a central uncertainty was whether the 7-7 would indeed be an all-new aircraft or a modified and stretched 737. The Japanese participants and MITI viewed a modification of the 737 as far less attractive, reflecting their interest in acquiring advanced design and systems integration skills through this project. Because of the uncertainties concerning the market for such an aircraft, Boeing announced unilaterally in early 1985 that the launch of the 7-7 aircraft would be delayed two to three years. Simultaneously, the firm began a major research effort with General Electric to develop an aircraft (the 7J7) utilizing unducted fan (UDF) turboprop engines, which promise dramatic improvements in fuel efficiency. Development of an airframe for a 150-seat aircraft with UDF engines involves complex issues of airframe-engine integration, as well as research on the extensive employment of composite (nonmetallic, carbon-based) materials in the wings or fuselage. Boeing's current plans for the 7J7 mean that the V2500 engine, to which the Japan Aero Engine consortium had made a large financial and engineering commitment (discussed later in this chapter), will be employed only on the A320 and possible 737 derivatives.

In March 1986 Boeing and the JADC signed another memorandum of understanding confirming the JADC's participation in the 7J7 project. The JADC is to provide 25 percent of the equity and will be involved in all phases of design, production, and marketing of the aircraft. Boeing also announced later in the month that Saab-Scania of Sweden and Short Brothers of the United Kingdom had agreed to participate in the 7J7 project as risk-sharing associates. Short Brothers will hold roughly 5 percent of the development program; Saab-Scania's share will be comparable or slightly greater.[18]

The 7J7 project represents a significant shift in the pattern of cooperation between Boeing and foreign aircraft firms. The involvement of foreign firms at an early point in the development and design cycle is likely to result in greater transfer of design concepts and technology to foreign firms. Boeing will gain as well, however, from the exploitation of foreign firms' technological assets, notably the considerable Japanese expertise in composite materials. Moreover, the initial claims (and expectations) that foreign participants will be involved fully in all phases of the 7J7 project are likely to be fulfilled in only a formal sense—the managerial requirements of this complex project will force members of the joint venture to specialize in a narrowly defined area or function. Nonetheless, the Japanese contribution of capital to finance sales of the aircraft will bolster Boeing's resources in an area that is critical to international competition in this industry. Despite the criticisms of the 7J7 agreement voiced by Robert Reich,[19] therefore, the greater technology transfer that will undoubtedly occur within this venture is not likely to result in Japanese (or Swedish or Northern Irish) entry into the commercial aircraft industry as independent prime contractors.[20] The 7J7 venture continues the development of the alliance of Boeing and Japan in commercial aircraft, but Boeing remains the senior partner in this alliance. As Boeing managers have acknowledged, however, component suppliers are excluded from partnership in the 7J7 venture, so as to encourage competition among these firms. The 7J7 venture thus is likely to increase foreign competition for U.S. supplier firms in the aerospace industry.[21]

McDONNELL DOUGLAS: THE MERCURE 200 AND THE MDF100

McDonnell Douglas Aircraft entered into two joint ventures during the 1970s and early 1980s, both of which failed to produce a new aircraft. Neither failure can be attributed to a lack of demand for the proposed aircraft, which would have served the large market for a 150-seat aircraft several years earlier than the Airbus A320 or the Boeing 7J7. In the case of the MDF100, a venture involving McDonnell Douglas and Fokker, the inability to synchronize the airframe development program with the introduction of advanced engines contributed to severe market uncertainties and delays that Fokker could not sustain. Managerial factors also contributed to the demise of this venture, however, as McDonnell Douglas refused to make the major financial commitment that would support the continued participation of a European partner with fewer engineering resources. The McDonnell Douglas-Fokker venture also reveals the unique difficulties of product development partnerships between established firms in technologically dynamic industries. The evolution of the technology of materials, airframes, and engines during the early 1980s caused the existing McDonnell Douglas product line to encroach on the market for the MDF100. The Mercure 200 venture, in which McDonnell Douglas's partners were Dassault, Breguet, and Aerospatiale, failed to reach even the advanced development phase. This venture appears to have unraveled largely because of the unwillingness of McDonnell Douglas to commit the resources to modify the aircraft design to make it more acceptable to potential purchasers.

The McDonnell Douglas Corporation was formed in 1967 through the merger of profitable McDonnell Aircraft with Douglas Aircraft, then caught in a financial crisis. The product lines and profitability of the two enterprises failed to converge after the merger. McDonnell Aircraft controlled central corporate management and continued to produce profitable military fighter aircraft. The Douglas Aircraft

Division, which produced commercial aircraft, performed poorly during the 1970s. The DC-10 faced direct competition from the Lockheed L-1011 and was not financially successful.[22] The decision to end production of the DC-8 in 1972 also deprived Douglas Aircraft of a product that would have been profitable in the late 1970s and 1980s.[23] Production of the DC-9, which had brought Douglas to the brink of bankruptcy, took a number of years to become profitable.

As a result of the poor financial performance of the Douglas Aircraft division through the 1970s, the corporate management of McDonnell Douglas was loath to commit huge sums of money to develop a new commercial aircraft. This reluctance of corporate management caused McDonnell Douglas to withdraw from several commercial aircraft development programs.[24] Other U.S. aircraft firms, notably Boeing, were also unwilling to undertake new development programs without some form of participation by one or more other firms. Boeing consistently refused, however, to accept anything less than a leadership position in any such consortium. For Boeing, joint ventures were a means to the end of new product development, while McDonnell Douglas's interest in joint ventures was motivated in part by the U.S. firm's desire to use its extensive product support and marketing network more fully, by acting as a marketing and servicing agent for products designed and produced largely by other firms. In addition, McDonnell Douglas employed the Mercure 200 venture as a means to win additional sales of DC-9s and DC-10s to European airlines. Reflecting its different motives, McDonnell Douglas did not insist on a controlling share in its joint ventures.

During the 1970s McDonnell Douglas conducted extensive negotiations with various European aircraft firms about joint development of a new aircraft. Along with Boeing and Airbus, McDonnell Douglas saw that the 150-seat segment of the market offered one of the last opportunities for a new commercial aircraft in the twentieth century. The major uncertainty clouding the outlook for such an aircraft was the availability of a new, fuel-efficient engine. Successful development of a 150-seat airframe depended on the availability of at least one, and preferably two, new engines with 20,000–25,000 pounds of thrust. While the General Electric-SNECMA joint venture was to produce such an engine, the existence and introduction date of an additional engine remained uncertain. This uncertainty dramatically increased when the JT10D venture between Rolls Royce and Pratt & Whitney, which had been developing such an engine, was dissolved in 1978.

The first major joint venture between McDonnell Douglas and a European firm was the Mercure 200. The Mercure 200 was designed to seat roughly 170 passengers and was a derivative of the commercilly unsuccessful Mercure 100 produced by Dassault–Breguet Aircraft of France. In an effort to support the development of a more successful derivative of the Mercure 100, an airframe that would utilize the CFM56 engine then being developed by General Electric and SNECMA of France, the French government sponsored discussions among Aerospatiale, Dassault–Breguet, Boeing, and McDonnell Douglas during 1975 and 1976. These talks led to the announcement in August 1976 of an agreement between McDonnell Douglas and the two French firms to develop the Mercure 200. Under the terms of the original agreement, McDonnell Douglas was to have a minor role in the development and production of the aircraft. Its share of the Mercure 200's production amounted to only 15 percent, although the U.S. firm was to design some of the components of the aircraft. Aerospatiale, which faced continuing financial losses due to the slow sales of the Airbus A300 and the termination of several military aircraft programs, had responsibility for the assembly of 40 percent of the aircraft, including final assembly. Dassault–Breguet was responsible for the overall design effort, as well as production of about 15 percent of the aircraft. While McDonnell Douglas had a secondary role in the design and production of the Mercure 200, the firm was responsible for marketing and providing product support for the aircraft. Moreover, according to one account, McDonnell Douglas was informally assured of orders from French and Swiss airlines for as many as seventy-five DC-9s and eight DC-10s in exchange for giving up the majority of the assembly work for the Mercure.[25]

The Mercure 200's wing design was identical to that of the Mercure 100, which constrained the range and other operating characteristics of the proposed aircraft and limited its potential market.[26] Despite strong support from McDonnell Douglas and a number of airlines for a new wing design, the costs of such a redesign made this alternative unattractive to the French participants.[27] McDonnell Douglas viewed a new wing design as essential to penetration of the U.S. market, which was critical to the commercial success of the Mercure 200. The U.S. firm was unsuccessful in its efforts to alter the design, however, and the Mercure 200 finally was abandoned, largely because of insufficient demand. The weak market for the Mercure 200 was not due solely to its wing design, but this flawed design clearly reduced the aircraft's appeal. Although McDonnell Douglas personnel were well aware of the problems in the Mercure 200 design, the firm was apparently unwilling to invest further in the costly development program that would have been necessary to produce a commercially successful Mercure 200 design.

A similar lack of financial commitment to match the firm's considerable technological assets characterized McDonnell Douglas's participation in the MDF100 project. McDonnell Douglas and Fokker began joint design and engineering work on a 150-seat aircraft, the MDF100, in May 1981. A serious difficulty with the project from the outset was its timing—there was no all-new engine available for the MDF100, the project having begun prior to the announcement of the V2500 venture and well after the introduction of the CFM56. Moreover, because any engine development program would take roughly one year longer than the airframe development, prospective purchasers of the MDF100 were faced with a choice between two derivative engines, the CFM56 or the JT8D.[28] Other aircraft producers deal with timing problems of this sort by extending the design definition phase, developing numerous variations on a few basic design concepts and constantly consulting with airlines and engine manufacturers as to the likely course of both propulsion technology and customer demand. This technique reduces commercial uncertainties, but requires a large and sustained commitment of engineering resources.

The uncertain market for the MDF100 dictated a prolonged period of design definition. The length of this gestation period, as well as its demands on Fokker's limited pool of engineering and design talent, were the critical factors in the demise of the joint venture. Fokker was producing two successful aircraft, the F27 commuter turboprop and the F28 short-range passenger jet. Product support, production engineering, and design modifications for these products required considerable engineering resources, and a substantial commitment by Fokker of engineering resources to the joint venture could jeopardize these ongoing, profitable programs. Any expansion of Fokker's engineering staff would have been temporary and eventually would have required costly layoffs. Faced with the likelihood of an indefinite period of preliminary design activity, uncertainty concerning the commercial prospects for the MDF100, and growing risks to the firm's successful product line from continued work on the MDF100, senior management of Fokker elected to withdraw from the MDF100 venture in May 1982.

While Fokker's reluctance to continue stemmed from the uncertain market for the MDF100, McDonnell Douglas's interest in the venture also diminished because of the remarkable potential of the DC-9 for additional stretching and re-engining. Renamed the MD-80, the aircraft fuselage seemed capable of being stretched to accommodate as many as 150 passengers (with a new engine). Moreover, a stretched DC-9 could be sold profitably for less than the MDF100, the price of which was expected to be $25 million dollars in 1981. Engine developments and technical possibilities unforeseen at the outset of the joint venture contributed to growing conflicts of interest between McDonnell Douglas and Fokker, as McDonnell Douglas's existing product line increasingly encroached on the market for the jointly developed product.

The total costs of launching the MDF100 were roughly $2 billion—Fokker's share of this was $1 billion, of which nearly $700 million was supported from public funds, $326 million in credits and $367 million in guaranteed loans.[29] The Dutch firm was to repay the loans out of a royalty on each aircraft sold prior to the achievement of a profit and a fixed share of total program profits following that point.

Since both firms were involved in the preliminary design phases of the MDF100 project, considerable exchange of proprietary data and design skills took place. Although the terms of the original memorandum of understanding provided that in the event of termination of the joint venture all design data would be returned to the original provider, the MDF100 venture almost certainly resulted in one of the most extensive transfers of technology of any venture discussed in this chapter. According to senior McDonnell Douglas personnel, for example, the wing design of the MDF100 was a hybrid of Fokker and McDonnell Douglas concepts.[30] Fokker also brought expertise in metal bonding to the joint venture. Neither participant in this project, however, was anxious to maximize the amount of technology transfer within the venture, in contrast to the Japanese participants in the 7J7 venture with Boeing.

The MDF100 venture was managed by a small project office staffed by employees of both firms, reflecting the equal status of

McDonnell Douglas and Fokker in the joint venture. This management structure proved somewhat unwieldy. Although the bulk of design work and all production management, marketing, and product support functions were carried out by the firms, rather than by an independent entity, the small size of the project office meant that fundamental decisions on design and other issues had to be resolved by senior peronnel from one or both firms. Since each partner had a full voice in all matters of design and management, each partner effectively held a veto over these decisions. As a result, both the time and the costs of the design phase of the MDF100 project were substantially higher than those of an independent project. Had the partner firms committed the resources to build up a separate engineering staff dedicated to the MDF100, some of the difficulties in decision-making and design might have been ameliorated.

The experience of McDonnell Douglas in the Mercure 200 and MDF100 joint ventures suggests some of the difficulties inherent in ventures in which a technologically or financially senior firm is unwilling to take a senior position within the joint venture. Had McDonnell Douglas been willing to adopt the more costly senior role in either joint venture, a technically and commercially successful aircraft might have been produced.[31] Certainly, the unwillingness of the French participants in the Mercure 200 project to address McDonnell Douglas's design concerns contributed to the failure of that venture. McDonnell Douglas's modest role in the venture, however, meant that the firm was not in a position to make its wishes and design philosophy prevail. In the case of the MDF100, a larger commitment of McDonnell Douglas funds and personnel might have supported Fokker's continued participation. Fokker's unwillingness to absorb the drain on its engineering resources during a lengthy period of design definition, rather than the prospective length of this period, was the central factor in the project's collapse. Balanced against the reluctance of McDonnell Douglas to undertake such a commitment, however, is the evident unwillingness of Fokker to assume a junior role in the MDF100 joint venture. Similar resistance to a subordinate role would have been raised by the French partners in the Mercure 200 project, judging from the statements of French aerospace industry managers and policy makers.[32]

GENERAL ELECTRIC-SNECMA

The joint venture between General Electric and SNECMA (Société Nationale d'Etude et de Construction de Moteurs d'Aviation) is centered on the production of the CFM56, a high-bypass ratio engine of 22,000–25,000 pounds of thrust. The collaboration of these two firms is managed formally by a separate entity (CFM International) in which each partner owns 50 percent of the equity. In contrast to the McDonnell Douglas-Fokker joint venture, however, which operated as an alliance of financial and technological equals, the technological senior partner within CFM International is General Electric. CFM International also has operated successfully under Defense Department controls on the transfer of engine technology from General Electric to SNECMA through the joint venture.

CFM International is a response to the factors discussed in chapter 2 that caused the gradual withdrawal of major engine producers from various segments of the commercial engine market. General Electric had long been involved in the production of commercial jet engines, but by the late 1960s this market was dominated by Pratt & Whitney. GE had produced several successful and profitable military engines, however, including the TF39 for the C-5A and the F101 for the B-1 bomber. These military engines, along with GE's partnership with SNECMA, formed the basis for GE's return to the commercial market. SNECMA, which had throughout the postwar period concentrated exclusively on military engines, used the joint venture as a vehicle for diversification away from reliance on the military market.[33]

The CFM joint venture originated in the early 1970s when engine producers on both sides of the Atlantic recognized the market for a high-bypass engine of 20,000–30,000 pounds of thrust, to be employed on medium- and short-range aircraft. A major market for such an engine was Europe, with its dense short-haul route structure. Both General Electric and Pratt & Whitney sought European participation in the development and production of this engine in order to enhance their market access. Simultaneously, SNECMA had developed a design concept for such an engine. (The French government owns 90 percent of the equity in SNECMA; the remaining 10 percent is owned by Pratt & Whitney.) SNECMA held talks with both General Electric and Pratt & Whitney, and ultimately chose General Electric as a partner in the development and production of the so-called ten-ton engine. SNECMA's choice of General Electric built on a relationship established through SNECMA's major sub-contracting role in the production of the CF6-50 and CF6-80 engines, employed on the Airbus A300 and A310 (SNECMA also undertook the final assembly of the CF6 engines for the Airbus, in an agreement with a strong resemblance to military offsets).

The General Electric design for the ten-ton engine continued the firm's reliance on military-civilian technology spillovers in developing commercial engines (the CF6 had employed high-bypass engine technology developed for the TF39 military engine). General Electric's proposal for the CFM56 utilized the engine core compressor developed by the firm for the military F-101 engine. In the eyes of the U.S. Air Force, however, this engine core compressor constituted a considerable technological advance and national security asset, developed with public funds. As a result, the Defense Department opposed the transfer of this technology from General Electric to a foreign firm. After lengthy negotiations that reached the highest levels of the French and U.S. governments (the issue was raised in a letter from French President Pompidou to President Nixon in 1972), the Pentagon approved the use of the F-101 compressor technology in the CFM56 under restrictive conditions. These included the shipment of the engine core by General Electric in a sealed "black box" module for installation by SNECMA on its CFM56 assembly line, a delay of eighteen months before the compressor could be shipped to France for testing, and the payment of a royalty on each engine to the U.S. government. These negotiations, although ultimately successful, delayed the introduction of the CFM56 by at least one year.

Such a delay would normally have a disastrous impact on the commercial prospects for a new engine. The CFM56 was, if anything, aided by this hiatus because its market was for several years quite unpromising. The expected reequipment programs of European and other airlines failed to materialize in the late 1970s. Despite the considerable efforts of the French government to support the launch of an aircraft that could use the CFM56 engine, sales of the engine were slow until the early 1980s, when the re-engining of the DC-8 and the KC-135 military tanker produced orders for nearly 2,500 engines. More recently, the introduction of the Boeing 737-300 and the development of the Airbus A320, both of which do or will employ versions of the CFM56 (respectively, the CFM56-3 and -5), has expanded potential sales considerably.

Several aspects of this joint venture are noteworthy. Although the efforts of the Defense Department to restrict technology transfer through CFM made the development of this engine more difficult and more costly, the imposition of restrictions on technology transfer ultimately did not jeopardize the program. The relative ease with which the central compressor could be manufactured separately and shipped to SNECMA from General Electric in a sealed black box reflected the modular design of the CFM56, which also reduced maintenance costs. The success of the modular design philosophy and its capacity for minimizing technology transfer have led to its application in other engines, including the International Aero Engines V2500. In addition, General Electric did most of the overall development and systems integration for the engine, reducing the requirements for information and data exchange between the two partners. Nonetheless, some observers have suggested that the CFM56 has incurred performance penalties, because much of the engine development took place without extensive sharing of technology and design data by the parties responsible for the compressor and the rear sections of the engine.[34]

The slow pace of development of the CFM56 simplified the management of this process. Had the CFM56 been a tightly time-constrained program (such as the JT9D for the Boeing 747), project management would have been more difficult because of the absence of a clear veto power by either partner and of a well-staffed independent project management office. Although neither firm held a formal veto, General Electric was the acknowledged technological senior partner within the venture, receiving a fee from SNECMA for project management. As such, major design decisions typically were made by General Electric personnel, with input from SNECMA. The nature of the General Electric role within CFM International also can be inferred from the fact that GE provides virtually all of the product support for the engine. That the financial equality of the two partners is not reflected in the technological relationship of General Electric and SNECMA seems to have prevented problems in decision making. The technological asymmetry between General Electric and SNECMA, as well as the greater length of the development cycle, thus seem to have prevented difficulties of the sort that plagued the MDF100 and Mercure 200 projects.

SNECMA shares with General Electric the responsibility for final assembly of the engine, with production lines operating in both France and the United States. Thus far, the CFM partnership appears to have avoided the difficulties in the management of production fluctuations that have created problems in some military offset and coproduction programs. Within the CF6 program, for which SNECMA is a major supplier, General Electric has absorbed problems associated with the fluctuations in demand by varying production rates on its assembly line and by shifting labor to other products. Fluctuations in demand for the CFM56 have not yet been significant—since production began, demand for the engine has been sufficient to keep both assembly lines fully occupied.

The CFM venture has been a commercial success. SNECMA was one of the leading French exporters of aerospace products in 1984, and the CFM56 engine accounted for nearly 50 percent of total orders for large commercial aircraft engines in 1984. General Electric also has benefited: SNECMA contributed 50 percent of the development costs of the CFM56, which totaled more than $1 billion. But the importance of SNECMA's financial contribution goes beyond its magnitude. In the view of senior personnel at General Electric's Aircraft Engine Group, SNECMA's financial contribution prevented termination of the CFM56 program in the mid-1970s. Moreover, the adoption of the CFM56-5 for the Airbus A320 undoubtedly was aided by the engine's substantial French content, providing a good example of enhanced market access through the strategic choice of joint venture partners. Estimates of the French government's share of the SNECMA contribution to the development of the CFM56 vary, but the government contribution, much of which took the form of low- or no-interest loans, has probably amounted to at least several hundred million dollars over the life of the project.[35]

The CFM venture has proven financially rewarding for SNECMA, but the technological benefits are less visible. SNECMA gives no signs of undertaking the development of a commercial engine without General Electric's participation, either independently or in cooperation with other European producers. Indeed, it is possible that the CFM venture prevented the development of an all–European consortium, conceivably led by Rolls Royce, in commercial jet engines.[36] SNECMA's participation in the engine business as a prime contractor is unlikely, but it has almost certainly become more competitive as a supplier of spare parts. Spare parts sales for the CFM56 are regulated by the GE-SNECMA agreement, but the possibility remains that SNECMA could enter the market for other military or civilian engine spare parts.

The agreement between General Electric and SNECMA covers only the CFM56 engine. General Electric and SNECMA recently have extended their alliance, however, to include the development of an unducted fan (UDF) engine, which has been proposed by Boeing for its 7J7 aircraft. SNECMA now holds a 35 percent share in a partnership developing the UDF engine. Like the CFM56, the UDF draws on an engine core technology developed for military applications, in this case the F404 fighter engine. Nonetheless, the financial burdens of the UDF undertaking potentially dwarf those of the CF6 or the CFM56. rendering the partnership attractive to General Electric.

The amount of technology transfer that is likely to occur between the partners in the UDF joint venture is difficult to determine because two opposing factors operate within the project. On the one hand, SNECMA's proposed share in the UDF project is smaller than its share in the CFM56 program.[37] On the other hand, the UDF program will involve both firms as partners at an earlier stage in the development process, and inevitably will generate significant flows of knowledge and expertise between the partners. Technology transfer also may be increased by the fact that the UDF cannot be developed in the modular fashion that characterized the CFM56, because it is a relatively unproven technology and because the technology of the engine itself is less amenable to such an arm's-length arrangement.[38] Like the 7J7 venture between Boeing and the Japanese consortium, the UDF project suggests that the SNECMA-General Electric alliance is likely to continue, and technology transfer within the partnership is likely to increase. Nonetheless, General Electric will remain the senior partner.

The CFM International venture also illustrates the costs and benefits of efforts by the U.S. government to regulate technology transfer. Controls on technology transfer did not jeopardize the technological or commercial success of the joint venture and reduced the amount of technology transferred within this joint venture. Nonetheless, developing and negotiating these controls with groups in the

Defense and State departments, as well as the White House and National Security Council, consumed a great deal of time, seriously delaying the CFM56 project. In addition, the restrictions on technology transfer may have resulted in some performance penalties. At a minimum, the CFM56 experience suggests that any federal policy structure regulating technology transfer must have as an overriding goal the development of an expeditious and internally consistent evaluation process.

THE SAAB-FAIRCHILD 340

The Saab-Fairchild 340 (SF340) is the only commuter aircraft introduced since the deregulation of U.S. domestic air transportation that was developed and produced in part by a U.S. firm. Moreover, the aircraft is the first civil aircraft produced by Saab-Scania of Sweden in more than thirty years and briefly expanded Fairchild Aircraft's civil aircraft product line. The Saab-Fairchild joint venture resembled CFM International in that it was intended to serve as a vehicle for entry into new markets for both firms. Unlike CFM International, however, Saab-Scania and Fairchild were technologically equal partners, and their joint venture involved significant technology exchange. The Saab-Fairchild joint venture recently has collapsed with the withdrawal of Fairchild from the partnership. While Fairchild will remain involved as a major subcontractor and supplier for the SF340 for several more years, the U.S. firm has proven unable to bear the financial and technological burdens of partnership.

The SF340 venture was initiated by Saab-Scania Aircraft in the late 1970s as part of the firm's efforts to diversify its production of aircraft beyond exclusively military products.[39] Saab-Scania's design and manufacture of military aircraft for the Swedish Air Force during the previous forty years had developed strong design and production capabilities within the firm. For a number of reasons, however, the Swedish military aircraft market in the late 1970s presented limited and unstable growth prospects, creating strong incentives for Saab-Scania to diversify out of the exclusive production of military aircraft. Production of components for other commercial aircraft afforded one means for the preservation of employment, production capacity, and some design skills. Saab-Scania's role as a subcontractor expanded considerably during the early 1980s, as the firm manufactured components for the McDonnell Douglas MD-80 and the British Aerospace BAe 146. Subcontracting alone, however, would not preserve Saab-Scania's design and systems integration capabilities. These could be maintained only through the development and production of a commercial aircraft for which Saab-Scania had significant responsibilities for overall design and systems integration.

The decision to pursue development of a commuter aircraft followed attempts to design and develop a "Europlane" in cooperation with MBB (Messerschmitt-Boelkow-Blohm) of Germany, the British Aircraft Corporation, and CASA (Construcciones Aeronautics, S.A.) of Spain in the mid-1970s. The Europlane consortium had as its goal the design and production of a short-range transport with a capacity of 100–140 passengers. Europlane foundered in the face of the depressed aircraft market of the early 1970s and was hampered as well by a lack of new engines that could provide significant reductions in operating costs. Because participation as a lead design firm in other large civil transport consortia was not feasible (for example, as a partner with Boeing or Airbus Industrie), Saab-Scania's prospects were confined largely to the commuter aircraft market.[40] The commuter aircraft market was expected to grow rapidly in the late 1970s, and commuter aircraft development projects were less costly than large commercial transports. Deregulation of U.S. domestic transport and continued economic growth in industrializing nations (many of which had limited substitutes for air transportation) contributed to buoyant forecasts of future markets for commuter aircraft. The commuter aircraft designs considered by Saab-Scania were relatively sophisticated in their incorporation of cabin pressurization and advanced flight management systems. Consistent with its earlier experiences in military aircraft, Saab-Scania set out to design a high-performance commuter aircraft.

Saab-Scania's interest in a U.S. partner for the development, production, and marketing of the aircraft was motivated by several considerations. Penetration of the U.S. market was essential to the commercial success of any commuter aircraft. Access to this market would be aided greatly by the presence of a U.S. partner. In addition, Saab-Scania had no foreign marketing or product support network for nonmilitary aircraft. Teaming with an established U.S. producer could provide such a network for Saab-Scania in the U.S., the largest single market for the aircraft. Finally, the financial and engineering requirements for the development of the SF340 meant that a partner was necessary for the aircraft to be introduced in a timely fashion. Significantly, access to technological expertise was not a major concern for the Swedish firm in evaluating potential U.S. partners.

The major U.S. producers of general aviation and business aircraft, including Beech, Cessna, and Piper, were unwilling to participate in the proposed joint venture when approached by Saab-Scania in the late 1970s. Fairchild Aircraft seemed to be an attractive partner, because of its ownership of Swearingen Aircraft, producers of the nineteen-passenger Metro. In the course of producing and marketing the Metro to commuter airlines and business firms, Fairchild-Swearingen had developed an extensive U.S. marketing and product support network, the key corporate asset of interest to Saab-Scania.

The terms of the agreement signed by the two firms in 1980 required that each partner contribute 50 percent of the costs of developing the aircraft, which was to be assembled in Sweden by Saab-Scania. Part of the Swedish firm's development costs were underwritten by a loan from the Swedish Industry Fund of SKr 350 million ($60–80 million at 1982 exchange rates). Fairchild's primary production responsibility was the wing, assembled at Fairchild-Republic Aviation, a producer of military aircraft and a major sub-contractor on earlier Boeing aircraft. Marketing and product support for the aircraft in the United States were the responsibility of Fairchild-Swearingen. A jointly owned entity, Saab Fairchild International, was created, but its responsibilities did not include design or project management, being limited to marketing and product support outside the United States. Management of the development and production phases of the project was controlled by a special board, with equal representation from senior management of both partner firms. In its financial and technological composition, then, the SF340 venture was a partnership of equals, and had no project management office that was independent of the partner firms.

The small independent staff of the SF340 project frequently needed to take design and technical issues to the full management committee for resolution—both major and trivial decisions on design and technological issues were made at the most senior levels of both firms. This process consumed considerable time. Saab-Scania's inexperience in the civil aircraft market also contributed to the Swedish firm's acceptance of several key design features proposed by Fairchild, including the three-seat cross section and the thirty-four-seat capacity of the final design. Undertaken in order to make the aircraft attractive to corporate aviation customers, these decisions placed the SF340 in a crowded segment of the commuter aircraft market, one served by products manufactured by both de Havilland of Canada (the DHC-8) and Embraer of Brazil. Although the SF340 can be stretched to serve the forty-passenger market, this operation is costly and might reduce sales of the smaller version of the aircraft.

The protracted discussions and disputes over design features, as well as technical difficulties in mastering the new bonding technologies and wing design incorporated in the aircraft, contributed to delays in the development of the SF340. As a result, the SF340's lead time over several competing commuter aircraft was reduced considerably. Moreover, the development of the aircraft was substantially more costly than expected: development and startup costs mounted to over $400 million.[41]

A number of the important technological advances in the SF340 were contributed by neither firm. The aircraft wing, for example, is based on a design developed by NASA. Saab-Scania's access to the wing design and performance data was facilitated by its partnership with Fairchild. As a U.S. firm, Fairchild Aircraft has immediate access to any data released by NASA; access to these data by Saab-Scania is prohibited for one year after their domestic release. The construction of the fuselage of the SF340 also employs high-temperature bonding technologies, which were developed by Lockheed and Boeing and utilized by Fairchild Aircraft in its role as a major subcontractor for Boeing. The technological parity of the partners in the SF340 venture meant that the net "outflow" of U.S. aircraft technology within this joint venture was modest. The aircraft is assembled in Sweden, but the U.S. content of the final product, which uses General Electric engines, is high—the landing gear and the propeller are the only non-U.S. components. This joint venture is unlikely to hurt U.S. supplier firms.

The SF340 was introduced in 1984 and has sold well. Current orders for the aircraft total at least seventy-nine, and the Swedish assembly line has an order backlog extending through 1986. The aircraft is not yet profitable, however, and the unexpectedly high financial burdens of its production have exacted a toll on the U.S. partner. Moreover, the aircraft has experienced recurrent operating problems in its first two years of service.

Severe financial difficulties during 1984 and 1985 led Fairchild Industries, corporate parent of the aircraft firm, to withdraw from its partnership with Saab-Scania in September 1985. The firm's withdrawal followed a succession of managerial and technical problems, ranging from wing assembly to marketing the aircraft in the United States.[42] Under the terms of the dissolution agreement negotiated with Saab-Scania, Fairchild will manufacture wings for the SF340 as a subcontractor through the first half of 1987.[43] During 1986–1987, Fairchild is to transfer the wing design, manufacturing tooling, and design data to Saab-Scania, which will assume full responsibility for wing production in 1987. Fairchild will also withdraw completely from marketing and product support for the SF340.

In contrast to Fairchild Industries, the corporate parent of Saab-Scania Aircraft has not suffered financial losses as a result of the SF340—the costs of the venture have been partially defrayed by public funds and the robust profits of Saab-Scania's automotive operations. Withdrawal of Fairchild from the joint venture does not mean the end of the SF340. Fairchild's technical and financial weaknesses had for some time forced the Swedish firm to play a more substantial role within the joint venture than originally planned, as in the reorganization of the U.S. marketing network. Nonetheless, if Saab-Scania is to remain profitably involved in civil aircraft production, the firm will have to introduce additional products in the commuter or business aircraft markets to take full advantage of the marketing and product support network established for the SF340. Because of the high costs of independent development projects, Saab-Scania will have to seek other partners in any future product development venture.

Despite its initially promising sales, the financial returns from the SF340 are not likely to be substantial. Fairchild provided considerable funding, but ultimately proved to be a weak partner. Saab-Scania faces a large additional investment to sustain the market for an aircraft that will have to be produced in considerable quantity (more than 200–250 units) before it returns a profit. The SF340 has achieved a substantial presence within the U.S. market, however, aided initially by the involvement of a U.S. partner in the aircraft's development and production. Saab-Scania's strategy of reducing its financial exposure by undertaking the development of such an aircraft in a partnership has been a mixed success at best.

In addition to its sobering implications concerning the importance of choosing a strong partner in joint ventures, the SF340 venture suggests some guidelines for the management of international joint ventures between technological and financial equals. This joint venture was hampered by the lack of either a clearly designated senior partner or an autonomous group charged with managing the design, development, and production of the aircraft. Although such independent entities may duplicate some of the functions and many of the costs of senior management of the partner firms, the inability of the personnel in the SF340 venture to resolve issues at lower levels considerably delayed the design of the aircraft, thereby delaying its introduction in a market in which early delivery is critical and contributing to cost overruns.

THE INTERNATIONAL AERO ENGINES V2500

The V2500 joint venture involves Pratt & Whitney, Rolls Royce, Fiat, MTU, and Japan Aero Engines Corporation (JAEC, itself a consortium of Kawasaki Heavy Industries, Mitsubishi Heavy Industries, and Ishikawajima–Harima Heavy Industries), in one of the most ambitious joint ventures in the commercial aircraft industry. Announced in 1983, the joint venture has as its goal the development and production of a new 25,000-pound thrust engine, for employment in the 150-seat aircraft of the 1990s (currently, the Airbus A320 and McDonnell Douglas MD-89). International Aero Engines (IAE), an entity incorporated in Switzerland, coordinates development, production, marketing, and product support for the V2500. Ownership of IAE equity is divided as follows: Pratt & Whitney (30 percent), Rolls Royce (30 percent), Japan Aero Engines (19.9 percent), MTU (12.1 percent), and Fiat (8 percent). While the formal structure of the V2500 venture appears complex, the venture more nearly resembles an alliance of two multifirm groups, centered on Rolls Royce (partners with Japan Aero Engines) and on Pratt & Whitney (teamed with MTU and Fiat). Both the identities of the member firms and the division of production and design activities among the participants in International Aero Engines reflect the experiences of each of the two groups in joint development and production of other engines.

The decision by Rolls Royce and Pratt & Whitney to join forces followed a previous, unsuccessful joint venture between the two firms, the JT10D project. The JT10D was a high-bypass engine generating 28,000 pounts of thrust intended for the Boeing 757. The

1976 agreement between the two firms provided that Pratt & Whitney would handle overall project management, with 54 percent of the work, while Rolls Royce would handle 34 percent, Fiat 2 percent, and MTU 10 percent of the design, development, and production work. Inasmuch as overall management of the venture was to be handled largely by Pratt & Whitney, no independent management structure was envisioned in the original agreement. The JT10D partnership lasted less than a year, breaking up "amicably," according to the participants, in the spring of 1977.[44]

Several factors contributed to the dissolution of the JT10D partnership. By far the most important was the evolution of the Boeing 757 from an aircraft with 150 seats to one with 180 seats; as a result, the aircraft needed a larger engine, with a thrust rating of nearly 35,000 pounds. Growth in the 757's thrust requirements diminished the attractiveness for Rolls Royce of participation in the development of a new engine, since the British firm was developing independently an engine of 38,000 pounds of thrust, the RB211-535. Rolls Royce accordingly proposed to Pratt & Whitney that the venture be reorganized, with Pratt & Whitney operating as a junior partner in a venture that would develop and optimize a version of the RB211-535 for the 757; the U.S. firm was not interested. In addition, several observers have suggested that transatlantic cooperation in the development of this engine was complicated by the restrictions on transfer of engine core technology that were imposed on Pratt & Whitney by the U.S. Defense Department.[45] The JT10D was to be a true joint design, requiring a more extensive exchange of technology and design data than was true of the CFM56, and restrictions on technology transfer accordingly were more onerous. In the wake of the dissolution of this joint venture, Pratt & Whitney enlisted Fiat and MTU as risk-sharing subcontractors in the development of the PW2037, an engine generating 37,000 pounds of thrust that now competes directly with the Rolls Royce RB211-535 for deployment on the 757.

Prior to its discussions with Pratt & Whitney on the JT10D, Rolls Royce had joined Japan Aero Engines in the early 1970s in the development of the RJ500, a high-bypass engine producing 20,000 pounds of thrust. The Rolls-Japanese consortium built on the JAEC's previous work on the smaller FJR710. The FJR710 was funded by the Japan National Aeronautics Laboratory as an experimental development project. Lacking high-altitude engine testing facilities within

Japan, the JAEC consortium used those of Rolls Royce, which led to the decision to cooperate in the development of the larger RJ500. Although test versions of the RJ500 were running successfully in early 1982, airframe manufacturers did not exhibit great interest in the engine. The RJ500 was intended to power the 737-300, but Boeing preferred the CFM56-3, which would be available sooner. Moreover, the uncertainties that clouded the design discussions of McDonnell Douglas, Boeing, and Airbus Industrie over the configurations and engine requirements of future 150-seat transports caused the Anglo-Japanese consortium to delay a commitment to a specific engine thrust rating.[46] Despite the uncertainties, it gradually became apparent that any engine for a 150-seat aircraft would require more than 20,000 pounds of thrust and would have to incorporate new technologies in materials and controls to increase fuel efficiency. Faced with these costly requirements, in 1982 the RJ500 group began exploring the possibilities for cooperation with either General Electric or Pratt & Whitney.

The other major group within the V2500 venture consists of Pratt & Whitney and the two European firms with whom Pratt & Whitney has worked closely in developing and producing the PW2037. During the late 1970s Pratt & Whitney undertook the development of two new engines, the PW4000 and the PW2037, from a "clean sheet of paper"—neither engine had a military antecedent, and neither was a derivative of a previous civil engine design. The technological and financial burdens of these development projects were and remain immense, particularly in view of the modest pace at which the Boeing 757 is selling. Fiat and MTU account respectively for 4 percent and 11 percent of the value of the PW2037.[47] Reflecting an emerging pattern of specialization, Fiat produced the gearbox for the PW2037, while MTU developed the low-pressure turbine section at the rear of the engine.

Pratt & Whitney's ambitious development agenda largely precluded the firm's unaided launch of yet another multibillion dollar program to develop an engine with a thrust capacity in the 20,000–25,000-pound range, a market segment that appeared increasingly attractive as the Airbus A320 was finally launched and McDonnell Douglas announced its intention to develop the MD-89 to serve this market. The U.S. firm accordingly reentered negotiations with Rolls Royce. An alternative partner for Rolls Royce was General Electric. CFM International's participation in this segment of the market (with the CFM56), however, reduced General Electric's interest in teaming with the Rolls Royce-JAEC group in the development of a competing engine. In 1982 the existing Rolls Royce and Pratt & Whitney groups formed an alliance to develop an all-new engine with 25,000 pounds of thrust.[48]

Significant technological contributions to the V2500 are being made by both of the senior partners. Rolls Royce and JAEC are responsible for the forward section of the engine (the low- and high-pressure compressors), using the advanced technology for fan blade fabrication developed by Rolls Royce for the RB211 family of engines. The Pratt & Whitney group is responsible for the rear sections of the engine, employing technologies developed and applied in the PW2037. Pratt & Whitney is responsible for the engine core, while MTU and Fiat respectively will develop and produce the same components that these firms developed and produced for the PW2037, the low-pressure turbine and the gearbox. Assembly of the engine will take place in both the United States and Great Britain. Marketing is to be carried out by International Aero Engines, which also has responsibility for systems integration and project management. The managerial and marketing role for an independent IAE is important, in part because of the numerous possibilities for conflict of interest if either Rolls Royce or Pratt & Whitney were given primary responsibility for marketing the engine. Such conflicts between jointly developed and wholly owned products, after all, undermined the JT10D venture.[49] Product support, however, will be delegated by IAE to the member firms best able to provide it. These firms are likely to be Pratt & Whitney and Rolls Royce.

The governments of the nations in which the foreign participants in the V2500 venture are based all have provided significant financial assistance. Rolls Royce, for example, requested funding from the British government in the amount of $170 million, or 50 percent of its estimated costs of participation, and eventually received slightly less, roughly $150 million. These funds were granted in the form of a no-interest loan, to be repaid out of a royalty on each engine sold. The Japanese consortium, responsible for a smaller share of the total program, has received annual financial payments since the inception of the FJR710 project of roughly $20-25 million, covering 75 percent, 66 percent, and 50 percent respectively of the fundamental development, testing, and production tooling and nonrecurring start-up costs. Japanese government support is to be repaid with interest to the Ministry of International Trade and Industry upon the achievement of a profit. Comparable figures are more difficult to obtain for the other foreign participants, but the levels of government support for MTU and Fiat participation with Pratt & Whitney in the PW2037 project provide a general indication. Fiat requested from the Italian government a grant of $23 million for its PW2037 and other turbine technology research during 1981,[50] while MTU received public funding in the form of a loan of $80 million for 50 percent of the costs of its participation in the PW2037 project.[51]

The senior partners in the V2500 venture have devoted considerable attention to minimizing technology transfer. Some of these efforts were motivated by U.S. government scrutiny of Pratt & Whitney's role in the consortium and the desire of the Pentagon to prevent transfer of the U.S. firm's high-pressure engine core technology to foreign firms. Much of this concern, however, reflects the individual commercial interests of the member firms. In order to minimize technology transfer, the V2500 program emphasizes the separate development of engine components by member firms, with minimal exchange of technical or proprietary data among the partners.[52] Interfaces among these components have been negotiated and designed to facilitate the assembly and testing of the entire engine without the need to know a great deal about the internal mechanics or technology of the individual components. Like the CFM56, the V2500 relies heavily on modular design and construction principles.

While a development program organized in this fashion reduces technology transfer among the participants, it complicates the resolution of the systemic problems that inevitably arise in the course of testing an engine. Efforts to minimize technology transfer within the V2500 program may reduce the ease and speed with which the engine can be tested and brought to market.[53] Indeed, the experience of both the CFM56 and the JT10D suggests that the construction of barriers to technology transfer may result in performance penalties. The desire of both Pratt & Whitney and Rolls Royce to minimize technology transfer within the joint venture also conflicts with the desires of other participants to improve their technological and marketing skills. Japanese participants in the V2500 project, for example, are unlikely to gain the broader knowledge of marketing, product support, and development engineering to support their entry into the engine industry as a prime contractor.[54] A clearly delineated and narrowly defined division of labor within the con-

sortium thus imposes costs on individual firms and may create difficulties in systems integration. Nonetheless, the ability of individual
participants to exploit their specialized skills and technologies in the
development and manufacture of specific components (for example,
Fiat and the gearbox) should yield efficiency gains.

The U.S. Department of Justice reviewed the V2500 venture and
approved it in September 1983. It is difficult to think of another
U.S. industry with a comparably concentrated market structure
(three firms account for virtually 100 percent of total sales of large
transport engines in the noncommunist world market) in which a
joint venture among two of the three major competitors would be
approved. Moreover, as the above discussion makes clear, one of the
two alliances that have joined forces in IAE (Rolls Royce and the
JAEC) had a product, the RJ500 engine, that might have supported
separate entry into this segment of the engine market. The approval
of the IAE proposal by the Department of Justice provides some
evidence to support the view that joint ventures between U.S. and
foreign firms receive less thorough scrutiny than those involving only
U.S. firms.

The V2500 project contrasts with the other joint ventures discussed in this chapter in several ways. There exists no clearly defined
or designated technological or financial senior partner—the multinational groups respectively assembled by Rolls Royce and Pratt &
Whitney are each making significant contributions of capital and
technology. The technological and financial contributions of the participants in each group, however, vary substantially. Nonetheless,
International Aero Engines A.G. clearly departs from the usual practice of entrusting management of the joint venture to an ad hoc
committee (as with the SF340, a thinly staffed, separate corporate
entity) or to the financially or technologically senior firm (as with
the Boeing 767 and, to a lesser extent, GE-SNECMA ventures). Unlike these ventures, IAE has a substantial staff of managers specifi-
cally charged with control of overall development and marketing. As
the discussion in chapter 4 suggests, this structure resembles that of
Airbus Industrie, for good reasons.

The V2500 venture's emphasis on specialization and barriers to
technology transfer also distinguish this project. Unfortunately, it is
too early to assess the effectiveness of such barriers to technology
transfer or to reach conclusions about the outcome of the clash in
incentives between technologically junior and senior partner firms in

this venture. The efforts of the senior firms in the V2500 to establish and enforce barriers to technology transfer clearly suggest that the management of these firms is concerned about the longer-term competitive implications of unrestricted technology transfer. The potentially detrimental effect of these barriers to technology transfer on the integration and testing of the numerous components that are necessary to yield an optimal design cannot yet be determined. Nonetheless, these tasks are made more difficult by the interposition of barriers to technology transfer.

CONCLUSION

The multinational joint ventures discussed in this chapter are a limited sample of a rapidly growing phenomenon in the commercial aircraft industry. Even these cases form a remarkably diverse collection about which generalizations are difficult. The structure of the ventures, the amount of technology transfer occurring within them, and the relative importance of U.S. and foreign firms as participants within each venture all differ greatly. Among other things, this diversity suggests that any general policy aimed at controlling or otherwise regulating these ventures will be uneven and arbitrary in its effect. Nonetheless, some general themes, many of which are relevant primarily to managers of such ventures, are clearly discernible within this collection of contrasts.

The nature of the "glue" binding together the partners is complex, with implications for the organization and management of such undertakings. One of the most important bonding agents is the technological disparity among the participant firms. This disparity creates the basis for an exchange of technology for capital or market access. The structure of joint ventures of this variety does not seem to be an issue of great moment, since the more advanced firm typically assumes responsibility for overall management and design. Ventures founded on the existence of technological disparities have operated reasonably well as a partnership of financial equals (CFM International) or as a partnership between a prime contractor and a risk-sharing subcontractor (the 767 and possibly Japan Aero Engines, Fiat, and MTU, producers of components for Rolls Royce and Pratt & Whitney, within the V2500 project).

A critical source of tension between technologically junior and senior partners, however, involves the amount of technology transfer that is acceptable to the participants. Thus far, technology transfer within these joint ventures has involved none of the key components of the senior firms' most advanced technologies. In other words, the quality and quantity of technology transfer has been insufficient to enable the junior partners to become serious threats to the senior firms within any reasonable time horizon. This characteristic of joint ventures between technological leaders and followers means that the aspirations of technologically junior firms for extensive learning and technology acquisition may not be realized. Firms interested primarily in establishing a specialized subcontracting capability, or in stabilizing their work force and production capacity, are more likely to be satisfied with the limited technology transfer operating within joint ventures than are firms interested in entering the airframe or engine industry as a prime contractor, responsible for comprehensive management, design, and systems integration. As the discussion in chapter 4 indicates, the aspirations of various European firms, such as Volvo Flygmotor of Sweden, MTU of West Germany, and Fiat and Aeritalia of Italy, all of which have pursued specialized roles, may be more compatible with the realities of technology transfer within these ventures than are the goals of the Japanese participants in the Boeing and V2500 ventures.

Ventures involving firms of comparable technological endowments require greater attention to organization and management. The cases discussed here suggest several sources of difficulty within such partnerships. In both the MDF100 and Saab–Fairchild ventures, the resolution of design disputes between the partner firms proved to be difficult and time-consuming. Because these ventures had no strong, independent design staff such issues had to be resolved at senior levels of the partner firms. The structure of the V2500 venture, in which the high-level systems integration and overall design activities are the responsibility of an independent staff that works with the participant firms as subcontractors and suppliers, seems to have great advantages in this regard.

In addition, of course, an organizational structure like IAE's, in which systems integration is combined with marketing and the management of product support, reestablishes an essential link that was severed or greatly weakened in both the MDF100 and SF340 ventures. The history of such projects as the Boeing 757 and 767 or the Airbus Industrie A310 and A320 demonstrates that close consultation between potential customers and the marketing and design personnel of the airframe producer is crucial to successful introduction of a new product. Joint venture organizations without this link between marketing, product support, and design are more likely to make inappropriate design compromises and decisions.

An additional problem in joint ventures among technological equals is the emergence of competition between the product being developed within the joint venture and those produced independently by participant firms. This problem was particularly important in the unsuccessful JT10D venture between Pratt & Whitney and Rolls Royce and contributed to the demise of the MDF100 project. The degree to which aircraft and engines may be substitutes for one another varies greatly across customers and markets, reflecting the influence of financial terms, route structure, and characteristics of the potential purchaser's existing aircraft fleet.[55] Some competition between independently manufactured products and those developed and produced jointly therefore is always present in a joint venture and may confront the partners with a conflict of interest if marketing is not handled by an independent management organization. There are no obvious solutions to this problem; its prevalence reflects the technologically dynamic character of this industry as well as the advanced capabilities of technological equals. The frequency with which the problem has occurred, however, suggests that firms contemplating joint ventures as a means of obtaining financial support or market access are ill-advised to enter a joint venture with a partner of comparable technological capabilities.

NOTES

1. "This trend toward subcontracting for services and renting or borrowing talent also is part of the [Boeing Company's] desire to avoid the huge buildup of manpower that marked the late 1960s and the subsequent wholesale layoffs that rocked the entire state of Washington. . . . An interesting trend is revealed by a chart comparing Boeing sales in constant dollars with total manpower. From 1957 through the late 1960s the curves traveled closely together. Since then, a wide gap has opened indicating the company is achieving more total sales with considerably fewer employees." Richard G. O'Lone, "Boeing Cools on Cooperative Programs," *Aviation Week and Space Technology*, June 6, 1977, pp. 48–49.

2. Risk-sharing subcontractors for the 767, who include the JCAC and Aeritalia, are required to amortize nonrecurring costs over the first 500 units, a

significant increase from the demands on risk-sharing subcontractors within the 747 project, where nonrecurring costs were amortized over the first 200 aircraft. E.H. Boullioun, president of Boeing Commercial Airplane Company, noted in 1978 that "We learned on the 747. . . . People were crying about the risk, but we had sold 200 before the contracts were signed. There was no risk." Quoted in O'Lone, "United's Purchase Launches 767," *Aviation Week and Space Technology*, July 24, 1978, p. 14.

3. MITI's interest in the aircraft industry is based on the industry's utilization of high technology inputs, links with other R&D-intensive industries, the high value-added characteristics of commercial aircraft production, the opportunities afforded by the aircraft industry to utilize production capacity built up under the auspices of coproduction programs, and the potential of aircraft industry employment to absorb workers from such declining businesses in the Mitsubishi and Kawasaki groups as shipbuilding.

4. A third design, for a three-engine transport known as the 777, was discussed widely during this period but ultimately was dropped as both the 757 and 767 expanded in size.

5. "According to Boeing, Japan was considered for the 'risk-sharing subcontract' only after U.S. companies had been approached and showed no interest in the program. The U.S. companies were either unable or unwilling to risk the investment." U.S. General Accounting Office, *U.S.-Military Co-production Agreements Assist Japan in Developing Its Civil Aircraft Industry* (Washington, D.C.: U.S. Government Printing Office, 1982), note, p. 16.

6. "It is a ground rule that Boeing will own 51% and will control any collaborative effort on a new Boeing airplane. 'We have looked at programs that were 50–50, and we don't think it works very well,' the [Boeing] official said, 'You get hung up on the decisions, and it costs you money.'" *Aviation Week and Space Technology*, "Joint U.S. Foreign Efforts Pushed," February 2, 1976, p. 24.

7. "BAe might be given an important place in the design process, but overall responsibility for the vital integrating functions would remain with Boeing. In effect, BAe would be a subcontractor to a dominant and perhaps unreliable partner, a status which might threaten the long-term health of BAe's civil capability. BAe feared that its ability to design, produce, and market a complete civil aircraft would be progressively eroded by the contract with Boeing." Keith Hayward, *Government and British Civil Aerospace* (Manchester, England: University of Manchester Press, 1983), p. 170. I have relied on Hayward's excellent account in this discussion of the byzantine negotiations between Boeing and various potential European participants.

8. "Transport Minister Marcel Cavaille said the [French] government rejected possible cooperation with Boeing because of what he called the risk that the French industry would become a subcontractor under Boeing's

terms." *Aviation Week and Space Technology*, "French Pick U.S. Firm," August 16, 1976, p. 12.

9.   The nonrecurring costs for both the 757 and 767 amounted to more than $2 billion, and the 767 accounted for well over half that amount. As much as 95 percent of the hydraulic systems in the two aircraft are identical; commonality in other major areas, such as the cockpit, nose, and electrical power systems is roughly 70 percent. See "Commonality Stressed in New Aircraft," *Aviation Week and Space Technology*, November 12, 1979, p. 67.

10.   The terms of the Boeing contract with the JCAC were described as "severe" by officials at MITI and the participating firms, requiring considerable efficiency and productivity improvements. Moreover, " . . . a Mitsubishi Heavy Industries executive said openly early in the program that the 767 is 'not an effective program—because the investment is too large and the profit is small.' " See "New Efforts Task Japanese Firms," *Aviation Week and Space Technology*, October 2, 1978, p. 31.

11.   " . . . the new design and manufacturing technology, especially computer-aided design, places much more accurate data in the hands of the subcontractors. It eliminates intermediate steps and provides less chance for error." *Air Transport World*, March 1981, p. 22.

12.   R.G. O'Lone, "Japan Setting Higher Aerospace Goals," *Aviation Week and Space Technology*, November 21, 1983, p. 16.

13.   Much of the reluctance of British Aerospace to undertake a venture with Boeing reflected the British firm's concern that it would be held to very stringent, perhaps impossible, financial and performance standards: " . . . BAe was being asked to meet targets which Boeing itself would find hard to meet. For instance, BAe would have to design and produce the newest element in the 757 design, the wing section (most of the remaining aircraft was derived from existing technology) at prices based on estimates derived from Boeing's calculations of *total* programme costs thereby hiding the true cost of developing the wing. According to BAe's calculations, Boeing and BAe differed by 30 percent on estimates of the cost of producing the wing section. BAe's analysis of comparative costings showed that American firms, even with their generally higher productivity, would be unable to produce a new wing at the prices demanded by Boeing." Hayward, *Government and British Civil Aerospace*, p. 176.

14.   The Japanese partners in the 767 project are making an extra payment of $143 million to Boeing as a royalty for the U.S. firm's production and design experience, as well as its global sales and product support network. See "Japanese Doubts Rising over F-15, P-3C," *Aviation Week and Space Technology*, June 6, 1977, p. 201.

15.   Aeritalia's participation in the 767 project has not yielded comparable market access to the European market, because of the superior political

saliency and strength of Airbus Industrie, whose A310 competes directly with the 767.

16. A similar argument may be found in Richard W. Moxon, Thomas W. Roehl, and J. Frederick Truitt, *Emerging Sources of Foreign Competition in the Commercial Aircraft Manufacturing Industry* (Washington, D.C.: U.S. Department of Transportation, 1985), pp. 53–54.

17. The JADC also insisted, however, that Boeing commit to provide at least 51 percent of the equity in the 7J7 project so as to ensure the U.S. firm's participation as project manager.

18. Interestingly, Short Brothers and Saab-Scania currently are participating only in the design of the 7J7, with no explicit commitment to produce portions of the aircraft. According to senior Boeing management, "The associates [Saab-Scania and Short Brothers] must be able to produce the components they design in a cost-competitive manner, however, if they are to get the production business. . . ." See David A. Brown, "Short Brothers, Saab-Scania Join Boeing 7J7 Program," *Aviation Week and Space Technology*, March 31, 1986, p. 32.

19. Robert B. Reich, "A Faustian Bargain with the Japanese," *The New York Times*, April 6, 1986, p. 2, section 3.

20. Reich's critique of the 7J7 joint venture is consistent with his earlier work in viewing manufacturing process technology as the central competitive asset in the commercial aircraft industry. This assessment is somewhat distorted for this and other high-technology industries, as is the belief that foreign participants in joint ventures with U.S. firms contribute no technological assets.

21. According to David Brown, Thomas Albrecht, executive vice-president of Boeing Commercial Airplane Company, " . . . ruled out equipment and subsystem suppliers as associate members of the [7J7] group, however, saying that Boeing wanted to retain the advantages of competition in the selection of component suppliers." ("Short Brothers, Saab–Scania Join Boeing," p. 32).

22. One account estimates that the Douglas Aircraft division of McDonnell Douglas lost $70 million in 1979 and more than twice that, $144 million, in 1980. *The Economist*, "Aircraft Industry: Tomorrow's Pterodactyls?" May 30, 1981, p. 4.

23. The DC–8, with its robust airframe design, can accommodate new, fuel-efficient engines and serve long-distance routes with modest traffic levels quite inexpensively.

24. See *Business Week*, "The Big Deal McDonnell Douglas Turned Down," December 1, 1980, pp. 81–82, for one case.

25. See Robert Ropelewski, "Mercure 200 Pact Sparks Uproar," *Aviation Week and Space Technology*, August 23, 1976, p. 12.

26. Among other problems, the original wing design was not well-suited to the high-bypass CFM56 engine, the diameter of which was much larger than the Mercure 100's engine.

27. According to one estimate, the development costs for the Mercure 200 of roughly $250 million would double or even triple if the wing was redesigned. See Ropelewski, "Mercure 200 Pact," p. 12.

28. Commenting on the demise of the MDF100 venture, one account noted the " . . . lack of a new fuel-efficient engine in the 23,400-lb. range to power the MDF100. Economic difficulties have forced engine manufacturers to delay launching new engines, and Fokker had little expectation a new engine would have been certificated by late 1985 to meet an in-service schedule requirement of 1987 for the 150-seat aircraft" (*Aviation Week and Space Technology*, February 15, 1982, p. 34). Frans Swarttouw, managing director of Fokker, commented in retrospect that "It should have gotten better as the months went by, but it got worse. The market crumbled, and we ended up by just talking to Delta. United made it clear that they were not in a position to order. The engine was not available. If the market had been there, all these problems could have been solved; but it was not there, and we soon wondered what the heck we were doing." (Reed, 1983, pp. 20–25).

29. See *Aviation Week and Space Technology*, "Industry Observer," September 21, 1981, p. 15.

30. The launch by Fokker of the F100 jet aircraft in 1983 drew on some of the design developments of the MDF100 joint venture, as well as the unexpended government development funds. See *Aviation Week and Space Technology*, "Dutch, Swedes Use Innovative Financing," September 6, 1982, p. 172.

31. The current collaborative agreements between McDonnell Douglas and foreign firms that center on the development of derivatives of the MD–80, including technical cooperation with Saab-Scania and Aeritalia, as well as the licensed production in China of the MD-82, all appear to give the dominant technological managerial role to McDonnell Douglas, in contrast to these earlier ventures.

32. As was noted in the discussion of the negotiations between French firms and Boeing, French airframe enterprises historically have been reluctant to accept a subordinate role in any joint venture.

33. A venture with Rolls Royce in the early 1970s to develop and produce a small turbofan engine, the M45H, had produced disappointing commercial results due to modest sales of the aircraft for which the engine was intended (the Fokker/VFW 614, less than thirty of which were produced).

34. One account of the subsequent negotiations between the U.S. government and Pratt & Whitney over technology transfer within the JT10D venture with Rolls Royce cited David Pickerell, a Pratt & Whitney executive: "If

the restriction [on technology transfer] is not lifted and the European partners are forced to operate under the same conditions as Snecma on the CFM56—Snecma is not permitted access to GE core engine technology on the program—you can be certain the JT10D will not be as good an engine as it could be,' Pickerell said," *Aviation Week and Space Technology*, "Rolls Confident of Major JT10D Task," September 6, 1976, p. 109.

35. Estimates of French government support for SNECMA's CFM56 program may be found in the National Academy of Engineering *Background Paper* for the NAE Roundtable Discussion on the U.S. Civil Aviation Manufacturing Industry, as well as in the study by the Aerospace Industries Association, *The Challenge of Foreign Competition* (Washington, D.C.: Aerospace Research Center, 1976). These estimates run to as much as $500 million.

36. Such a consortium would have required considerable British government pressure on Rolls Royce. As Hayward noted, the firm historically has been extremely reluctant to undertake cooperative programs with European engine firms: "Rolls saw Anglo–American cooperation as being 'between equals.' In certain areas, according to Rolls' Chairman, Sir Kenneth Keith, 'they are better than us, and in certain areas, we are better than them.' The problem with European collaboration, he said, was that it was usually in a 'one-way direction, with Rolls-Royce on the giving end.'" Hayward, *Government and British Civil Aerospace*, p. 157.

37. A SNECMA official was quoted in a recent article as saying, "On the CF6, Snecma's role is basically that of a subcontractor, for the CFM56, the company is an equal partner, and on the UDF the company's role will be between the two." Jeffrey M. Lenorovitz, "Snecma Takes Share of GE Unducted Fan, Talks with Rolls on Smaller Engine," *Aviation Week and Space Technology*, May 27, 1985, p. 20.

38. "'The Unducted Fan is much more difficult than a turbofan engine to "cut up" for work-share distribution because the pod and thrust reverser, for example, are integral parts of the powerplant,' a Snecma executive said. 'Therefore, I don't know whether a 50% share would be too much for us. Even if it is below the 50% level, we'd still want to take a significant share in the program,'" Jeffrey M. Lenorovitz, "Snecma, General Electric Consider Joint Development of Unducted Fan," *Aviation Week and Space Technology*, February 25, 1985, p. 41.

39. See chapter 4 for a more detailed discussion of Saab-Scania's history.

40. The firm's recent decision to enter cooperative product development agreements with both Boeing and McDonnell Douglas suggests that the preservation of these broader capabilities now may be a less central objective. See chapter 4 for further discussion.

41. See *Aviation Week and Space Technology*, "Fairchild Withdrawing from 340 Aircraft Project," October 21, 1985, p. 23.

42. U.S. marketing and product support, originally the sole responsibility of Fairchild, were reorganized in 1984 and placed under the control of Saab Fairchild International.

43. See *Aviation Week and Space Technology*, "Fairchild Withdrawing," October 21, 1985, p. 23.

44. See *Aviation Week and Space Technology*, "Rolls Royce Leaves JT10D Turbofan Development Program," May 16, 1977, p. 17.

45. See especially, J.E. Steiner, "How Decisions Are Made" and David Pickerell's comments in *Aviation Week and Space Technology*, September 6, 1976, p. 109.

46. One account of the RJ500 venture written in 1981 noted that "Development of a definitive version of the engine has been delayed indefinitely by the British and Japanese, pending clarification of the market for a 150-seat aircraft and indications that an airframe manufacturer is prepared to proceed," *Aviation Week and Space Technology*, "Anglo-Japanese Engine Go-Ahead Awaits 150-Seat Aircraft Decision," November 2, 1981, p. 26.

47. Significantly, in view of the greater profitability of the large-engine segment of the market, Pratt & Whitney's partners in the PW4000 project account for no more than 11 percent of this engine.

48. The share of IAE equity controlled by the Pratt group is precisely 50.1 percent, giving Pratt & Whitney a formal controlling share.

49. According to one account, "IAE already is facing potential conflicts of interest among its members, Keen [J.M.S. Keen, executive vice-president of International Aero Engines] said. There could be a 'clear conflict of interest for a manufacturer,' he said, if an airline were trying to decide between a Boeing 757 equipped with Rolls-Royce RB 211-535 engines and a 150-passenger aircraft equipped with the IAE V2500, for example. 'That is one reason we believe we have to have our own marketing organization,' Keen said." Michael Feazel, "Large Engine Design Costs Dictate Consortium Efforts," *Aviation Week and Space Technology*, June 18, 1984, p.108.

50. See *Flight International*, "Fiat Seeks Italian Government R&D for Civil Engines," October 24, 1981, p. 1275.

51. *Military Technology*, "MTU—German Funding for PW2037 Participation," July 1982, p. 81.

52. " 'Technology transfer questions were raised by both Pratt & Whitney and Rolls–Royce early in the consortium negotiations,' according to Samuel L. Higginbottom, chairman and president of Rolls–Royce, Inc. Both companies feel there will be a minimum of exchange of proprietary data in the final assembly process. 'We will have to know the interfaces, and there obviously will be some exchange of data involved in that,' Higginbottom said. 'But we will not have to get into the details of technology . . .' It took a lot of work to match the technology split to the work-sharing for-

mula, one official said. But now that it is completed, final assembly essentially will involve bolting together the separate modules." Donald E. Fink, "Pratt, Rolls Launch New Turbofan," *Aviation Week and Space Technology*, November 7, 1983, p. 29.

53. Despite these potential problems, development of the V2500 thus far has proceeded slightly ahead of schedule; initial testing of the entire engine began in late 1985. Prompt delivery of the V2500 is essential to the engine's prospects against the competing CFM product, the CFM56–5, which will be introduced six to eight months earlier.

54. "Some consortium partners remain dissatisfied with that [specialized participation], however, because they develop expertise in only one area of engine design. Keen said the Japanese, for example, may be unwilling to participate in future consortiums because they want to develop the ability to design and produce entire engines." Feazel, "Large Engine Design Costs," p. 108.

55. Referring to the marketing efforts of Airbus Industrie for the A300, the managing director of Airbus Industrie noted that "'It's misleading to believe that an aircraft is just right for a certain market slot,' Airbus Industrie Chairman Bernard Lathiere conceded recently. 'Our principal competitor for the Indian Airways order was the Boeing 737, and in South Africa it was the 747.'" *Aviation Week and Space Technology*, "Eastern Lease," p. 241.

4 COUNTRY STRATEGIES

The formation of joint ventures and other alliances between U.S. and foreign firms has been influenced heavily by the policies of foreign governments, including support of development costs for local aircraft or components firms, demands for offsets as part of procurement contracts, and financial support for research in the public or private sector. Simultaneously, changes in the technological environment of the commercial aircraft industry, including growing international trade in components and the increasing need for prime contractors to spread costs and risk among other partners, have opened up new possibilities for government industrial policies. How have increased international technology flows altered the ease with which other nations can either enter the commercial aircraft industry or significantly enhance their competitiveness within the industry? This chapter considers the policies of several industrialized and industrializing nations—Japan, Sweden, and Brazil—in supporting the development of a domestic aircraft industry. One of the most important government-supported multinational consortia in large commercial aircraft, Airbus Industrie, also is examined.

Several themes unify this discussion of foreign government policies. The first is the distinction between "catch-up" and "keep-up" policies. Catch-up policy strategies support entry into the world aircraft industry by national firms with modest technological or production capabilities—both government and domestic firms are concerned with technology transfer and learning. By contrast, a number of European nations are more concerned with maintaining their technological and production capabilities in aircraft and engines. These keep-up strategies often are the result of a desire to retain production capabilities and a design for military aircraft and have very different implications for the strategies adopted by governments and the firms within their borders in the aircraft and engine industries.

The choice between a catch-up and keep-up strategy influences the technological learning and capabilities that governments and firms wish to support. The discussion in this chapter describes examples of strategies intended to support entry by firms into specialized "niches" of the aircraft industry, producing specific components or sections of an engine. This strategy contrasts with one supporting entry or participation by firms as prime contractors able to carry out design, systems integration, production, marketing, and product support activities. The size of the domestic market for aircraft also influences government strategies. Where the domestic market is very large, import-substitution or infant industry policies, supporting firms during an initial period of learning and cost reduction, may be feasible, albeit costly. Where the domestic market is small relative to the minimum efficient scale of airframe or engine production, however, such policies are exorbitantly expensive. Since the domestic market in most countries is too small to support an indigenous aircraft industry, and rising development costs favor long production runs, export or international collaboration are increasingly essential components of national development strategies.

The discussion of the Airbus Industrie consortium in the last section of this chapter describes the combination of keep-up and catch-up strategies that motivated the formation and affected the evolution of this venture. The evolution of Airbus Industrie has also been influenced heavily by the often conflicting interests of the participants in the consortium, clashes that yield insights into the incentives that hold such consortia together. The examination in this section of the structure of the Airbus consortium sheds additional light as well on chapter 3's discussion of principles of organizational design for joint ventures.

THE JAPANESE AIRCRAFT INDUSTRY

The emergence of a Japanese commercial aircraft industry has attracted considerable attention recently within the U.S.[1] The discussion in chapter 3 of cooperation between Boeing and Japanese firms in the development and production of the 767, as well as the analysis of Japanese participation in the V2500 engine project, suggests that much of the alarm expressed in some discussions concerning Japanese entry into the large commercial aircraft industry is misplaced. The characteristics of commercial aircraft technology and the Japanese and world markets for commercial aircraft are such that development strategies for the Japanese aircraft industry cannot follow the pattern of Japanese industrial policy in other successful export industries, such as automobiles or steel. Moreover, the current participation of Japanese aircraft and engine firms in multinational consortia seems unlikely to result in their rapid acquisition of the capabilities in marketing, systems integration, and design that will support independent entry into the world airframe and engine industries.

History and Development

Before and during World War II, the Japanese aircraft industry was both large and technically sophisticated.[2] After World War II, it was completely dismantled by the occupation forces, and production of aircraft was prohibited. The Korean War supported a vast expansion in military aircraft repair and service activities, areas in which U.S. military authorities encouraged Japanese firms to become active. Following this early stage of reconstruction, the end of military occupation in 1952 effectively removed the prohibition on aircraft manufacture in Japan.

An important component of the Mutual Defense Assistance Agreement signed by the United States and Japan in 1954 was the provision for Japanese production of U.S. military aircraft for use by the Japanese Self-Defense Forces. Mitsubishi Heavy Industries began licensed production of the T-33 trainer and F-86 fighter aircraft in the 1950s and now manufactures the F-15 fighter under license (the Japanese aircraft is known as the F15J).[3] U.S.-Japanese coproduction agreements transferred considerable production and technical knowledge from U.S. firms to the major Japanese aircraft firms. However, for reasons discussed in chapter 2, the *design* capabilities of Japanese firms do not appear to have benefited appreciably; nor is a great deal of the technology employed in fighter aircraft applicable to commercial aircraft.[4]

The Nippon Aircraft Manufacturing Company (NAMC)—a consortium of Mitsubishi Heavy Industries, Kawasaki Heavy Industries, Fuji Heavy Industries, Showa Aircraft, and Shin Meiwa Industries— was established in 1958 and undertook the development of the YS-11, the first Japanese commercial transport of the postwar era. The Japanese government provided considerable funding for this project, acquiring a 50 percent equity share.[5] The sixty-four-passenger, two-engine turboprop was a short-range aircraft, designed for short takeoffs and landings. As such, the aircraft was well-suited to the domestic market, and approximately 120 were sold to Japanese airlines, Foreign sales of the YS-11, however, failed to meet expectations. The sales and marketing network of the NAMC consortium was modest, and product support capabilities were weak. The YS-11 also faced strong competition in the U.S. and European commuter airline markets from European aircraft. Despite exports of roughly sixty aircraft out of a total production history of 182, the YS-11 was a financial failure. The Japanese home market proved to be too small to support the profitable introduction of an aircraft designed primarily for that region. The NAMC was dissolved in 1982.

During the late 1960s and early 1970s, major Japanese producers of military aircraft (primarily Mitsubishi Heavy Industries and Kawasaki Heavy Industries) expanded their subcontracting for U.S. commercial aircraft firms, producing small assemblies and components for the Boeing 737 and 747 and for the McDonnell Douglas DC-9 and DC-10. In an effort to encourage more extensive cooperation between Japanese and foreign aircraft manufacturers, MITI sponsored and helped fund two consortia of Japanese firms, the Japan Commercial Transport Development Corporation (succeeded by the Japan Commercial Aircraft Corporation and the Japan Aircraft Development Corporation) and Japan Aero Engines Corporation. These two consortia are participating in the Boeing 767, 7J7, and V2500 projects discussed in chapter 3.

Structure

The small Japanese domestic market for commercial aircraft is a key factor in explaining industry structure and government policy. Japanese scheduled carriers operate an aircraft fleet that constitutes no more than 7–10 percent of the total number of large commercial transports operated by scheduled trunk airlines. The domestic market for other types of aircraft is even more underdeveloped relative to the population and income levels of the country.

The Japanese aircraft industry is highly concentrated. Mitsubishi Heavy Industries accounts for 49 percent, Kawasaki Heavy Industries produced 21 percent, and Ishikawajima–Harima Heavy Industries produced 21 percent of the value of total shipments of aircraft and engines in 1981. The aircraft sales of these firms are dominated by the domestic military market. Military sales during the late 1970s and 1980s have accounted for at least 80 percent of total industry sales, substantially greater than the military share of total sales by the U.S. aircraft industry of 50–60 percent. The military market is profitable but faces severe constraints to growth. These limits stem from both the informal but thoroughly established ban on Japanese weapons exports and the equally informal but binding ceiling of 1 percent on the share of gross national product devoted to defense spending. Any growth in the market for the products of Japanese aircraft firms must come from an expansion of the commercial aircraft market.

The major Japanese aircraft firms spend substantially less on R&D, relative to their size, than do U.S. aircraft producers. Self-financed R&D amounts to 4–5 percent of the sales of the major U.S. firms but is generally less than 2 percent of the sales of Japanese producers.[6] Low levels of firm-financed aircraft research within Japan are not offset by large government research expenditures. Indeed, a key weakness of the Japanese aircraft industry is the lack of large-scale, sophisticated test apparatus and facilities.[7]

Government Policy

In its "vision" of industrial structure in the 1980s, MITI identified commercial large transports as a key future industry for the Japanese economy.[8] A particularly attractive feature of this industry, according to MITI's analysis, is that a strong Japanese capability in commercial aircraft design and production would not be undercut by Asian competitors such as South Korea or Taiwan as rapidly as was true of other industries (for example, steel). Obviously, this argument cuts in two directions—the prospective difficulty faced by South Korea or Taiwan in acquiring aircraft production and design skills also may impede Japanese acquisition of these skills from U.S. or European producers.

Largely because of the small size of the Japanese domestic market, however, the modified infant-industry strategies employed in such other Japanese export industries as steel, automobiles, or electronics are less feasible in commercial aircraft. The policy framework applied by MITI and the Ministry of Finance historically combined support of the market for the products of these industries with support for the technological development of industry. Policies supporting market demand included the protection, through tariffs or administrative suasion, of the domestic market in the industry's early years.[9] MITI also played a major role during the 1950s and 1960s in the identification of foreign industrial technologies for import into Japan, the negotiation of favorable terms for the licensing of the technologies from foreign patentholders, and, of central importance, the liberal licensing of these technologies within Japan.[10] The goal was the provision of a pool of technological knowledge that was relatively accessible to firms throughout an industry.[11]

The YS-11 experience demonstrated the limitations of this strategy in commercial aircraft, limitations that stemmed from the small size of the Japanese domestic market. The small size of the Japanese market for military aircraft also has limited the impact of coproduction of military aircraft on the development of a significant aircraft industry. Reflecting the deficiencies of the infant industry strategy, the 767, YXX (now the 7J7), and V2500 projects represent an alternative strategy. The goals, revealed most clearly in the YXX program, are the acquisition of expertise in all phases of aircraft design, manufacture, and sales through joint ventures with established U.S. and European producers of aircraft and engines.[12]

A central question in evaluating Japanese government policy in the aircraft industry concerns the reasons for its focus on large commercial transports. Commuter aircraft face a rapidly growing market and have less demanding technological and financial requirements for design and product. Business and general aviation aircraft are another market, in which one Japanese firm was able to introduce and win foreign orders for two products (Mitsubishi Heavy Industries, producer of the MU-2 and the Diamond 300).[13] Nonetheless, all available evidence suggests that MITI policy makers remain committed to large commercial transports. This commitment reflects the belief of MITI policy makers and industry personnel that technological supremacy is less significant as a competitive weapon within the general aviation, business aircraft, and commuter aircraft segments of the industry than within the large transport market. According to this view, unit profitability is likely to be lower and technological spillovers less significant in the production of commuter aircraft. General aviation and commuter aircraft design also demand less technological expertise, meaning (among other things) that a Japanese technological lead in design and production of these aircraft is likely to be less enduring.[14]

In their joint ventures, Japanese firms have expressed a desire to be involved in all aspects of research, development, manufacture, and marketing. The Japanese participants did not originally intend to develop specialized capabilities in either the production of particular components of engines and airframes or specialized design and testing functions. Nonetheless, if the near-term goal of government and industry managers is continued participation in future product development and manufacturing consortia, specialization is likely to be far more effective. The incentives of the technologically advanced senior partners in the Boeing 767 and the V2500 ventures do not support transfer of the technological and managerial capabilities that are necessary for Japanese firms to be significant independent competitors in the world aircraft and engine industries in the near future. Indeed, Japanese participation in these ventures has been narrowly delimited thus far, and transfer of advanced technologies has been fairly limited. Participation by Japanese firms in the Boeing 7J7 project will be less restricted, but the managerial incentives to limit this participation to specific, delimited areas remain very strong.

Current Japanese government policy toward the commercial aircraft industry places little emphasis on the funding of basic aeronautical research. Despite the availability of loans from MITI for as much as 75 percent of the costs of the earliest stages of the design and development work in the V2500 engine and the 767 ventures, public funding for nonmission-oriented aeronautics R&D within Japan is very modest. Neither the National Aeronautics Laboratory nor the Japanese Defense Agency are significant sources of research funding, and the number and sophistication of engine and airframe test facilities within Japan are low. MITI policy in aircraft thus displays some similarities to previous Japanese catch-up strategy, in focusing on the acquisition from foreign sources of product and production technologies, rather than the development of a strong indigenous R&D base. Within the large commercial aircraft and engine industry, however, the pace of technological change is sufficiently rapid that this strategy is unlikely to bring Japanese firms up to the technological frontier.

Summary

The Japanese government's strategy for the development of a domestic aircraft and engine industry by obtaining technology from foreign sources through joint ventures is a clear case of a catch-up strategy. Within the historical structure of Japanese industrial policy, however, commercial aircraft may represent a transitional case. The aircraft industry continues to rely on foreign sources of technology, but the small Japanese domestic market, as well as the characteristics of the technology of commercial aircraft and engines, mean that imported technology cannot be employed initially within a protected domestic market. The historically successful Japanese policy framework for infant industries is inapplicable. International joint ventures thus may be a compromise between the strategy applied in other Japanese export industries and a more novel policy aimed at the strengthening of indigenous technological resources. Nonetheless, Japanese firms are not likely to acquire a broad range of technological capabilities in aircraft and engine design and manufacture through such multinational joint ventures. Independent entry into the aircraft or engine industries by Japanese firms is a remote prospect.[15]

BRAZIL: DEVELOPMENT WITH A LARGE DOMESTIC MARKET

The Brazilian aircraft industry, which has grown rapidly and registered impressive penetration of foreign military and commercial commuter aircraft markets, is an interesting contrast to the Japanese aircraft industry. Unlike Japan, Brazil has a large domestic market for commuter and general aviation aircraft. In addition, the segment of the aircraft industry in which Brazilian firms have achieved considerable success is one in which Japanese policy makers and industry executives have expressed little interest. While joint ventures with foreign firms have influenced the development of the Brazilian industry, alternative mechanisms for technology transfer, as well as indigenous technological development within the protected domestic market, have been of equal or greater importance.[16] Like the Japanese aircraft industry, however, the Brazilian industry is developing through a catch-up strategy.

Industry Development

Despite its recent prominence, the Brazilian aircraft industry has a long history. Manufacture of small military and civilian aircraft was first undertaken by Brazilian firms during the 1930s. Nonetheless, Brazil's recurrent attempts to establish an indigenous aircraft design and manufacturing capability were unsuccessful prior to the foundation of Embraer (Empresa Brasileira de Aeronautica, S.A.) in 1969. Embraer, manufacturer of the Bandeirante and Brasilia commuter aircraft and the Tucano military trainer, as well as agricultural and general aviation aircraft, has grown rapidly. Since 1971 Embraer has produced more than 3,200 planes of various types, of which more than 350 (primarily the Bandeirante and the Tucano) have been exported or produced under license in foreign markets. Another important institution in the development of the Brazilian aircraft industry is the Centro Tecnico Aerospacial (CTA). Established by the Brazilian Army in the late 1930s, CTA is responsible for aeronautics research and education.

Embraer was established in 1969 as a mixed public-private enterprise in which the Brazilian government owns 49 percent of the equity. The founding of Embraer was a response to pressure from the CTA to develop a manufacturing installation for the production of an aircraft design developed at the CTA. Another important influence on the decision of the Brazilian government to commit resources to Embraer was the desire of the Brazilian armed forces, then ruling the nation, to reduce Brazil's historical dependence on U.S. sources of military equipment. This government goal was a response to the restrictions imposed by the U.S. government on military aid and weapons sales in the wake of the military seizure of power in 1964. Embraer's founding was one part of a broader effort to develop a significant Brazilian weapons industry (an industry that has expanded dramatically in military field transports and personnel carriers, in addition to aircraft).

The Embraer product line now includes several commercial aircraft, most notably the Bandeirante, a nineteen-passenger, unpressurized commuter aircraft based on the CTA design. More than 400 of these were produced from 1973 to 1983, with exports accounting for 225. The Brazilian military was the original customer for the Bandeirante and has purchased more than half of those sold in Brazil. The Brazilian content of the Bandeirante is approximately 60 percent. Since 1979, Embraer also has produced a second major line of small single- and two-engine aircraft under license from Piper Aircraft beginning in 1974. More than 2,000 of these aircraft have been manufactured, entirely for the domestic market. Two other aircraft produced by Embraer, the Xingu and the Brasilia, are advanced derivatives of the Bandeirante design. The Xingu was a pressurized corporate aircraft, production of which began in 1977. Despite the sale to the French armed forces of forty-one aircraft, the Xingu was a commercial failure and ceased production in 1984. The Brasilia, production of which began in 1985, is substantially larger than the Bandeirante (thirty passengers) and pressurized, but contains many identical components.

Embraer also produces military aircraft. It designed the Tucano as a trainer for the Brazilian air force in 1983. Orders from the Brazilian, Egyptian, and Honduran air forces have been received for more than 100 aircraft, and arrangements have been made to license the production by Short Brothers of Great Britain of an additional 130 aircraft for the British Royal Air Force. The Xavante is a lightweight fighter and trainer produced under license from Aermacchi, an Italian producer, beginning in 1971. More than 180 of these aircraft were produced prior to the cessation of production in 1981. Aermacchi, Aeritalia, and Embraer are now collaborating as equal partners in the development of the AMX, a fighter aircraft that has been ordered by the Brazilian and Italian air forces.

International Technology Flows and the Brazilian Industry

The penetration by the Brazilian aircraft industry of markets in the advanced industrial nations, such as the U.S. commuter aircraft and British military aircraft markets, suggests that Brazilian firms have developed design and production capabilities that span several types of aircraft. How has the competitive and technological environment of the global aircraft industry affected the dramatic growth of the aircraft industry within Brazil?

International technology flows have been important to the development of the Brazilian aircraft industry, but differ from those associated with the Japanese or Swedish aircraft industries. In particular, joint ventures between Brazilian and foreign firms in aircraft design and development did not lead, but followed, the development of indigenous technological capabilities. Cooperation with Aermacchi in the design and development of the AMX occurred after, rather than before, the development by Embraer of a military trainer (the Tucano). The early civil aircraft products of Embraer, including the Bandeirante, were indigenous designs.

Military coproduction and licensing of civil aircraft designs have been more important than joint ventures in transferring technology to Brazilian firms. The licensing agreement with Aermacchi for production of the Xavante allowed for increases in the amount of fabrication and assembly (but not design) activity undertaken in Brazil increased over the life of the agreement. Offset agreements with Northrop were negotiated as a part of the Brazilian purchase of the F-5 military fighter. These agreements transferred important metal bonding technologies to Brazil. The agreement signed by Embraer and Piper Aircraft in 1974, providing for licensed production by Embraer of a wide range of Piper general aviation aircraft, also involved significant transfers of design data and production technology.[17]

None of these three licensing and offset agreements transferred the engineering and design skills necessary to support independent entry into the airframe industry. In excluding design and product development activities, these agreements resembled military coproduction agreements, which have not resulted in the development of significant aircraft industries in other countries. Moreover, the Piper-Embraer agreement was reached only after the introduction by Embraer of the Bandeirante. Indeed, both Moxon et al. and Crane and Gilliot suggest that the licensing agreement between Piper and Embraer was sought by the Brazilian firm as a means of quickly developing a general aviation aircraft, so as to reduce the demands on Brazilian foreign exchange reserves resulting from large imports of these aircraft. In other words, the ability to design, develop, and produce such aircraft was already present in Brazil—licensing simply hastened the introduction of a Brazilian aircraft.

How has the Brazilian aircraft industry been able to develop significant design and systems integration capabilities in the absence of technology transfer through joint ventures? First, Brazilian government policy has emphasized the development of a strong indigenous technological base, largely through public funding of research and training of aeronautics engineers. The level of public-private cooperation in research and development in the Brazilian aircraft industry contrasts with Japan, where the National Aeronautics Laboratory's research proceeds largely independently of the country's major aircraft producers. The CTA's role as an educational institution also contrasts with the activities of similar institutions in both the United States and Japan and has aided in the diffusion of aeronautical design and research skills in Brazil. Its interactions with industry and its function as a source of personnel have given the CTA a major role in product development within the Brazilian aircraft industry. Second, Brazil has a large domestic market for aircraft, something lacking in both Sweden and Japan.

The Role of the Domestic Market

The Brazilian aircraft industry has benefited in a number of ways from the large and protected character of its domestic market. Military support for development, as well as military purchases of early models of the Bandeirante in the 1970s, were important in defraying development costs, supporting incremental design modifications based on operating experience, and lowering production costs through movement down the learning curve. Moreover, imports of aircraft deemed to be competitive with Brazilian designs were virtually prohibited. Private sector demand for commuter aircraft, which was substantial in a country of Brazil's large size and primitive internal road network, therefore was channeled largely to Embraer. Unlike the Japanese experience with the YS-11, the domestic market within Brazil was sufficiently large to support the early production of the Bandeirante, which aided substantially in the subsequent sales of the aircraft in export markets. Because of the size and the protected character of its internal market and the major military role in procurement of civilian aircraft designs, the Brazilian aircraft industry was able to enjoy the fruits of a Japanese-style catch-up industrial policy. Where the domestic market has not been large, as in the case of the Xingu, Embraer aircraft have not been successful in export markets.

The Export Market

The export market for Embraer products has developed gradually but steadily. The deregulation of U.S. domestic air transportation opened a large market for commuter aircraft. Penetration of the U.S. market had been difficult for several reasons, including the staunch opposition of established U.S. manufacturers of commuter aircraft. This opposition may have influenced the slow pace at which the Federal Aviation Administration certified the Bandeirante for operation in the United States, although direct evidence of any connection is lacking.[18] Penetration of the U.S. market also required the establishment of a major U.S. service and product support network. With the introduction of the Brasilia, the Embraer product strategy resembles that of producers of large commercial transports. Embraer now focuses on the development of a "family" of commuter aircraft to enhance the attractiveness for airline purchasers of any single design within the family. Finally, the product strategies of Embraer in both civilian and military aircraft markets around the world have been aided by the rapidly growing market for these aircraft in developing countries, where rugged, low-maintenance designs have considerable utility.

Summary

While Embraer's development has been remarkable, potential problems remain. The introduction of the Brasilia was delayed, and the aircraft is encountering intense competition from such products as the Saab-Fairchild SF340 and the de Havilland Dash 8. Moreover, the development of the Brazilian aircraft industry is largely confined to the development of Embraer. Growth in the Brazilian engine and components industries has been much less dramatic. Indeed, no Brazilian firm in the engine business has systems design and integration or product support skills comparable to those of Embraer in airframes. Celma, another government-owned firm, is gradually expanding its role in engine maintenance and overhaul and has begun to produce engine components; but Brazilian participation in the engine market is likely to be modest for the foreseeable future.

The contrasting development of the Brazilian airframe and engine industries is influenced by the relatively unprotected nature of the market for aircraft engines in Brazil. One reason for the high foreign content of the Embraer Bandeirante, after all, is the aircraft's use of Canadian or U.S. engines rather than Brazilian engines. Many of the other components employed in Embraer aircraft, such as the avionics and flight management systems, are also of foreign manufacture, further shrinking the market for Brazilian manufacturers of such products. The Brazilian aircraft industry has benefited from the changing structure of the world aircraft industry through its ability to procure advanced technological systems from foreign sources for incorporation into Brazilian designs. Technology transfer has been very important to the Brazilian industry, but it has been uneven and has largely assumed an "embodied" form. The transfer of advanced aircraft technologies to Brazil has occurred primarily through the purchase by Brazilian firms of advanced components.

The Brazilian aircraft industry's development illustrates the limited role played by interfirm joint ventures in transferring the technological and design capabilities necessary to enter the aircraft industry. Had the licensing and offset agreements with Piper, Aermacchi, and Northrop not been accompanied by a vigorous indigenous program of research and engineering education, the Brazilian industry would probably not have experienced its current success. The contemporary technological environment of the aircraft industry affords numerous opportunities to gain production and management experience through coproduction and licensing agreements, while the liberal trade regime in aircraft components and engines provides ample "embodied" technology transfer. The development of key design and systems integration skills, however, requires investment in indigenous sources of research and training. The development of the Brazilian aircraft industry also benefited from the nation's peculiar political circumstances in the late 1960s and 1970s, as well as from its large domestic market. Technology transfer through joint ventures, licensing, or coproduction thus appears to be a necessary, but not a sufficient, condition for the development of a national aircraft industry.

SWEDEN: "KEEP-UP" POLICY WITH A SMALL DOMESTIC MARKET

Sweden is pursuing an industrial development strategy in aircraft that contrasts with those of both Japan and Brazil. The Swedish firms are better established and more technologically advanced producers of airframes (Saab-Scania Aircraft) and engines (Volvo Flygmotor), primarily for military applications. Faced with a changing market for military aircraft and engines, these firms have resorted to joint ventures as a means of maintaining employment and technological capabilities. Although many aspects of the Swedish case are unique, some of the problems faced by the Swedish aircraft firm resemble those of the aircraft industries of other European nations: escalating costs and declining markets forced them to undertake joint ventures. Airbus Industrie, discussed in greater detail later in this chapter, is one example.

The Development of the Swedish Aircraft Industry

The Swedish aircraft industry was influenced heavily by Sweden's neutrality during World War II[19] and the sharp increase in cold war tensions that enveloped the Baltic during the Korean War. The industry was largely created in response to the 1936 decision of the Swedish government to pursue rearmament. One firm was designated by a consensus among public and private sector decision makers to be the producer of military aircraft engines, and one was to manufacture military airframes. Engines were produced by Volvo, which had been involved in the production of engines under license from foreign firms since 1930. A new firm, SAAB (Svenska Aeroplan Aktiebolaget) was founded in 1937 out of the aircraft division of a firm controlled by the Wallenberg interests and began the production of airframes. Before the war, intensive negotiations were undertaken for additional licenses to produce foreign aircraft and engine designs within Sweden, while Swedish purchasing missions attempted to obtain additional military aircraft from foreign producers.

As international tensions grew, military aircraft became increasingly difficult to obtain or to license from major European and U.S. producers, and Swedish air power in 1939 remained weak.[20] The infeasibility of rapid rearmament during a period of severe international tension led to the decision in 1942 to rely on Swedish firms for aircraft design and production. Sweden's progress in developing a world-class aircraft industry was remarkable, albeit aided by the emigration of a number of German aircraft engineers to Sweden after World War II. By 1948, Saab (since 1969, Saab-Scania) had produced 1,000 aircraft. Only 204 aircraft within this total output were Swedish versions of foreign airframe designs—the remainder were Swedish designs—and Sweden introduced a jet-powered fighter aircraft in 1948.[21] While airframe designs during and after World War II were overwhelmingly Swedish in origin, engine production continued to rely on Swedish production of licensed foreign designs.

In the aftermath of World War II, Saab faced a decline in the market for its exclusively military product line and undertook the development and production of the Scandia, a two-engine commercial aircraft. Eighteen of these aircraft were produced from 1948 to 1950. Production of the Scandia and Saab's involvement in commercial aircraft ceased with the outbreak of the Korean War in 1950. This conflict sparked another major rearmament drive, forcing Saab to commit all of its production capacity to the manufacture of military airframes. By 1955 Sweden fielded the largest air force in Western Europe, and Saab and Volvo respectively were dedicated to the production of military airframes of Swedish design and of foreign engines under license. While Saab's fighter and strike aircraft (the Draken, introduced in 1960; the Viggen, introduced in 1971; and the Gripen, to be introduced in 1992) were sophisticated airframe designs, Volvo also became adept at modifying foreign civilian engines for military applications, developing expertise in afterburner and advanced engine technologies.[22]

Diversification in the 1970s and 1980s

The parent firms of the two Swedish companies involved in aircraft production are large, but the aircraft divisions of these firms are remarkably small by world standards. Total employment in Swedish airframe and engine production is no more than 30 percent of the work force of the largest U.S. producer of commercial airframes (Boeing). In 1984 Saab-Scania Aircraft employed 6,165 persons, down from 7,700 in 1965 and 7,200 in 1968. Volvo Flygmotor employed 3,326 persons in 1984, an increase over its work force in the late 1960s, which totaled slightly more than 2,000 persons. The Swedish domestic market for commercial aircraft is also small by world standards. Like the Japanese aircraft industry, Swedish commercial airframe and engine products cannot achieve commercial success without significant exports; but unlike the Japanese industry Swedish firms can design and produce advanced airframes and sophisticated modifications of foreign engines.

From 1950 to 1975, Volvo and Saab were fully occupied with the design, modification, and production of airframes and engines for military applications. These firms faced growing difficulties in the Swedish military market, for several reasons. The first was declining military export markets, due to increased competition from other European suppliers (as well as the increasing protection by some governments of their military markets), and tighter Swedish government controls on exports of military equipment. Not only was the export market declining in size and importance, but so was the domestic military market. Smaller Swedish procurement programs in military aircraft reflected the growing unit costs of the advanced aircraft produced by Saab and Volvo, as well as intense competition for public funds between military and other programs.

As the military market entered a period of slower growth, management of the design and development cycle, involving substantial buildups of human and physical capital investment in the development phase, followed by a gradual decline during production, became more difficult for Volvo and Saab. Their ability to employ fully their engineering and production staffs and the production facilities that had been developed to serve the needs of the Swedish military required the development of alternative markets. These were found in commercial aircraft.

Beginning in the late 1970s, Volvo Flygmotor expanded its subcontracting activities for European engine producers, including Rolls Royce and MTU. In addition, Volvo entered an agreement with General Electric in 1980 that calls for the firm's participation as a risk- and revenue-sharing partner (with a share of 10 percent) in the manufacture of the CF6-80 engine employed on the Boeing 767 and Airbus A310. Volvo's activities in the CF6-80 production team (which also includes SNECMA) are focused on the production of turbine and compressor disks, engine frames and casings, and some development work, which primarily takes the form of advanced design studies. Volvo is the exclusive supplier for the components that the firm produces for the CF6-80.

In addition to teaming with General Electric in the production of commercial engines, Volvo Flygmotor is producing a significant share of the engine chosen for the Gripen fighter aircraft (the RM12), a modified version of the GE F404 fighter engine. Volvo will produce 50 percent of the components for the RM12 and is the sole foreign source for 20 percent of the components in all versions of the F404. The firm is also a partner in the production of several smaller jet engines with Garrett Corporation, a partnership in which Volvo's share of risk capital and profits stands at 15–30 percent. The firm's participation in this venture is based on its expertise in thermal coatings. Finally, Volvo is participating with Pratt & Whitney, with a 9 percent share, in the production of components for the JT8D-200 series of engines. Volvo Flygmotor's new activities have been profitable (net income increased by 43 percent during 1984) and have supported diversification away from the military market (1984 was the first year in Volvo Flygmotor's history for which military sales were less than 50 percent of total revenues).

Although Volvo's strategy of specialized participation in joint ventures for advanced commercial engines has been financially successful, the firm is not an important participant in multinational product *development* ventures. Virtually all of Volvo's ventures in civilian engines, with the possible exception of the CF6-80, involve little new product development. Volvo's current joint ventures consist largely of components production for well-established products. The firm is investing in the development of specialized capabilities, notably in advanced design, analysis, and testing technologies, that should enable Volvo Flygmotor to participate as a risk-sharing partner in future engine development ventures. Specialization can be carried too far, however. Although the development of specialized technological capabilities supports participation in future joint ventures, the preservation of a broad-based design and production capability is also essential for the development of both these specialized R&D capabilities and the technical skills to support the firm's existing military products.[23]

Whereas Volvo Flygmotor has been concerned primarily with the preservation of its team of production engineers and specialized technological capabilities, Saab-Scania has developed strategies to preserve the firm's ability to perform the design and systems integration functions that are the province of prime contractors in military and commercial aircraft. Subcontracting activities are insufficient to achieve this goal. It was essential for Saab-Scania to become a prime contractor, involved in all phases of the design, production, marketing, and support. Saab's strategy, centered on its joint venture with Fairchild in the production of the SF340, contrasts sharply with that of Volvo, in that Saab cannot afford the luxury of specialized participation in product development joint ventures. The discussion of the SF340 joint venture in chapter 3 makes clear the risks faced by Saab in pursuing this strategy of entry as a prime contractor, risks that have increased in the wake of Fairchild's withdrawal from the joint venture. The recent entry by Saab-Scania into joint ventures with both McDonnell Douglas and Boeing, however, suggests that the firm may undertake a specialized role in future large commercial transport ventures, possibly as a complement to its activities in commuter aircraft.[24] Nonetheless, in the Boeing 7J7 venture Saab-Scania will use only its design staff, rather than the global marketing and product support network it used for the SF340. The 7J7 project also does not sustain Saab-Scania's systems integration and project management capabilities.

Government Policy

In spite of the importance of Saab-Scania and Volvo Flygmotor for the preservation of an independent Swedish military aircraft design and production capability, the Swedish government has not adopted a particularly interventionist policy stance toward these firms. The formal Swedish military aircraft procurement process emphasizes regular cycles of development and production, in order to increase the stability of the market for Volvo and Saab and to ease the management of fluctuations during the development and production phases. In fact, however, the decisions to proceed with the Viggen and the Gripen were controversial political issues in Sweden, creating considerable uncertainty about the future of the programs that persisted well into the development phase. The instability of the Swedish military aircraft market in the late 1970s was impressed upon these firms when the Gripen program, a mainstay of Saab-Scania's and Volvo Flygmotor's military business well into the twenty-first century, was briefly cancelled during this period.

126   ALLIANCE POLITICS AND ECONOMICS

The Swedish government provides financial support for the costs of developing commercial airframes and engines to both Saab and Volvo in the form of loans of up to 50 percent of these costs. A modest research program is also supported with public funds (roughly 10 million kroner, or $1–1.5 million) through the Swedish Aeronautical Research Institute. In addition, training in aeronautical engineering and design is supported with public funds at the Royal Institute of Technology, the only institution of higher education in Sweden that offers advanced training in aeronautical engineering.

Summary

Swedish airframe and engine firms within the global aircraft industry largely employ a keep-up rather than a catch-up strategy. In the face of declining military markets, both Volvo Flygmotor and Saab–Scania have little choice but to diversify into commercial products if the firms are to retain technological and production capacities that are applicable to military aircraft. Given the exorbitant costs and risks of independent entry into the world commercial aircraft market, both firms have chosen to diversify through joint ventures. The specific teaming strategies chosen by Volvo Flygmotor and Saab–Scania are quite different, however, reflecting the historic differences in the technological capabilities and role within the Swedish aircraft industry of each firm. While Volvo is developing highly specialized technological skills, Saab-Scania is attempting to enter the commercial aircraft industry as a systems integrator and designer. Saab's latest initiatives with Boeing and McDonnell Douglas suggest that the firm may also participate in a specialized capacity in large transport development projects.

The prospects for both firms' strategies are uncertain. The Saab-Fairchild joint venture has been dissolved by the withdrawal of Fairchild, facing the Swedish partner with the prospect of substantial increases in its financial commitment to the SF340. Moreover, the SF340 alone is not likely to sustain Saab over the long term. The development of other aircraft, or participation by Saab as a significant risk-sharing partner in the development of a large commercial aircraft design, will almost certainly be necessary if the firm's commitment to commercial aircraft is to be sustained. Saab's prospective specialized participation in large transport development projects may

be insufficient to sustain the firm's general design and systems integration capabilities, while the risks of the more independent strategy
exemplified by the SF340 are also high.

The concerns raised by Japanese managers and officials about the
level of technological sophistication necessary to compete in the
commuter aircraft market also suggest hazards in the Saab-Scania
strategy. On the one hand, Saab's SF340 aircraft faces competition
from less technologically advanced but cheaper products. On the
other hand, the design and manufacture of commuter aircraft may
allow Saab's production staff and work force to remain fully employed; but the technological requirements of this product will not
support the retention by Saab of the advanced design and fabrication
capabilities necessary to produce and support high-performance military fighter aircraft.

The Volvo Flygmotor strategy also contains risks, although they
may be more modest than those confronted by Saab-Scania. While
Volvo Flygmotor has joined several multinational consortia for established engine products, the firm has yet to establish a major position
within a commercial engine development project. Volvo Flygmotor
thus may not be able to retain indefinitely its technological superiority over such prospective competitors as Japan Aero Engines, and
the firm's participation in future consortia could be called into question. In addition, Volvo has thus far avoided a long-term commitment to any single producer of engines, unlike SNECMA and General
Electric, or Fiat Aviazone, MTU, and Pratt & Whitney. This strategy
allows Volvo to maximize its short-term flexibility and profitability,
while simultaneously reducing prospects for long-term technological
development.

The prospects for Sweden's retention of an independent military
aircraft design and development capability seem dim at best. Although the successor to the Gripen might be produced in Sweden,
the costs of independent development and design are likely to preclude the development of an all-Swedish design for such an aircraft.
Indeed, national self-sufficiency has already been reduced in the case
of the RM12 engine, only 50 percent of the components for which
are produced in Sweden. The design and fabrication of the airframe
for the Gripen also draw on foreign engineering resources. The wing
for the Gripen was designed jointly by Saab-Scania and British Aerospace, and BAe is responsible for producing the first two sets of
wings. In the case of engines, increased dependence on U.S. sources

reflects the operation of U.S. restrictions on foreign production of some engine components, such as controls. Nonetheless, in the absence of other policy changes, such as a relaxation of export controls, future Swedish military aircraft development projects are likely to be multinational joint ventures involving Saab, Volvo Flygmotor, and foreign firms.

AIRBUS INDUSTRIE: A JOINT VENTURE OF "NATIONAL CHAMPIONS"

Airbus Industrie is one of the most durable joint ventures in the commercial aircraft industry. The longevity of the Airbus Industrie consortium suggests that its structure and management have implications for the management of other joint ventures. These implications must not be overdrawn, however—Airbus remains essentially a consortium of governments, or firms largely controlled by its governmental participants. When considered as an example of government policy in the aircraft industry, Airbus combines dimensions of both the catch-up and keep-up strategies. Indeed, the need to combine these two strategies within a single joint venture, because of the contrasting goals and technological capabilities of the major participants, has served alternately as a source of strength and as a crippling weakness within the consortium.

The development and financing of Airbus Industrie have been extensively analyzed elsewhere.[25] This discussion of the consortium therefore is selective, focusing on themes in the development of Airbus Industrie that illustrate the tensions among the shifting goals of the various national participants. A brief historical description is followed by an assessment of the implications of the Airbus consortium for the management and organization of joint ventures.

Four Phases in the Development of Airbus Industrie, 1966–1986

The history of the Airbus consortium may be divided into four phases. During the first phase (1966–1969), Britain, France and West Germany all participated in the design discussions. When these collapsed in the wake of Great Britain's withdrawal, France and West

Germany became the primary participants in the second phase (1969–1975), culminating in the introduction of the A300B. During the third phase (1975–1979) the French participants seriously considered abandoning Airbus Industrie in order to pursue other joint venture opportunities. A series of negotiations between French and foreign firms followed, many of which involved cooperation with U.S. firms in product development and manufacture. The final phase (1978–1986) has witnessed the maturation of Airbus Industrie, with the readmission of Great Britain and a substantial rationalization and expansion of the consortium's product line.

One of the central tensions running through this history is the use by both the British and the French governments of Airbus Industrie as the basis for a keep-up strategy for these two nations' aircraft industries. Both Britain and France had aircraft industries of great technological sophistication and achievement. Great Britain, for example, produced the first jet-powered passenger transport. By the 1960s, however, the aircraft industries of both nations faced a situation similar to that of the Swedish aircraft industry. Domestic military and civilian aircraft markets were too small to support independent product development and manufacture efforts, while competition from U.S. producers of military and commercial aircraft, as well as "tied" military aid from the U.S. and the Soviet Union to potential military aircraft purchasers in the third world, had reduced military export markets.

Participation in aircraft development or production consortia had become major issues of public policy within the industrialized European democracies by the 1960s. Their governments had become increasingly involved in the operation of aircraft producers through the nationalization of firms, government intervention in supporting and forcing mergers, and the reliance of privately held enterprises on public subsidies for aircraft and engine development programs. The history of the Airbus consortium has been punctuated by clashes between the engine and airframe "national champions" of France and Great Britain (SNECMA and Aerospatiale in France, Rolls Royce and British Aerospace in Great Britain). Sporadic conflicts have erupted not only between French and British industrial policies, but also between the engine and airframe firms of each nation. Throughout the 1970s, for example, Rolls Royce was interested primarily in cooperation with U.S. airframe firms, especially Boeing, while British Aerospace gradually became a supporter of Airbus. Particularly in situations in which Boeing and Airbus were manufacturing competing products, the interests of the two British firms clashed directly, requiring complex negotiations involving both firms, the British government, and various European governments.[26] Similarly, SNECMA's financial and technological prospects during the 1970s were tied to the CFM56 engine project with General Electric, while Aerospatiale was concerned first and foremost with Airbus.

In 1966 the West German, French, and British governments began to discuss the design and production of a wide-body aircraft. The French and German governments previously had collaborated on several military weapons systems. British participation was new, however, and followed the cancellation by the British government of funding for a number of military and civilian aircraft projects. While the British and French governments viewed the joint venture as a means of sustaining their aircraft industries, for West Germany the consortium presented an opportunity to rebuild its aircraft industry, which had been destroyed during World War II and remained moribund.

The 1967 agreement among the three governments outlined a joint venture in which Great Britain and France each held shares of 37.5 percent, with Germany contributing 25 percent in the development of the airframe. As a concession to Great Britain, France agreed that a new Rolls Royce engine, the RB207, would be developed to power the aircraft.[27] Great Britain acquired a 75 percent share in the engine development, with West Germany and France each accounting for 12.5 percent. In exchange for accepting the development of an all-new engine, rather than employing the JT9D of Pratt & Whitney or the CF6-50 of General Electric, the French won responsibility for design leadership and final assembly of the airframe. The consortium partners also agreed that the Airbus would employ as many European components as possible.

During this early phase of the Airbus project, the British and French firms developed a design that was unacceptable to the national airlines of the sponsor nations (capacity expanded from an original target of 250 passengers to 300–350, far above the levels desired by British, French, or German flag carriers) and much more costly than originally planned. The conflicting design objectives of the participant firms and the various national carriers had by late 1967 produced an aircraft design with virtually no orders. The final blow to this phase of the Airbus project, however, came when Rolls

Royce canceled development of the RB207 because of its greater interest in developing another engine (the RB211) for the Lockheed L-1011 and its inability to fund and staff both projects. As Rolls Royce became less enthusiastic about the Airbus project, the project's attractions for the British government faded (the British Aircraft Corporation, predecessor of British Aerospace, had resisted the concession of design leadership on the airframe to France), and Great Britain withdrew from the consortium in 1969.

Following the withdrawal of Great Britain, the design philosophy and formal organization of the consortium were revised extensively. West Germany and France initially attempted to continue developing the aircraft, now known as the A300B, on a bilateral basis. The Spanish and Dutch governments soon were brought in as partners: as of 1971, Fokker of the Netherlands provided 6.6 percent of the development funds, while CASA of Spain contributed 4.2 percent. France and West Germany each contributed 44.6 percent of the development costs. Although the British government had ended its formal participation and funding, Hawker Siddeley Aircraft, then a private firm (now part of British Aerospace) continued to participate in Airbus as a risk-sharing subcontractor responsible for the design and fabrication of the wing for the A300B.

After the 1969 collapse of the Airbus consortium, the incentives of the participants and the design philosophy changed as well. Before 1969, the Airbus venture had been influenced (or immobilized) by the desire of both France and Great Britain to utilize the venture in a keep-up strategy as a support for their aircraft, engine, and components industries. The tensions created by the participation in Airbus Industrie of the technologically equal British and French firms were replaced after Britain's withdrawal by the binding agent of technological inequality between the two remaining major participants. Cohesion in the reorganized venture was provided by the desire of the West German government to employ Airbus in a catch-up policy for its domestic aircraft industry in a partnership with the more advanced French industry. Thus, the West German government was initially willing to underwrite a large share of the costs of the Airbus in exchange for a modest design and production role, which consisted largely of assembling and fabricating several sections of the fuselage.[28]

This shift in the incentives of the major participants was also reflected in the design philosophy of the reconstituted Airbus consortium. The consortium dropped its earlier goals of maximizing European content and simultaneously developing an engine and airframe.[29] Design considerations came to be dictated largely by the preferences of established national flag airlines, which meant, among other things, a shrinkage of the aircraft's passenger capacity to 250, and the adoption of components employed on other (mainly U.S.) aircraft, in order to reduce the maintenance and inventory requirements for carriers purchasing the aircraft. As a result of these changes in design philosophy, the early A300B aircraft had a U.S. content of nearly 50 percent. The A300B used for its engines a version of the General Electric CF6-50 that was assembled by SNECMA, with a German and French content of roughly 35 percent.

While transfers of production technology within the consortium, primarily from the French to the German participants, remained significant, Airbus no longer had as a central goal the advancement of European commercial aircraft and engine technology. The post-1969 Airbus project contrasts in this regard with many European collaborative military aircraft projects, most of which have pursued ambitious performance and technological goals. Development of the Airbus A300B was therefore completed more rapidly and cheaply. Reflecting the reduced level of direct governmental involvement in the Airbus project after the British withdrawal, Airbus Industrie also began to develop an independent administrative structure, albeit one that was dominated by French personnel and subject to the vetoes of participant governments.

During the third phase of the Airbus project, spanning the mid-1970s, the commitment to the consortium of the French government and its nationalized airframe firm, Aerospatiale, wavered. In negotiations undertaken by French government and Aerospatiale officials with U.S. aircraft firms over the development of a short-haul aircraft that would be smaller than the A300B, the French indicated their desire to maintain employment and technological capabilities within the French aircraft industry. These goals required the development of a new aircraft in order to utilize the underemployed design and production capacity of Aerospatiale. As one account during the mid-1970s noted:

> Even with an increase in the pace of Airbus sales and the eventual development of new versions of the A-300, this program by itself would not be substantial enough to occupy all of France's commercial transport development and production resources.

Most of these resources are concentrated within the aircraft division of Aerospatiale, which is faced this year with employment cutbacks and reduced work schedules for remaining employees because of a dwindling workload.[30]

In addition to its concern over the utilization of airframe production and design capacity, the French government was anxious to find an airframe on which to employ the CFM56 engine, which was scheduled to enter service in the late 1970s. Just as the British commitment to Airbus had been undercut by conflicting goals for the nation's airframe and engine firms, so France entered a period of tortuous maneuvering among U.S. airframe and engine firms, the Airbus partners, and (occasionally) the British aircraft industry, in evaluating a number of independent and joint development projects. The 1977 agreement between the French government and McDonnell Douglas concerning the Mercure 200, discussed in chapter 3, created considerable concern among the French government's partners in Airbus Industrie.

Following the failure of the McDonnell Douglas agreement, the sale of A300s to Eastern Airlines in the United States, and the sale of CFM56 engines to the U.S. Air Force for employment on the KC135 tanker, Airbus Industrie entered into a new phase. The consortium rationalized and expanded its product line and strengthened its product support capabilities, and Great Britain rejoined Airbus Industrie. The French government's renewed commitment to the consortium was closely linked with the eventual development of a market for the CFM56, which reduced the need to launch a new aircraft that would use the engine. At the same time, reentry of the British government into the consortium reflected the gradual alignment of the interests of that nation's airframe and engine firms.

The introduction of the A310 and the simultaneous rationalization of the A300 product line in 1981-1982 were decisions of great strategic importance for Airbus Industrie, since they effectively committed the consortium to the production of a broad family of aircraft serving clearly distinguishable market segments. Before 1980 modifications in the design of the A300 had produced several modest variations of the original design that closely resembled one another. In 1982, however, the introduction of the long-range A300-600 and the A310, a wide-body aircraft with a passenger capacity of 210-220, gave Airbus Industrie the ability to produce two broadly similar aircraft for different markets. Before 1981 the proliferation of modi-

134 ALLIANCE POLITICS AND ECONOMICS

fications of the A300 design had effectively reduced the market for any single A300 design. But in 1986, with a three- and potentially a five-aircraft family of products (the A300-600, the A310, the A320, and the longer-range A330 and A340), Airbus Industrie has expanded its activities considerably and has greatly enhanced the appeal of its entire product line. The consortium's expansion of its product line may be due in part to an increase in the independence of Airbus Industrie management from government control.

The longer-term prospects for the Airbus consortium also have been enhanced by Great Britain's 1979 decision to rejoin the venture for the production of the A310, as well as Britain's decision to participate in the A320 project. While the conflicting attractions of cooperation with U.S. airframe firms for Rolls Royce and cooperation with the European consortium for British Aerospace remain, these tensions have been reduced somewhat by several factors. Rolls Royce engines (the RB211-524) are now an option on the A300-600 and the A310, a technical change made by Airbus Industrie to accommodate one of Great Britain's conditions for rejoining the consortium.[31] In addition, similar incentives for cooperation in airframe development between British and U.S. firms have vanished in the wake of the breakdown of negotiations between Boeing and British Aerospace over British participation in the 757 project. Finally, the fact that Rolls Royce is now involved in an engine development project that will benefit directly from the successful introduction of the A320 (the V2500) has enhanced the attractiveness of Airbus Industrie for the British government.

Evaluation

The mere survival of Airbus Industrie is a considerable achievement in the turbulent atmosphere of European cooperation in high-technology industries. In contrast to other European high-technology ventures, Airbus Industrie has achieved trans-European cooperation and technological parity with U.S. products. The success of Airbus owes a great deal to the fact that the independent development of a national aircraft industry was beyond the financial capacity of any single European government. In this regard, aircraft are quite different from electronics or telecommunications, and the political success of Airbus may not prefigure successful European cooperation in

ESPRIT or EUREKA. Airbus also benefited, however, from the structure of its management organization, which gradually developed considerable independence from both sponsor governments and participant firms.

Despite its political and technological success, the Airbus venture certainly cannot be judged a commercial success. Estimates of the development costs of the A300 suggest that 350–400 of these aircraft must be sold to recover the initial investment of the various partners in Airbus Industrie. By 1982 only 200 A300s had been delivered, and at least one projection of total sales of the A300 through 1990 suggests that only 310–320 aircraft will be sold, well below the estimated break-even point.[32] While these projections, which are similarly gloomy for the A310 and A320, may be incorrect, they suggest that Airbus Industrie has not been and is unlikely to become a successful financial investment for its member governments.[33]

Financial returns are, however, only one of several criteria that should be employed in any evaluation of this investment. Much of the motivation for the Airbus Industrie venture stems from the desire of European governments to maintain, for reasons of national security and economic development, a substantial aircraft design and production capability. Airbus Industrie is a means to this end and, as such, cannot be evaluated on narrowly economic grounds any more than the U.S. investment in aeronautics R&D by the National Aeronautics and Space Administration or the Defense Department can or should be so evaluated.[34]

The modest sales forecasts for the Airbus consortium are due in part to the limited ability of the consortium to manage production fluctuations to meet the demands of the market. Inasmuch as a primary reason for government financial support of Airbus Industrie was the preservation or expansion of skilled employment, the consortium has been constrained in its ability to shed and hire labor. Airbus has been unable in recent years to promise rapid deliveries of the A300-600 and A310, thereby benefiting the Boeing Company, which has developed a far larger production capacity and is able to vary production rates over a wide range without incurring severe financial penalties.[35]

The Airbus consortium has relied on specialization by member firms in different aspects of airframe design and production. British firms have designed and built the wings for the aircraft. The German participants have concentrated on the fabrication and assembly of fuselage sections, and the French participants have been responsible for the majority of the cockpit and fuselage design work, as well as final assembly. Such specialization limits the prospects for substantial technology transfer within the Airbus consortium. Moreover, as the various national participants become increasingly specialized, participation in Airbus Industrie is a less effective means for the preservation of general design and systems integration capabilities.[36] A key issue in the negotiations between the various participant governments over British participation in the A320 project was the strong desire of the British to undertake more of the technologically sophisticated tasks of cockpit design and fabrication, which would involve computer, avionics, and advanced communications technologies.[37] Britain's reentry into Airbus Industrie may eventually rekindle some of the disputes over the division of the technological gains from Airbus design and production. Thus far, however, the greater efficiency of stable patterns of specialization within the consortium appears to have dominated the outcome—Aerospatiale has retained the primary responsibility for the cockpit.

Summary

Airbus Industrie illustrates a number of the general propositions concerning the organization and management of joint ventures: the dangers of encroaching product lines; the need for a strong technological or financial senior partner under some circumstances; and the importance of a strong, autonomous entity for the management of the joint venture under other circumstances. The development of Airbus Industrie also illustrates the potential for conflicts between managerial or commercial feasibility and technology transfer and learning.

The development of an autonomous management structure for Airbus Industrie has been of great importance, for at least two reasons. Much of the prior conflict and breakdown in Anglo–French cooperation through this consortium reflected the fact that the position of each government resembled that of a partner in a joint venture that also manufactures a competing product. The Rolls Royce "subsidiary" of the British government had independently developed products (the RB211-535 and RB211-524) that could face indirect competition from the products of the joint venture—if, for example, CF6-powered A300Bs were sold instead of L-1011s or Boeing 747s powered by Rolls Royce engines. The British government consistently favored the interests of its engine firm over those of its airframe firm and therefore was not interested in participating in the consortium before the late 1970s. The adoption of the RB211-524 as an option for the A300-600 reduced the threat posed by Airbus aircraft sales to Rolls Royce engine sales, thereby increasing the incentives for the British government to participate in the consortium. Nonetheless, the great potential for continued conflicts of interest between the British government's interests in additional sales of Rolls Royce engines, which power the Boeing 757 and 747, and Airbus Industrie's interests in sales of the A300-600 and A310, make it imperative that a strong, independent marketing and sales staff be developed within the consortium's management organization.[38]

Design and engineering issues also are best handled by an autonomous organization in the wake of British reentry into Airbus Industrie. Whereas the design of the A300B was handled by a partnership of technologically unequal firms from France and West Germany, development of the A310, A320, and future aircraft has been and is likely to be undertaken in a partnership involving British and French firms with comparable technological capabilities. As such, the assignment of leadership on design issues to one or another firm raises difficult issues, which are resolved most effectively by an autonomous management group. Achievement of consensus between the senior management of the key partner firms is difficult and impeded development of the McDonnell Douglas-Fokker and Saab-Fairchild aircraft.

The contrast between the structure of Airbus Industrie and the organization of the previous major Anglo-French joint venture, the Concorde, is instructive.[39] Despite its duration and complexity, the Concorde project never developed an autonomous management structure. Daily management was handled by the British and French prime contractors, while high-level oversight was loosely provided by the Concorde Management Board, composed of senior managers from Aerospatiale and British Aircraft Corporation. The results closely resembled the experience of the MDF100 and Saab-Fairchild ventures. Design and management disputes flourished and created delays, exacerbated by the need to seek intervention by senior management of the two "cooperating" firms. Among other things, the loose coordination of the design efforts of the British and French firms meant that for the first two years of the Concorde project the British participants designed a long-range, and the French a medium-range, aircraft.[40]

A closely related difference between Concorde and Airbus is that Concorde operated on a strict cost-sharing basis. The original Anglo–French agreement specified unambiguously that the two nations would share equally the costs of development and production. The modest incentives for cost containment provided by such an agreement led to dramatic cost escalation over the life of the project: development costs rose from the original estimate of roughly $450 million in 1962 to $770 million in 1964, to $1.4 billion in 1966, and to more than $4 billion by 1978.[41] By contrast, the organization of Airbus Industrie as an independent *groupement d'interêt économique* means, among other things, that the relationship between Airbus and the partner firms resembles that of a prime contractor and suppliers, in that fixed-cost contracts are employed for the procurement of aircraft components and assemblies. As a result, the Airbus partner firms face strong incentives to minimize costs, in contrast to the Concorde experience.[42] The Concorde venture also had no procedure for withdrawal by either partner, an omission that contributed to Britain's perseverance in the venture long after its disastrous financial consequences were well known. The Airbus consortium has developed procedures for withdrawal by partner firms, exploited thus far only by Great Britain.

The Airbus consortium's history also illustrates the managerial difficulties inherent in the employment of joint ventures for advancing the technological capabilities of participants. The change in Airbus design philosophy that occurred after Britain's withdrawal in 1969 meant that the development of this European aircraft would yield smaller technological spillovers and learning effects than those associated with a more advanced design, which would use a new European engine and employ components from European, rather than U.S., sources. Despite these greater learning advantages, however, the difficulties, costs, and delays attendant upon the advanced technology strategy led to the decision to pursue a simpler design that employed standard, largely U.S., components. The attractiveness of this less ambitious strategy was enhanced by the withdrawal of Great Britain, which stood to benefit from the policy of employing European components wherever possible.

Increasing specialization among the Airbus partners also reduces technology transfer within the consortium. Less-advanced firms may not increase their capabilities in the areas of design and systems integration, and specialization has implications as well for the keep-up strategies of more advanced firms. Even these technologically advanced participants may weaken their design and engineering capabilities outside of the narrow area for which they are responsible. The managerial requirements of consortium operations thus may reduce the chances that Airbus Industrie will support the development or retention by member firms of technological capabilities sufficiently broad and well-developed to support their entry as prime contractors in aircraft design and manufacture. Nonetheless, the Airbus consortium has enabled the French, West German, and British governments to maintain employment, capacity utilization, and to a limited extent, technological and engineering capabilities, in their aircraft industries.

CONCLUSIONS

Like the case studies in chapter 3, the country strategies examined in this chapter represent a small subset of the development policies employed by industrialized and newly industrialized nations for their domestic aircraft industries. Moreover, there are striking contrasts between national strategies and occasionally, as in Sweden, important differences between the strategies of individual firms within a single nation. With the possible exceptions of Airbus Industrie and Brazil, the effects of these strategies have yet to reveal themselves because they have been in place for only a short time. This difficulty is particularly acute in assessing the effect of joint ventures on the competitiveness of foreign aircraft industries.

The cases discussed in this chapter make clear the difference between strategies intended to support the development of a national aircraft industry—catch-up policies—and those designed to maintain an existing (often military) airframe and engine design and production capability—the keep-up strategies. Although a number of firms, including those in Sweden, Great Britain, and France, have pursued keep-up strategies through joint ventures, the results are unclear. The requirements for specialized collaboration within Airbus Industrie, as well as the consortium's prior technological conservatism (primarily in the development of the A300-B2 and A300-B4), may have reduced the utility of that venture for the maintenance of advanced capabilities in aircraft design and systems integration. The joint venture strategy being pursued by Volvo Flygmotor is also highly specialized and does not push the state of the art in engine design and fabrication, which reduces the utility of this strategy for the maintenance of the firm's technological assets. In contrast, Saab–Scania chose a joint venture as a means of retaining its generalized design and systems integration capabilities. Saab–Scania has had to do so, however, in a segment of the aircraft market characterized by modest technological complexity and now confronts its partner's withdrawal from the venture. Among other things, these consequences may lead to a shift by Saab to specialized participation in joint ventures.

Need catch-up strategies rely exclusively on joint ventures? The recent history of the Brazilian aircraft industry in particular suggests that joint ventures are by no means the only feasible mechanism for the development of a strong domestic airframe industry. Liberalized trade in aircraft engines and components and the stability of the technological interfaces in piston-, turboprop-, and even turbofan-powered aircraft mean that import substitution policies, which may rely on licensing rather than joint ventures, are feasible strategies for the development of commuter and general aviation aircraft producers. Such strategies are extremely costly, however, in nations without a large domestic market for such aircraft. Recognizing the different sizes of the Brazilian and Japanese domestic markets for aircraft is essential for understanding the contrasting catch-up strategies of these nations.

While international flows of aircraft and engine technology in embodied form are abundant, the exploitation of these flows for the development of a domestic aircraft industry requires much more than simply importing knock-down kits and bolting together the components. Entry into the world aircraft or engine industries depends above all else on the development of sufficient design and management capabilities to support entry as a prime contractor, or the development of specialized capabilities in the design, testing, and manufacture of specific components of an engine or airframe. The strategies of nations and their domestic firms vary substantially in pursuing specialized or more general modes of entry. The development of design and production skills in airframes and engines requires a considerable public and private investment in domestic research, development, and educational facilities on which the technology transfer occurring through joint ventures and other channels can build.

How effectively do joint ventures operate to transfer the technological and other knowledge necessary to support entry, in either a specialized or a more general fashion? The experiences of Japanese participants in the Boeing 767 or the International Aero Engines venture, or Embraer's reliance on local, versus external, sources of technological expertise, suggest that joint ventures are not the main channels for the transfer of the essential know-how. Both the incentives of technological leaders and the managerial requirements of joint ventures work against the use of interfirm cooperation to develop design and engineering capabilities sufficient to support entry as a prime contractor into the world airframe or engine industries. The development of specialized capabilities through participation in joint ventures appears to be feasible, however. Any foreign competitive threat to U.S. industry resulting from joint ventures between U.S. and foreign firms is not likely to be directed at the prime contractors, but at suppliers of components. Component design and manufacture, rather than the design and integration of systems into complete engines or airframes, are the key technologies transferred through existing joint ventures. The second tier of the U.S. aircraft industry, made up of the producers of parts and assemblies for fabrication by U.S. prime contractors, bears the brunt of competitive pressure resulting from the improvement of foreign capabilities in the aircraft industry.

NOTES

1.   The florid description of the Japanese industry contained in a recent congressional report is representative: "The Japanese aerospace industry appears to be preparing for takeoff. MITI is the pilot, urging and cajoling in order to raise the domestic industry from a technologically backward assembler industry of U.S.-designed military hardware to a full-fledged independent maker of commercial jet transportation. . . . Once Japan has her own commercial aircraft to sell . . . sales to Japan will probably be cut drastically and U.S. producers will face another major competitor." U.S. Congress, House Committee on Ways and Means, Subcommittee on Trade, *United States–Japan Trade Report*, 96th Congress, 2d session (Washington, D.C.: U.S. Government Printing Office, 1980), pp. 44–45.

2. Mowery and Rosenberg provide a more detailed analysis of several of the
    topics discussed in this section in "Government Policy, Market Structure,
    and Industrial Development: The Japanese and U.S. Commercial Aircraft
    Industries, 1945–85," U.S.–Northeast Asia Forum on International Pol-
    icy, Occasional Paper (Stanford, Calif.: Institute for Strategic and Interna-
    tional Studies, 1984) and in "Competition and Cooperation: The U.S. and
    Japanese Commercial Aircraft Industries," *California Management Review*
    27, no. 4, pp. 70–82.

3. Kawasaki Heavy Industries currently manufactures the P–3C patrol air-
    craft and the Chinook helicopter under coproduction agreements, while
    Ishikawajima–Harima Heavy Industries is manufacturing the Pratt & Whit-
    ney jet engines for the F–15. Other military aircraft manufactured on a
    coproduction basis in Japan include the F–104 and F–4 fighter aircraft.

4. A less sanguine view of the impact of the coproduction program may be
    found in the U.S. General Accounting Office study *U.S. Military Co-pro-
    duction Agreements Assist Japan in Developing Its Civil Aircraft Industry*
    (Washington, D.C.: U.S. Government Printing Office, 1982). Certainly, the
    fact that aircraft produced under license in Japan frequently cost as much
    as 100 percent more than identical aircraft produced in the United States
    (e.g., the F–15) because of the small size of Japanese production runs, sug-
    gests that one motive for Japanese participation in these coproduction
    agreements is the development of a stronger Japanese aircraft industry.

5. See R.W. Moxon, T.W. Roehl, J.R. Truitt, and J.M. Geringer, *Emerging
    Sources of Foreign Competition in the Commercial Aircraft Manufacturing
    Industry* (Washington, D.C.: U.S. Department of Transportation, 1985)
    for a more detailed discussion.

6. Ministry personnel, interview with author, Ministry of International Trade
    and Industry, Tokyo, Japan, June 1983.

7. As noted in the discussion of the V2500 project, the initial impetus for the
    RJ500 joint engine venture stemmed from the need for the Japanese con-
    sortium to utilize the test facilities at Rolls Royce in England. No compar-
    able installation existed in Japan.

8. "The aircraft industry is a typical knowledge-intensive industry, charac-
    terized by high added value and far-reaching technological spin-off. It will
    play an important role in the national plan to remold Japan's industrial
    structure into an innovative knowledge-intensive type.

    "At present the aircraft industry is smaller in scale in Japan than in ad-
    vanced Western countries and relies excessively on demands for defense
    industry. It should direct more attention to the manufacture of planes for
    civil transportation which has a big future.

    "It seems realistic that the private sector should bear the ultimate risks
    involved in an aircraft development project, but for the time being the

government will subsidize projects on the condition that a percentage of profits be contributed to the government, contingent on success.

"It is hoped that Japan will build up a system for basic research and development of aircraft engineering so that it may be fully ready for the expected technological innovation in the 1990's for the manufacture of the next generation aircraft. Development of aircraft engineering must be conducted on the initiative and assistance of the government as it involves highly sophisticated and complex technology." Ministry of International Trade and Industry, Industrial Structure Council, *The Vision of MITI Policies in the 1980s* (Tokyo: Industrial Bank of Japan, 1980), pp. 291–92.

9. The importance of the Japanese domestic market as a launch base for export industries has been noted by Myohei Shinohara, former director of the Economics Research Institute within the Economic Planning Agency, in *Industrial Growth, Trade, and Dynamic Patterns in the Japanese Economy* (Tokyo: University of Tokyo Press, 1982), pp. 22–23:

> One of the basic factors which made export promotion easier in Japan was the huge domestic market of approximately 100 million people. If the domestic market expands in line with or ahead of export expansion, a product with a higher rate of expansion would be subject to a considerable reduction in unit cost through mass production, thus allowing an increase in exports. In other words, even though the relationship between the expansion of the domestic and export markets might have been that of a trade-off on an extremely short-term basis, it proved to be highly complementary for the mid- and long-term. The existence of a feedback relationship between expansion of domestic demand and exports resulted in high growth in Japan.

Other policy instruments for the encouragement of markets include the Japan Electronic Computer Corporation, founded in 1962 to purchase and lease computers produced by Japanese firms, as well as the more recently established leasing firm for industrial robots.

10. In the aftermath of the restoration of convertibility of the yen, the incomplete liberalization of the Japanese capital market continues to give considerable powers of moral suasion to the Ministry of Finance and MITI in their dealings with the major Japanese banks, allowing for some influence over the allocation of investment. Leonard Lynn, *How Japan Innovates: A Comparison with the U.S. in the Case of Oxygen Steelmaking* (Boulder, Colo.: Westview Press, 1982), provides a detailed account of MITI's involvement in the acquisition by Japanese steel firms of basic oxygen furnace technology.

11. MITI recently has encouraged domestic sources of industrial technology, as in its support of joint research programs in VLSI and computer technologies. This policy shift reflects growing Japanese scientific and technological strength, as well as a decline in the availability of "off-the-shelf" industrial process technologies for purchase of licensing by Japanese in-

dustry. The goal of this new policy remains the same, however: the nurturing of an industry-wide knowledge base that will support vigorous interfirm competition in product development and manufacture. Okimoto and others have suggested that the system of lifetime employment and other obstacles to interfirm labor mobility in Japanese industry restrict interfirm diffusion of knowledge and technology, thus increasing the importance of such policies. See, for example, Daniel I. Okimoto, *Pioneer and Pursuer: The Role of the State in the Evolution of the Japanese and American Semiconductor Industries* (Stanford, Calif.: Northeast Asia–United States Forum on International Policy, 1983).

12.   Political obstacles to foreign sales of an all-Japanese large commercial transport almost certainly would be raised by other industrialized nations, creating an additional motive for international collaboration.

13.   While MHI has successfully marketed these aircraft in the U.S. and other foreign nations, the financial success of the venture has been adversely affected by the severe depression in the market for these products during the past four years. Mitsubishi sold its Diamond business aircraft program to Beech Aircraft in December 1985. See *Aviation Week and Space Technology*, "Beech Acquires Mitsubishi Diamond Program," December 9, 1985, p. 26.

14.   Interview with MITI personnel, June 1983.

15.   Recent changes in Japanese policy toward the aircraft industry appear to acknowledge the inability of Japanese firms to pursue an independent path in the aircraft industry. According to Yoder, the law establishing government financed support for the commercial aircraft industry is to be revised " . . . to require all government-funded projects for developing civilian aircraft to include foreign partners." Stephen Kreider Yoder, "Japan is Abandoning Its Dream of Developing Airplanes Alone," *Wall Street Journal*, February 7, 1986, p. 34. Yoder's account, however, differs from recent indications that the next Japanese military fighter may be a Japanese design, rather than being produced under license from the United States. See "Japan's New Jet Fighter Will Be Homemade," *Business Week*, November 17, 1986, p. 82.

16.   This discussion draws on the recent report by Moxon et al.; *Emerging Sources of Foreign Competition*, Crane and Gilliot (1985); Ravi Sarathy, "High-Technology Exports from Newly Industrializing Countries: The Brazilian Commuter Aircraft Industry," *California Management Review* 27, 1985, pp. 60–84; R.A. Hudson, "The Brazilian Way to Technological Independence: Foreign Joint Ventures and the Aircraft Industry," *Inter-American Economic Affairs* 37, 1983, pp. 23–43; and Jack Baranson, *North–South Technology Transfer* (Mt. Airy, Md., Lomond, 1981) and *Technology and Multinationals* (Lexington, Mass.: D.C. Heath, 1978).

17.   Crane and Gilliot argue that Embraer also gained considerable production know-how through this licensing agreement. The negotiations be-

tween the Brazilian government and U.S. producers of general aviation aircraft, as well as the Brazilian strategy of developing a significant indigenous technological capability, resemble the Indian government's policies toward the Indian computer industry, discussed in Joseph M. Grieco, *Between Dependency and Autonomy: India's Experience with the International Computer Industry* (Berkeley, Calif.: University of California Press, 1984).

18. Moxon et al. suggest such a link. U.S. firms also accused Embraer of predatory sales practices in marketing the Bandeirante, arguing that the firm was relying on publicly subsidized credits in offering lenient financing in aircraft sales. An extensive investigation of Embraer by the U.S. International Trade Commission concluded, however, that the Bandeirante was not winning orders in the U.S. due solely to the lenient financial terms offered by Embraer, and rejected the U.S. industry's petition. See U.S. International Trade Commission, *Certain Commuter Aircraft from Brazil*, publication #1291 (Washington, D.C.: U.S. International Trade Commission, 1982).

19. As Ingemar Dorfer noted, "Oslo was Sweden's Pearl Harbor. When General Engelbrecht's 163rd Wehrmacht Infantry Division took over Oslo airfield on the morning of April 9, 1940, it caused a shock among Swedish politicians that few of them ever forgot." This discussion of the Swedish aircraft industry draws on Dorfer's study, *System 37 Viggen: Arms, Technology and the Domestication of Glory* (Oslo: Universitetsforlaget, 1973), p. 27, as well as on Ulf Olsson, *The Creation of a Modern Arms Industry: Sweden, 1939-1974* (Gothenburg: Institute of Economic History, Gothenburg University, 1977.)

20. Dorfer estimates that in 1938, Sweden's total operational military air fleet consisted of ninety aircraft. Ibid., p. 48.

21. Saab began automobile production in 1949, while the production of Saab–Scania trucks and the designation of the firm as Saab–Scania followed the merger of the Scania and Saab firms in 1969. For expositional ease, the firm is occasionally referred to as Saab in this chapter.

22. Some idea of the magnitude of Volvo Flygmotor's modification of foreign engines is conveyed by the example of the RM8 engine, which powers the Viggen supersonic fighter. The RM8 is a modification of the Pratt & Whitney JT8D civil, subsonic engine. When equipped with a Volvo afterburner and other modifications, the RM8 is capable of supersonic speeds and generates 28,000 pounds of thrust, considerably greater than the 18–19,000 pounds of thrust for which the JT8D is rated in commercial applications. Swedish military applications of foreign engine designs also require that the front end of the engine be strengthened to withstand midair collisions with birds.

23. The requirement for after-sales service of the sophisticated aircraft and engines employed by the Swedish air force requires that both Volvo and Saab retain a sophisticated and broad-based technological capability. Ac-

cording to Simon Beavis, a key factor influencing the Swedish military's endorsement of the design and production of the Gripen, rather than the purchase of a foreign aircraft, was the need to retain the capabilities within Saab and Volvo to provide product support for the Draken and Viggen through the year 2000. See Simon Beavis, "JAS 39: Sweden Forges Ahead," *Flight International*, May 25, 1985, pp. 41–44.

24. See Brown (1986) and *Aviation Week and Space Technology*, "News Digest," February 24, 1986, p. 31, for a description of Saab–Scania's participation in Boeing and McDonnell Douglas projects. The Swedish firm's prospective share of either development project is likely to be small, not exceeding 10 percent.

25. See Mark A. Lorell, *Multinational Development of Large Aircraft: The European Experience* (Santa Monica, Calif.: The Rand Corporation, 1980); Michael Yoshino, "Global Competition in a Salient High-Technology Industry: The Case of Commercial Aircraft," presented at the Harvard Business School 75th Anniversary Colloquium, 1984; and John Newhouse, *The Sporty Game* (New York: Knopf, 1983); as well as the trade press.

26. The decision of British Aerospace to rejoin the Airbus Industrie consortium in 1978 is a good example, inasmuch as the simultaneous decision of British Airways to purchase Rolls Royce–powered Boeing 757s, rather than Airbus A300s or A310s, angered other participants in Airbus Industrie, caused concern at BAe lest the governments participating in Airbus move to block the British firm's readmission, and required the intervention of the British Prime Minister as an arbitrator between the British firms and a diplomat in negotiations with other European governments.

27. "The RB207 was chosen for the Airbus not because it was the best choice economically, commercially, or technologically, but because its choice had become a prerequisite to British participation." (Lorell, *Multinational Development*, p. 53). According to Hayward this decision reflected the British government's consistent policy since 1964 of favoring Rolls Royce over British airframe firms in international collaboration agreements. See Hayward, *Government and British Civil Aerospace*, pp. 80–81.

28. One account of the negotiations in the early 1980s over West German participation in the A320 project noted that "Soundings among West German aerospace leaders produced a consensus of opinion that there will not be anything like the desperation to be in on the launching of the A320 as [sic] there was ten years or more ago to be in on the launch of the original A300 project. At that time, industrial resources were desperately needed in West Germany, and the A300, with the French and the British passing over knowhow as partners, was seen as a superb way of building up the West German aerospace industry." Arthur Reed, "British, Germans Ponder Their A320 Participation," *Air Transport World*, September 1981, p. 38.

29. Hayward, in *Government and British Civil Aerospace*, p. 95, estimated that British withdrawal from the consortium cost the country's components industry more than $350 million in orders.

30. Robert Ropelewski, "Mercure 200 Pact Sparks Uproar," *Aviation Week and Space Technology*, August 23, 1976, pp. 12–13.

31. Despite their availability, there is no record of A300–600s or A310s being sold with Rolls Royce engines.

32. See Wolfgang Demisch, Christopher C. Demish, and Theresa L. Concert, *The Jetliner Business* (New York: First Boston Corporation, 1984), p. 39.

33. Estimates of the size of the public investment in Airbus Industrie vary greatly, but unpublished estimates from the Office of the U.S. Trade Representative suggest that over the period 1968–1982 Airbus received subsidies totaling nearly $2.5 billion. Paul R. Krugman, "The U.S. Response to Industrial Targeting," *Brookings Papers on Economic Activity* 1 (1984), pp. 77–102, 116.

34. The noneconomic nature of several of the goals of Airbus Industrie is readily apparent. Nonetheless, U.S. aircraft producers, who receive no direct public support for commercial aircraft development projects, and the Airbus consortium, which receives substantial public funding of development work, employ different criteria in evaluating investment and production decisions, which raises extraordinarily difficult issues for trade policy.

35. "Rapidly increasing orders have spurred some Europeans to criticize Airbus Industrie for what they contend is a production rate so low it threatens the financial success of the consortium. These critics argue the U.S. competition, namely Boeing Co., with its higher production rate, can promise faster deliveries. . . . Airbus officials believe they have made reasonable plans. Planning for too much production would be disastrous financially, they said.

"Manpower planning in Europe involves special problems. 'We can't just give people two weeks pay and tell them to go home if we suddenly find we don't have enough work,' one official said. 'Laying off people means paying out months of salaries, depending on the law of the country they are working in.' " Edward Bassett, "Airbus Gears for Production Increase," *Aviation Week and Space Technology*, November 12, 1979, p. 56.

36. Beteille notes that the consortium has pioneered the use of a new fabrication technique in which substantial sections of the fuselage are assembled to an advanced state of completion, and simply "plugged in" in the final assembly plant at Toulouse, in order to enable participant firms to gain experience in a variety of tasks: "The basic requirement was of a 'social' nature that is the importance for all partners to contribute to the entire range of tasks . . . leading to the concept of a 'plug-in' type of final assembly line matching large subassemblies delivered 'ready to fly' . . . " Although novel, this strategy maximizes the range of assembly rather than design tasks undertaken by participant firms and thus represents a partial solution at best. See Roger H. Beteille, "Developing Aircraft through Joint Venture Programs," speech delivered at the International Air Transportation Conference, Atlantic City, AIAA-81-0794, 1981, p. 3.

37.   "Continuing production of wings is seen here [in London] as very basic technology, and how much more demanding it would be to have the responsibility for the design and manufacture of the front end of the new airliner.

"This section would also mean that the British would have their hands on far more equipment than at present so that the British equipment and avionics industry would be in a better position to break what they are always complaining is the hold which their French industry counterparts and rivals have on the A300 and A310.

"Design of a whole new airliner cockpit and front end would also help to keep British design teams together. . . . " Reed, "British, Germans Ponder," p. 38.

38.   Concern by the other Airbus partners over the conflicts of interest in which the British government might find itself was raised in the discussion of British veto rights within the consortium: "As an example of why the major European partners in the Airbus consortium are fearful of British veto powers, one source said, 'Suppose they had those rights and there were two possible deals, one for the sale of the A310 and one for a Boeing plane with Rolls–Royce engines. The British might use their veto, say on the question of how much the A310 would cost, in order to let the Rolls–Royce deal go through. . . .'" *Aviation Week and Space Technology*, "Veto Issue Stalls A310 Talks," October 9, 1978, p. 26. In the event, Britain did receive full veto rights on all decisions concerning the A310.

39.   Hochmuth and Feldman provide brief surveys of the evolving structure and problems of the Concorde venture; Beteille provides an interesting discussion of the Airbus management organization from the perspective of a senior manager of Airbus Industrie. See Milton S. Hochmuth, "Aerospace," in Raymond S. Vernon, ed. *Big Business and the State* (Cambridge, Mass.: Harvard University Press, 1974); Elliot J. Feldman, *Concorde and Dissent* (Cambridge, Mass.: Harvard University Press, 1985); and Beteille, "Developing Aircraft."

40.   The proper spelling of the name of the aircraft was the cause of endless memoranda and negotiation, the British preferring to spell the name without the "e." Indicative of the level of direct involvement by senior political figures in the most prosaic management issues is the fact that the British decision to accept the Francophone spelling was announced by no less a personage than Anthony Wedgewood Benn, Minister of Aviation in the Wilson Cabinet, in a public speech in December 1967.

41.   See Feldman, *Concorde and Dissent*, and David Henderson, "Two British Errors: Their Probable Size and Some Possible Lessons," *Oxford Economic Papers* 29, 1977.

42.   Both CFM International and International Aero Engines utilize similar procurement procedures in dealing with partner firms.

5 CONCLUSIONS AND POLICY IMPLICATIONS

ARE INTERNATIONAL JOINT VENTURES A THREAT TO U.S. COMPETITIVENESS IN COMMERCIAL AIRCRAFT?

Commercial aircraft rely on a technology that exhibits considerable stability in the interfaces among components within and between an airframe and engine; that stability is likely to continue as long as turbofan engines remain the primary source of propulsion and metallic substances the dominant material of construction. Combined with substantial growth in technological and production capabilities in foreign firms, such stability means that U.S. firms can obtain many of the components and a growing share of the design tasks for a given aircraft from foreign sources. Joint ventures are one of the major channels through which these tasks and components can be obtained, but they are by no means the only one. Moreover, joint ventures are not the only channel through which design and production technology is transferred from U.S. to foreign firms. Regardless of the role of joint ventures, foreign competition in the commercial aircraft industry inevitably will increase in the long run as a result of the growing technological sophistication of foreign firms, as well as expanding international trade in aircraft components.

Although technological stability has made it easier for U.S. firms to obtain design services and specific components from foreign producers, the capabilities necessary to manage the processes of design, systems integration, marketing, and product support remain concentrated within a few enterprises, most of which are located in the United States. The concentrated distribution of managerial and systems integration capabilities and the dispersed production and component design capabilities interact with the spiraling costs of product development to create a strong basis for the exchange of intangible corporate assets through joint ventures involving product development and manufacture. Formal and informal restrictions on trade in high-technology products, such as government demands for offsets or other economic benefits as a prerequisite for market access by foreign firms, provide additional incentives for U.S. firms to seek out foreign partners for the development and production of aircraft.

Despite the fact that much of the joint venture activity in the aircraft industry is due to factors that are unique to this industry, both international and domestic joint ventures in research, product development, and manufacture have increased in number in many U.S. industries. Research cooperation among U.S. firms is widespread and growing, as is research cooperation between universities and industry. U.S. firms in numerous industries are relying increasingly on external sources of technological expertise for innovation.[1] The technologies of information processing and communication that are revolutionizing management in many U.S. firms also facilitate the transfer of technologies in various stages of development from external sources to the firm; this is particularly true of the design-intensive aircraft industry. Some of the forces giving rise to joint ventures in commercial aircraft thus are specific to this industry, while others affect all U.S. industry.

The increasing incidence of joint ventures in the U.S. commercial aircraft industry is a response to fundamental forces in the evolution of both the world economy and aircraft technology; in the absence of U.S. government intervention, joint ventures are likely to increase in number and significance. Indeed, several existing joint ventures in aircraft and engines, such as Airbus and Boeing-Japanese collaboration in aircraft and the CFM venture in engines, appear quite durable and are likely to undertake the development of additional aircraft and engines in the future. At the same time, a radical change in airframe or engine technologies, such as the development of a low-cost unducted fan turboprop engine, extensive employment of composite materials in wings and the fuselage, or a commercially viable supersonic transport, could revolutionize the technology of commercial aircraft. Radical technological advances by U.S. firms could work to the disadvantage of foreign firms, well versed in the design and production of components for engines or airframes using current technology, who may suddenly find their skills no longer relevant.[2] Discontinuous technological change in commercial aircraft therefore might reduce temporarily the growing reliance of U.S. firms on joint ventures. Nonetheless, the participation of SNECMA in General Electric's UDF engine development program and the JADC's involvement in the Boeing 7J7 program seems likely to result in sufficient technology transfer to allow these foreign firms to participate in future turboprop engine and airframe development programs.

The concerns of policy makers and others about the dangers posed by these cooperative ventures for the future competitiveness of the U.S. commercial aircraft industry seem overstated. U.S. prime-contractor firms do not appear to be threatened in the short run by foreign competitors that have been strengthened through joint ventures with U.S. firms. The characteristics of the technologies being transferred through such joint ventures are such that foreign firms will not be able to enter this industry as prime contractors in less than several decades.[3]

Independent entry of foreign firms into the commercial aircraft industry is unlikely for purely financial reasons as well. The costs and risks of independent entry are so great as to make such a strategy financially irrational. During the past twenty years U.S. and foreign firms with technological capabilities that were considerably greater than those of most potential foreign entrants have been forced to withdraw from the industry. Moreover, while foreign governments often are willing to defray all or part of the costs of participation in a joint venture, very few governments seem willing to risk the huge sums necessary for independent entry by a single "national champion."

The outlook for the major U.S. producers of engines and airframes thus seems fairly bright, although growing reliance by these firms on joint ventures with foreign partners does expose the second tier of U.S. suppliers and aerospace industry subcontractors to increased foreign competition. Foreign firms have gained expertise in the production of components and other subassemblies as a result of their participation in joint ventures with major U.S. firms. Since many of these U.S. supplier firms also produce components for military aircraft, continued high levels of joint venture activity in commercial aircraft and engines could eventually reduce the ability of U.S. domestic firms to provide the technological and production capacity necessary to sustain military aircraft procurement and preparedness.

This chapter examines the implications of the growing importance of joint ventures in the commercial aircraft industry for private sector managers and public sector policy makers. Lessons for managers from the case studies of chapter 3 deal largely with the organization and management of joint ventures. These new forms of interfirm cooperation also have implications for U.S. trade and industrial policy. While U.S. government policies have affected the motivation for U.S. firms to undertake joint ventures, and export controls have directly affected several projects, a policy of review or regulation of technology transfer through all joint ventures seems unrealistic and injurious to long-term U.S. economic interests. A review process already exists, in the form of Defense Department restrictions on technology transfer through joint ventures. Nonetheless, the role of U.S. policies toward the commercial aircraft industry in motivating joint ventures between U.S. and foreign firms deserves careful scrutiny.

ORGANIZATION AND MANAGEMENT OF JOINT VENTURES

The joint ventures discussed in chapter 3 (as well as Airbus Industrie, discussed in Chapter 4) range from risk-sharing subcontracting relationships in which the junior partner contributes a share of the tooling or other development costs, to a project managed in all respects by the senior partner, to independent corporate entities with a substantial staff and considerable autonomy from the partner firms. No single organizational principle distinguishes successful joint ventures from unsuccessful ones—the range of variables that can affect commercial success extends well beyond project management. Nonetheless, the problems encountered by McDonnell Douglas and Saab-Scania Aircraft, as well as the successes (defined as the introduction of a product, rather than the profitability) of the Airbus, CFM International, and Boeing joint ventures suggest the importance of tailoring the structure of a joint venture to the technological and financial positions of the partner firms.

Where participant firms are technological and financial equals, as in the V2500 and Airbus ventures, a separate management structure to control overall design, marketing, and production decisions seems essential. An independent management structure, while costly, reduces the difficulties of resolving disputes among equal partners and minimizes the conflicts of interest that are likely to arise between the sales of the jointly developed product and those produced independently by partner firms. Indeed, under some circumstances, the board of directors might consist of parties affiliated with none of the partner firms, as a means of ensuring that decisions reflect the interests of the joint venture, rather than the (potentially conflicting) interests of the partner firms.

Firms that are technologically more advanced than their partners are ill-advised to assume a junior role within a joint venture, as McDonnell Douglas did in the Mercure 200 project. The assertion of design preferences, however well-founded from a technical point of view, is far more feasible when such an assertion is accompanied by a significant financial contribution. The experience of CFM International, however, suggests that the reverse proposition is not true. The financial equality of the CFM partners masked General Electric's primary role in most of the overall design, production, marketing, and product support operations of the consortium. The influence of technological superiority or inferiority on the appropriate organizational structure for a joint venture thus seems more significant than the financial contributions of partners.

Joint ventures involving firms that are not technological equals— for example, Boeing-JCAC or CFM—are based firmly on a straightforward exchange between firms of intangible assets, such as technology for market access. This exchange provides a powerful cohesive force, reducing somewhat the importance of issues of management and organizational structure. The clear assignment to the senior partner of responsibility for overall project management, design, and marketing means that these joint ventures typically have less demanding managerial requirements. Nonetheless, the basis for the exchange that binds together the partners—the transfer of technology—is itself a very delicate process for the senior partner to manage so as to avoid the creation of a significant competitor, while at the same time retaining the participation of the technologically junior firm. Such ventures can yield significant financial benefits for the senior partner, however, in the form of additional fees for production experience or overall project management, and can effectively enable this firm to realize a financial return on portions of its portfolio of technological capabilities that otherwise could not be licensed or sold. Such financial returns are clearly discernible within the Boeing 767 and CFM International ventures.

The identification of one or another firm as a technological leader or as a follower, which is important in determining the structure and goals of a joint venture partnership, is more easily done in the abstract than in a specific instance. Nonetheless, assessments of the technological capabilities of competitors are an important part of the formulation of firm strategies in high-technology industries. Moreover, identifying specific technological, financial, and other strengths and weaknesses of a prospective partner is essential for the successful formation and management of a joint venture. An unlucky or inappropriate choice of partner (for example, Saab-Scania's choice of Fairchild Aircraft in the SF340 project) can impose great costs on all parties.

Management structure and partner choice have been clear sources of difficulty in the joint ventures examined in this study. Other potential sources of conflict, however, rarely have surfaced in the ventures examined here. The discussion in chapters 1 and 2 suggested that harmonization of production rates and practices between U.S. and European firms might be a problem, based on the experience of previous U.S.-European cooperative and coproduction programs in military aircraft. This problem contributed to the breakup of the MDF100 venture, because of Fokker's unwillingness to expand its engineering staff on a temporary basis. Evidence from the Boeing 767, CFM International, and SF340 ventures suggests, however, that an inability of European partners to invest sufficiently in tooling or to manage fluctuations in production volume has not been an issue. Indeed, the greatest single management and technological failure in any of these joint ventures is probably that of Fairchild Aircraft (a U.S. firm) in the SF340 venture.

Harmonization of production practices thus is not yet a major issue in these European-U.S. ventures. The programs in which it could emerge, however, the Boeing 767 and CFM International, have not confronted major fluctuations in production rates. The absence of this problem in civilian aircraft programs and its seeming prevalence in military programs may reflect the contrasting severity of the discipline of the market in the military and civilian sectors of the aircraft industry, rather than any inherent inflexibility in European management; where careful and efficient management of fluctuations in activity has been essential to private profitability, European firms do not appear to have had great problems. Nonetheless, the management of fluctuations in production volume has been a salient issue within the Airbus consortium (to which governments contribute much of the funding) and has arguably impaired the sales of Airbus aircraft. Transatlantic cooperation in managing production volumes thus may be a serious future problem, but it has not yet emerged in any of the joint ventures between U.S. and foreign firms that reached the point of production.

Another issue that has not been raised publicly within any current joint venture is the conflict between the desires of senior partners to restrict, and junior partners to maximize, the amount of technology transfer taking place. In most cases, considerations of managerial feasibility and efficiency and the incentives of the technological leaders have dictated specialized participation by the technologically junior firms and modest levels of technology transfer. Volvo Flygmotor has sought to develop a specialized role as a prospective participant in future engine development projects, and Saab-Scania may pursue a more specialized role in some future joint ventures. Specialization by the partner firms also is characteristic of Airbus Industrie, the junior partners of both Pratt & Whitney and Rolls Royce within the V2500, SNECMA within the CFM International venture, and the Japan Commercial Aircraft Corporation within the Boeing 767 venture. Specialized participation in joint ventures conflicts directly with the stated desire of Japanese firms to participate in the widest possible range of development, manufacturing, and marketing activities. Nonetheless, neither the Japanese nor the European junior partners in any of these consortia have withdrawn or raised the issue publicly. The apparent acquiescence of many European firms to such specialized roles may reflect the use of these joint ventures as a basis for a keep-up strategy, focused on the stabilization of skilled, high-wage employment. This issue, however, may well be a sore point in future joint ventures.

Existing joint ventures are not transferring all of the design and managerial skills necessary to enter the world aircraft or engine industries. This finding has clear implications for nations and firms using joint ventures as a catch-up strategy in developing a domestic aircraft industry. Joint ventures can support employment growth in

the production of components and assemblies, activities that mani-
fest the knowledge-intensive, high-skill characteristics viewed as
desirable by many nations. Catch-up strategies relying on joint ventures, however, will not develop a domestic prime-contractor design
and management capability in large commercial transports within a
reasonable time. Similarly, the limited transfer of generalized design
and management skills through existing joint ventures, coupled with
the highly specialized division of labor among the partners in these
ventures, means that even keep-up joint venture strategies may fail to
preserve the full range of design and management capabilities that
nations and firms deem essential for a complete domestic military
and commercial aircraft design and manufacturing operation.

The U.S. partners in these joint ventures, with the exception of
Fairchild Aircraft and McDonnell Douglas, have reaped substantial
benefits from their participation. In at least one case, and almost
certainly in others about which less is known, foreign partners provided significant infusions of capital, preventing the cancellation of
the entire development project. The CFM56, termination of which
may have been prevented by the infusion of capital from SNECMA,
has proved profitable for both partners.

The role of joint ventures in sustaining development projects
beyond the point at which they might be canceled if financed and
managed by a single firm raises interesting questions, in view of
the possibility that products manufactured independently may
encroach on markets for jointly developed products. The presence
of a foreign partner will lower the costs of continuing a project, and
may well raise the costs of withdrawal (in terms of negotiations,
indemnification of a partner, etc.). In certain circumstances, however, such as when a jointly developed product threatens to encroach
on the markets served by an independently developed (and presum-
ably more profitable) product, a firm's interests may be best served
by immediate withdrawal. The ability of joint ventures to prolong
development projects thus is potentially a mixed blessing. The evidence suggests, however, that U.S. and foreign firms (McDonnell
Douglas in the MDF100, Rolls Royce in the JT10D) have been quick
to withdraw from ventures that appeared to encroach on the markets
for their own products. The dangers posed by such encroachment
underline the importance of care in selecting partners in joint
ventures.

POLICY IMPLICATIONS

The greatest difficulty in deriving clear policy implications from this study stems from the fact that joint ventures in commercial aircraft have had little time to exert a significant influence on the structure or competitiveness of either the U.S. or foreign aircraft and engine industries. Some policy implications in two general areas, however, can be drawn. There appears to be little need for additional U.S. policies to restrict or control joint ventures and technology transfer. Policy makers nonetheless must recognize the cumulative effect on the U.S. commercial aircraft industry of the series of far-reaching policy shifts, affecting both military and commercial aircraft markets in the United States and abroad, that have taken place over the past thirty years. Rather than considering additional policy initiatives in narrowly defined areas, U.S. policy makers would be well advised to assess the effect and overall structure of existing federal policy on the military and commercial segments of this industry. Moreover, the likely near-term effect of joint ventures on U.S. suppliers of components may require more aggressive support of the technological development of these firms.

The foreign beneficiaries of the technology transfer occurring within joint ventures are likely to pose a competitive threat in the near future to U.S. suppliers of components and assemblies for both engines and airframes. Indeed, heightened competition within this second tier benefits the U.S. prime contractor firms undertaking the joint ventures. In many, although by no means all, cases these supplier firms are relatively small and invest little in R&D, having for many years produced components to the specifications of the prime contractors. Moreover, many of these firms are located in areas of the United States, notably the industrial Midwest, that are already suffering a decline in skilled manufacturing employment.

Although the plight of supplier firms thus is potentially serious, particularly if joint venture activity continues at its current pace, these firms are by no means innocent victims of short-sighted management decisions by U.S. prime contractors. In some cases, as the studies in chapter 3 noted, U.S. firms approached foreign firms for participation in product development projects only after U.S. supplier firms had expressed no interest in participating as risk-sharing subcontractors or as production associates.

The importance of this reluctance on the part of U.S. supplier firms should not be overstated. Local, or at least European and Japanese, content in engines and airframes marketed by U.S. producers is essential to the penetration of many foreign markets. Participation by U.S. supplier firms in these development projects thus almost certainly would have supplemented, rather than substituted for, that of foreign firms. Nonetheless, much of the responsibility for the increasing foreign competition through international joint ventures belongs to U.S. supplier firms. Restrictive trade policies aimed at this segment of the industry will impair the competitiveness of the major U.S. producers of engines and airframes, without necessarily making U.S. supplier firms more willing to participate as risk-sharing partners in future development projects.

Although U.S. supplier firms face an increasingly competitive environment, the growing international trade in components and other parts for airframes and engines that is associated with increasing international cooperation in development projects also has been a source of great benefit for these firms. This segment of the aerospace industry has experienced rapid export growth since the liberalization of the international trading regime in the aftermath of the Agreement on Trade in Civil Aircraft. Restrictive actions to reduce multinational joint ventures would assuredly invite retaliation, which would in turn harm the firms that the restrictions would be intended to help. Supplier firms thus are major short-term beneficiaries of liberalized international trade in aircraft components, even as they may be hurt by such trade in the long run.

Trade restrictions are an ineffective and counterproductive response to increased foreign competition in aircraft parts and components. Nonetheless other federal policy initiatives could go some way to restoring or preserving the competitiveness of supplier firms. In particular, the large public research investment that is channeled through the military budget and NASA might be reallocated to involve supplier firms more heavily in NASA and military-sponsored research. The track record of Pentagon contract research in reaching and supporting smaller firms is dismal, as the recent report of the National Academy of Sciences on the U.S. machine tool industry noted.[4] The program sponsored by the Air Force in aircraft manufacturing process technologies (the Technology Modernization program, Tech Mod), for example, has rarely involved component suppliers. Additional research funding from both NASA and military sources should be channeled into research programs yielding bene-fits for this segment of the aircraft industry.

The role of aircraft industry supplier firms as producers of compo-nents for both military and commercial aircraft and engines raises the possibility that increasing foreign competition in this segment of the industry may ultimately reduce the ability of U.S. industry to sup-ply national defense needs. Has the defense industrial base been impaired as a result of joint ventures between U.S. and foreign firms, and if so, what responses are appropriate? This is an area about which very little is known—the data necessary for a rigorous analysis of the health of the defense industrial base have not been collected, nor is it possible to monitor changes in the strength of this industrial base. Several studies by the Rand Corporation in the late 1970s on this subject, however, provide useful information.[5]

Baumbusch et al. concluded that the lower tiers of the defense industrial base, a segment that includes the supplier firms within the U.S. commercial and military aircraft industries, displayed little evi-dence of decline. That is, supplies of components or production capacity seemed adequate for peacetime or mobilization require-ments in the sectors examined.[6] Moreover, the authors concluded that the most important inducement to exit from the lower tier of the defense industry was Pentagon procurement practices, primarily insufficient support by the U.S. military for competitive procure-ment of components. In light of the substantial real increases in de-fense spending in the past five years, the current state of the defense industrial base is almost certainly more robust than it was in the late 1970s. Joint ventures may contribute to a gradual erosion of this industrial base, but no such erosion is yet apparent. Changes in the procurement policies of the U.S. Defense Department are likely to yield much larger payoffs than protection in supporting this sector of the defense industrial base.

While technology transfer through joint ventures appears to have been limited, some transfer clearly is taking place, and foreign pro-duction capabilities are being built up in the aircraft industry as a result of the actions of U.S. firms. Assuming that the long-term (that is, thirty to fifty years) consequences of these actions may be un-desirable for U.S. interests, what actions to influence the behavior of U.S. prime contractor firms are appropriate or likely to be effec-tive? This question cannot be addressed without considering U.S. policies in apparently unrelated areas, such as antitrust policy, that affect the incentives of U.S. firms to enter foreign joint ventures. Other policy areas that affect the behavior of the prime contractor firms include U.S. policy toward offsets and coproduction of military aircraft; U.S. trade policy toward foreign financial support for domestic producers of aircraft and engines; and foreign governments' resort to "directed procurement."

The role of U.S. antitrust policy in motivating joint ventures with foreign firms is a difficult issue. Antitrust policy clearly has nothing to do with the apparent reluctance of U.S. supplier firms to participate as risk-sharing subcontractors in development projects with prime contractors. U.S. antitrust policy is relevant only to joint ventures between U.S. prime contractors. Joint ventures among such firms involve collaboration between technological equals and are therefore less likely or feasible than joint ventures that exploit a technology gap. Antitrust policy therefore is relevant to a small share of the total volume of potential joint venture activity in the commercial aircraft industry. Moreover, there is little evidence that any of the major U.S. producers of either airframes or engines is seriously interested in teaming with another U.S. prime contractor.

The behavior of U.S. firms in the aircraft engine market does suggest, however, that joint ventures between U.S. and foreign firms do not receive the critical review by the Justice Department that one would see in joint ventures involving only U.S. firms. During the past three years, both U.S. producers of aircraft engines have employed joint ventures with Rolls Royce to reduce competition. General Electric and Rolls Royce announced an agreement in 1984 to cooperate in high-bypass turbofan engines, reducing competition in the 50,000–60,000-pound thrust segment of this market to two firms, General Electric (Rolls Royce having taken a 15 percent share in development and production of the CF6-80 and derivatives) and Pratt & Whitney, producer of the PW4000. In midsize engines (35,000–45,000 pounds of thrust), General Electric agreed to cooperate with Rolls Royce, taking a 15 percent share in the British firm's RB211-535 project.[7] Pratt & Whitney, producer of the PW2037, now faces only Rolls Royce in this segment of the engine market. A similar alliance between a U.S. firm and Rolls Royce has reduced competition in the 25,000-pound-thrust segment of the engine market, as Pratt & Whitney has teamed with Rolls Royce in the V2500 venture. Moreover, as chapter 3 noted, the decision by Rolls Royce and the JAEC to form an alliance with Pratt & Whitney meant the abandonment of a separate engine development project, the RJ500, that might have supported independent entry by Rolls Royce into this segment of the engine market.[8]

It is difficult to imagine the Justice Department's approving similar agreements in these or other industries that involved only U.S. firms. An alliance of Pratt & Whitney and General Electric in any segment of the engine market would invite a skeptical review by the Justice Department and might well encounter significant military and congressional opposition. A Pratt & Whitney-GE alliance, however, would have the same impact as the Rolls-GE and Pratt-Rolls ventures. Although direct evidence is lacking, it is difficult to avoid the conclusion that joint ventures between a U.S. and a foreign firm (Rolls Royce) have received a more lenient review by the Justice Department's Antitrust Division than a venture between U.S. firms would receive. In a unified world market such as that for airframes and engines, such distinctions are inappropriate. Moreover, to the extent that such discrimination encourages U.S. firms to seek foreign rather than domestic partners in joint ventures and thereby accelerates technology transfer to foreign firms, the distinction between domestic and international joint ventures may well be injurious to the longer-term economic interests of the United States. Nonetheless, U.S. antitrust policy has little effect on most of the joint venture activity in this industry.

Joint ventures between technological equals in a highly concentrated industry also create the possibility that competition in the industry might be reduced through collusion across different product lines. A similar network of research joint ventures involving major chemicals firms in the United States, Great Britain, and Germany during the 1920s and 1930s established an international cartel in petrochemicals and synthetic industries and may have reduced the diffusion of such technical advances as synthetic rubber.[9] A comparable restraint of competition in the engine or airframe market is unlikely, because of the unified world market and the absence of overlapping patent portfolios among the major firms. The potential for anticompetitive behavior and therefore the need for careful antitrust scrutiny of international competition, especially in jet engines, nonetheless remains significant.

Trade policy clearly affects the incentives of U.S. firms to undertake foreign joint ventures. If foreign governments provide extensive subsidies for domestic firms and restrict their procurement (and that of government-controlled airlines) to aircraft embodying a significant local content, U.S. firms seeking capital or market access face compelling incentives to enlist foreign firms as partners in development projects. Moreover, if U.S. firms must compete against heavily subsidized foreign firms, U.S. enterprises may have little choice but to tap public funds by enlisting other foreign partners. To the extent these foreign government policies unduly bias U.S. firms toward seeking foreign partners, they are legitimate targets for U.S. trade policy. These issues are difficult ones for U.S. trade policy as well as for the General Agreement on Tariffs and Trade (GATT), because of the historical focus of these instrumentalities on tariffs rather than on other trade-distorting policies. Tariffs, however, are now very low for most manufactured goods and are therefore irrelevant. As a result, trade negotiations repeatedly bog down in tedious specifications of acceptable and unacceptable policies. Inasmuch as the central concern of many foreign governments is outcomes (industrial development) rather than a specific type of conduct, new policies can be devised to circumvent restrictions.

Both the subsidization of the development costs of domestic firms and the practice of directed procurement are prohibited by the Agreement on Trade in Civil Aircraft. The GATT is unusual because of its multilateral nature and coverage of trading practices in a single industry. Indeed, the agreement is even restricted in its coverage of the aircraft industry, applying only to large commercial transports and engines. Although the agreement has no specific enforcement mechanisms and has been criticized for not preventing abuses, U.S. firms have benefited from it in several ways. The dramatic growth in trade in aircraft components supported by the agreement has benefited U.S. firms, even those in the second tier. Moreover, it specifies in considerable detail acceptable and unacceptable trading practices in aircraft and provides a basis for the enforcement of fair trade policies that frequently is lacking in other sectors.

The positive effect of this multilateral agreement on exports of U.S. aircraft components contrasts with the effect of bilateral trade restrictions in automobiles. Bilateral trade restrictions in automobiles do not appear to have led to increased use of U.S. components in foreign automobiles. Moreover, as Japanese auto producers increasingly resort to direct foreign investment to gain access to the U.S. market, their components suppliers are locating production capacity in the United States. Increasing use of bilateral quotas in the international automobile industry is likely to damage U.S. suppliers of automotive components more severely than joint ventures in aircraft have harmed the aircraft industry's supplier sector. Multilateral trade agreements, however limited in their sectoral coverage, seem to have considerable advantages over bilateral agreements that are no less limited in coverage. Because of the dynamic character of high-technology industries and the great influence that nontariff barriers may exert on the development of these industries, negotiation of multilateral agreements in other high-technology manufacturing industries deserves consideration by U.S. and foreign policy makers. Negotiations could complement broader trade talks, possibly in sessions following multilateral, multi-industry negotiations.

Foreign governments provide development funding to their domestic firms and frequently fund research in aircraft and engines. These foreign expenditures are dwarfed, however, by the level of federal research support for aeronautics and propulsion channeled through NASA alone in a given year.[10] Foreign funding generally is directed to specific programs and therefore constitutes a stronger source of support for the development of products. Nonetheless, this foreign financial support increasingly takes the form of loans, rather than outright grants, in part because of the Agreement on Trade in Civil Aircraft. U.S. policy has opposed subsidies for the development of products that compete with U.S. products developed with private capital—indeed, U.S. trade officials have increased significantly their scrutiny of foreign government financial support for domestic firms in recent years. The fact remains, however, that foreign governments view the support of domestic high-technology industry and employment as an important policy goal, and U.S. pressure is unlikely to prevent the pursuit of this goal. Sustained pressure may control flagrant abuses, but this source of tension will remain serious for the foreseeable future.

Foreign government financial support for product development also frequently subsidizes European and Japanese participation as suppliers and subcontractors in joint ventures with U.S. firms and thereby effectively defrays part of the costs of U.S. corporations' product development programs. In view of the importance of advanced technological capabilities for U.S. firms, however, one of the most effective U.S. responses to growing foreign support of aeronautics R&D is increased support for civil aeronautics research in NASA. Recent initiatives in research on supersonic and hypersonic transports may bring about some convergence in the research concerns and agenda of the currently separate NASA research programs in space transportation and aeronautics, thus strengthening aeronautics research considerably.

Joint ventures and the internationalization of this industry raise challenging issues for export finance agencies (for example, the U.S. Export-Import Bank).[11] As the foreign content of U.S. aircraft and engines increases, foreign export finance agencies increasingly play a role in supporting the sale of products with substantial U.S. employment effects. Similarly, as the U.S. content of foreign aircraft remains high, U.S. export finance agencies may be able to affect the sales of products with considerable employment effects on foreign (primarily European) nations.

The complexity of this situation can create dilemmas for the Export-Import Bank. The bank finances the sale of Boeing 757s, which may employ British engines (the Rolls Royce RB 211-535), and does not support export sales of the Airbus Industrie A300-600 and A310, both of which may employ Pratt & Whitney or General Electric engines (respectively, the PW4000 or the CF6-80). Export finance provided by the bank for Boeing's exports of the 757 favors U.S. airframe industry employment, but the lack of bank support of sales of Airbus Industrie aircraft exerts a moderate depressive influence on U.S. aircraft engine industry employment.

While these positive and negative employment effects are modest and are dwarfed by the positive influence use of exports of U.S. airframes that use U.S. engines (for example, the Boeing 747 with PW4000 engines), the fact remains that current policy favors one U.S. industry over another in the export arena. Just as domestic content restrictions are increasingly difficult to define in industries like automobiles, internationalization of the commercial aircraft industry complicates the implementation of export finance policies that treat domestic industries in an even-handed manner.

The dilemma created for export finance policy by internationalization of the aircraft and other industries affects other areas of trade policy. Although U.S. policy makers are strongly opposed to the financial aid provided to Airbus Industrie by member governments, this financial aid indirectly supports U.S. jobs, through Airbus Industrie's demand for U.S. components and engines. The number of U.S.

jobs supported by the export of Boeing aircraft with Rolls Royce engines is likely to exceed the number supported by sales of Airbus aircraft with U.S. engines and components, but these calculations are unreliable and the foreign or domestic content of aircraft will shift over time. Trade policy makers are operating in an uncertain arena in dealing with products whose financing and employment creation span national boundaries—perhaps the most that can be attained is agreement among export finance and other industrial development agencies within the industrialized nations on a common set of principles for export finance and other forms of financial support. Agreement on even these basic principles, however, has been elusive, as the "Commonline" negotiations among the OECD nations on export finance practices demonstrate.

In part because of the limited amount of technology transfer operating through the joint ventures, as well as the availability of alternative policy instruments to counteract undesirable effects of these joint ventures on the U.S. aircraft industry, an extensive program of federal oversight or direct controls on joint venture activities by U.S. firms seems unwarranted. Moreover, direct oversight of a great deal of joint venture activity and technology transfer is already exercised by the U.S. Defense Department. As the discussion in chapter 3 made clear, this oversight is most pronounced in the area of propulsion technologies, but may be extended to cover avionics, display technologies, and computerized flight management systems, all of which benefit from substantial military-civilian technological spillovers. The controls on technology transfer, which require Defense Department approval of even preliminary discussions between U.S. and foreign firms, have not prevented the successful completion of at least one joint venture (the CFM56), and did not prevent the inception of two others (the V2500 and JT10D). The controls have contributed to increased development costs, but U.S. firms have been able to live with them.

Inasmuch as such controls have implications reaching well beyond national defense, however, Pentagon decisions on such issues should take into account the concerns of other federal agencies and should consider a broader range of factors. Much of the motivation for the controls on the CFM56 engine core, for example, stemmed from the fact that the development costs of this technology had been borne largely by the military. While some arrangement to recoup development costs is appropriate, neither the Defense Department nor the

U.S. taxpaying public benefits from a blanket prohibition on joint ventures employing these technologies. Moreover, prohibitions cannot prevent advanced technologies from reaching foreign soil, particularly since they are employed on aircraft that operate throughout the world. Prohibitions on the transfer of civilian derivatives of military technologies through joint ventures thus are in many cases unrealistic. The logic of permitting the export of civilian technologies, while prohibiting their transfer through a joint venture (as in the CFM56), is murky. If a determination is made that specific technologies must be prevented from reaching potential adversaries, a blanket prohibition on their transfer through any channel, including export or deployment on U.S. aircraft operating overseas, should be imposed. If not, joint ventures involving such technologies should be allowed, especially in view of the strong incentives of U.S. firms to minimize the wholesale transfer of state-of-the-art technologies.

U.S. policy toward transfer technologies with potential military applications is inconsistent in another respect. While Pentagon controls on the transfer of civilian technological derivatives of military technologies are exercised in a great many joint ventures, the U.S. Defense Department has simultaneously encouraged or mandated the transfer of military technologies to foreign firms through its efforts to support the "two-way street" in defense procurement. The recent agreements between the United States and various NATO allies covering the Strategic Defense Initiative seem likely to result in additional transfers of test data and design specifications for military technologies. This policy produces a curious conjunction of controls on the export of civilian technologies with official encouragement or mandates for the transfer of military technologies to foreign firms.

Joint ventures between U.S. and foreign engine and aircraft producers have become attractive for both technical and financial reasons. U.S. government policy during the past thirty years has affected both sets of factors. Military coproduction programs contributed to the development of the components production and design capabilities of foreign firms. NASA and military research programs in the United States, combined with regulation of domestic air transportation, supported rapid innovation in the U.S. aircraft industry. The size of the combined U.S. military and civilian aeronautics research budget dwarfs any comparable program in Japan or Europe. Public funds have even been employed on several occasions to save failing U.S. aircraft producers. More recently, export controls on the sale of

U.S. aircraft, which also cover foreign-produced aircraft that contain significant U.S. content, have affected the market for U.S. aircraft, engines, and components in Europe and elsewhere.

For all of these reasons, a "hands-off" federal policy toward this industry simply is not realistic; U.S. government policy affects all aspects of industry operations. The key question is whether the various instruments of federal policy toward the aircraft industry are to be coordinated, so as to allow U.S. industry to employ joint ventures in ways that preserve U.S. technological superiority, allow for continued U.S. penetration of foreign markets, provide U.S. firms some protection against the high risks of innovation, and at the same time prevent the wholesale export of U.S. jobs. The export of U.S. aircraft industry jobs through joint ventures is not yet serious. Moreover, any decline in the U.S. employment content per aircraft or engine resulting from joint ventures must be balanced against the potential employment created by larger total sales of these products. Policies to enhance cooperation between supplier and prime-contractor firms within the industry, as well as initiatives strengthening the technical capabilities of supplier firms, could help prevent erosion of the aircraft industrial base. A prohibition of joint ventures is unrealistic— creative policies should be developed to increase the benefits of these ventures for U.S. industry and labor. Technology, especially the management of its creation and embodiment in new aircraft and engines, is the foundation of the U.S. comparative advantage in commercial aircraft. Public and private policy responses to the effects of increasing joint venture activity in the aircraft industry should support the creation and management of technology, rather than attempting to stem its diffusion.

NOTES

1. Many industries are facing rapid growth in development costs and risks, as well as the increasing importance of materials, molecular biology, and information processing technologies. Firms in these industries have sought external sources of research expertise as a means of gaining familiarity with new technologies more rapidly and inexpensively than would be possible through the development of in-house capabilities.

2. The reverse is, of course, also true. A major breakthrough by Japanese aircraft and materials firms in the design and fabrication of aircraft employ-

ing composite materials, for example, could shift the relative competitiveness of the Japanese and U.S. aircraft industries. Moreoever, insofar as a central motive for many foreign firms' participation in joint ventures is technology transfer, a sudden widening in the technology gap between U.S. and foreign firms might make foreign firms far more anxious to pursue such ventures.

3.   Even if they do not enter as prime contractors, firms may gain sufficient technological and other capabilities through joint ventures to displace U.S. firms as equal partners in joint ventures. The prospect for increased competitive pressures thus exists, although there is no evidence that any such displacement has occurred.

4.   The primary program supported by the Defense Department is the Manufacturing Technology (Man Tech) program, which primarily funds research in manufacturing processes. Man Tech now accounts for nearly $200 million annually and has been evaluated critically in a 1983 report by the National Academy of Sciences, which advocated a longer-term research orientation for the program and noted that the transfer to private firms of technologies developed within the program has consistently been difficult. Another DoD program, the Industrial Modernization Incentive Program (IMP), is concerned with the adoption of manufacturing technologies. See National Academy of Sciences, Committee on the Machine Tool Industry, *The Machine Tool Industry and the Defense Industrial Base* (Washington, D.C.: National Academy Press, 1983).

5.   See G. Baumbusch and Alvin J. Harman, *Peacetime Adequacy of the Lower Tiers of the Defense Industrial Base* (Santa Monica, Calif.: The Rand Corporation, 1977) and G. Baumbusch, P.D. Fleischauer, A.J. Harmah, and M.D. Miller, *Defense Industrial Planning for a Surge in Military Demand* (Santa Monica, Calif.: The Rand Corporation, 1978).

6.   A more recent and rather cursory interagency study of the impact of military offsets on the aerospace industrial base also concluded that surge capacity currently was more than adequate to accommodate any mobilization requirements. See the U.S. Office of Management and Budget, *Impact of Offsets in Defense-Related Exports* (Washington, D.C.: Office of Management and Budget, 1985).

7.   The General Electric–Rolls Royce agreement was abandoned as this book went to press, largely as a result of the unwillingness of Rolls Royce to forgo competition with General Electric for an order of large engines placed by British Airways in August 1986. Rolls Royce won the British Airways engine order of nearly $1 billion (for the Rolls Royce RB211-524) in the face of competition from General Electric. The breakup of the agreement, however, does not affect the argument concerning Justice Department review of the agreement in 1984.

8. Clearly, any assessment of the desirability of the Pratt & Whitney-Rolls Royce joint venture is critically affected by assumptions concerning the probability that the RJ500 would have been introduced separately, as well as the likelihood that Pratt & Whitney would separately have introduced a new engine in this thrust class. Nonetheless, the likely duration of the Pratt-Rolls Royce joint venture (as long as thirty years), as well as the joint venture's conferral of significant market power on International Aero Engines, suggest that this joint venture might violate even the relatively permissive criteria developed by Ordover and Willig (1985) for the analysis of R&D joint ventures and mergers. See James A. Ordover and Robert D. Willig, "Antitrust for High-Technology Industries: Assessing Research Joint Ventures and Mergers," *Journal of Law and Economics* 28, 1985, pp. 311–33.

9. George Stocking and Myron Watkins, in *Cartels in Action* (New York: Twentieth Century Fund, 1946), provide a detailed description of the cartel; Vernon notes the possibilities for collusion through modern international joint ventures in R.S. Vernon, "Coping with Technological Change: U.S. Problems and Prospects," Presented at the National Academy of Engineering Symposium on World Technologies and National Sovereignty, Washington, D.C., February 1986.

10. See B. Chandler, R. Golasewski, C. Patten, B. Rudman, and R. Scott, *Government Financial Support for Civil Aircraft Research, Technology, and Development in Four European Countries and the United States* (Washington, D.C.: NASA, 1980), who compared funding for civil aviation R&D in the Netherlands, Great Britain, France, and West Germany during 1974-1977. This study concluded that the combined civil aviation research budgets of these nations amounted to less than 40 percent of the annual expenditures on civil aeronautics R&D in the United States.

11. This discussion draws on J.B.L. Pierce, "The Global Airplane," presented at the meetings of the National Aeronautics Association, Washington, D.C., May 14, 1986.

BIBLIOGRAPHY

Aerospace Industries Association, Foreign Competition Project Group, Commercial Transport Aircraft Committee. *The Challenge of Foreign Competition.* Washington, D.C.: Aerospace Research Center, 1976.

Aerospace Industries Association. *Aerospace Facts and Figures 1983/84.* New York: McGraw-Hill, 1983.

____. *Aerospace Facts and Figures 1984/85.* New York: McGraw-Hill, 1984.

"Airbus Views 7-7 Pact As Response to A320." *Aviation Week and Space Technology.* March 26, 1984, 32.

"Aircraft Industry: Tomorrow's Pterodactyls?" *The Economist.* May 30, 1981, 3-12.

Alchian, Armen A., and Harold Demsetz. "Production, Information Costs, and Economic Organization." *American Economic Review* 62 (1972): 777-95.

"Anglo-Japanese Engine Go-Ahead Awaits 150-Seat Aircraft Decision." *Aviation Week and Space Technology.* November 2, 1981, 26-27.

Arrow, Kenneth J. "Economic Welfare and the Allocation of Resources for Invention." In *The Rate and Direction of Inventive Activity.* Princeton: Princeton University Press for the National Bureau of Economic Research, 1962.

Bacher, Thomas J. "International Collaboration on Commercial Programs." Paper presented to a conference sponsored by the Society of Japanese Aerospace Companies, Tokyo, Japan, 1983.

Baranson, Jack. *North-South Technology Transfer: Financing and Institution Building.* Mt. Airy, Md.: Lomond, 1981.

____. *Technology and the Multinationals.* Lexington, Mass.: D.C. Heath, 1978.

____. "Technology Transfer through the International Firm." *American Economic Review* 60 (1970): 435-40.

171

Bassett, Edward W. "Airbus Gears for Production Increase." *Aviation Week and Space Technology*, November 12, 1979, 56–58.

Baumbusch, Geneese, and Alvin J. Harman. *Peacetime Adequacy of the Lower Tiers of the Defense Industrial Base.* Santa Monica, Calif.: The Rand Corporation, 1977.

Baumbusch, Geneese, Patricia D. Fleischauer, Alvin J. Harman, and Michael D. Miller. *Defense Industrial Planning for a Surge in Military Demand.* Santa Monica, Calif.: The Rand Corporation, 1978.

Beavis, Simon. "JAS 39: Sweden Forges Ahead." *Flight International*, May 25, 1985, 41–44.

Becker, Gary. "A Theory of Marriage." In *Economics of the Family.* Edited by T.W. Schultz. Chicago: University of Chicago Press for the National Bureau of Economic Research, 1974.

"Beech Acquires Mitsubishi Diamond Program." *Aviation Week and Space Technology*, December 9, 1985, 26.

Beteille, Roger H. "Developing Aircraft Through Joint Venture Programs." Paper delivered at the International Air Transportation Conference, Atlantic City, AIAA–81–0794, 1981.

"The Big Deal McDonnell Douglas Turned Down." *Business Week*, December 1, 1980, 81–82.

Bluestone, Barry, Peter Jordan, and Mark Sullivan. *Aircraft Industry Dynamics: An Analysis of Competition, Capital and Labor.* Boston: Auburn House Publishing, 1981.

Boeing Commercial Airplane Company. *Potential Boeing-Japan Aircraft Industry Cooperation in Commercial Aircraft.* Seattle, Wash.: BCAC, 1984.

"Boeing Considers Two Configurations for 7J7 Advanced Technology Transport." *Aviation Week and Space Technology*, January 27, 1986, 32.

"Boeing, Japan Near Decision on 7-7 Work Share." *Aviation Week and Space Technology*, January 23, 1984, 30.

Booz, Allen, and Hamilton Applied Research, Inc. *A Historical Study of the Benefits Derived from Application of Technical Advances to Commercial Aviation.* Paper prepared for the joint Department of Transportation-National Aeronautics and Space Administration Civil Aviation R&D Policy Study. Washington, D.C.: U.S. Government Printing Office, 1971.

Bowen, Harry P. "Changes in the International Distribution of Resources and Their Impact on U.S. Comparative Advantage." *Review of Economics and Statistics* 65 (1983): 402–14.

Brodley, Joseph F. "Joint Ventures and Antitrust Policy." *Harvard Law Review* 95 (1982): 1523–90.

Brown, David A. "Short Brothers, Saab-Scania Join Boeing 7J7 Program." *Aviation Week and Space Technology*, March 31, 1986, 32–33.

Bush, Vannevar. *Science—The Endless Frontier.* Washington, D.C.: U.S. Government Printing Office, 1945.

Carroll, Sidney L. "The Market for Commercial Airliners." In *Regulating the Product*. Edited by R.E. Caves and M.J. Roberts. Cambridge, Mass.: Ballinger Publishing Co., 1975.

Caves, Richard E. *Multinational Enterprise and Economic Analysis*. Cambridge: Cambridge University Press, 1982.

Caves, Richard E., H. Crookell, and J.P. Killing. "The Imperfect Market for Technology Licenses." *Oxford Bulletin of Economics and Statistics* 45 (1983): 249–68.

Chandler, Alfred D., Jr. *The Visible Hand*. Cambridge: Harvard University Press, 1977.

Chandler, Beth, R. Golasewski, William C. Patten, Beverly Rudman, and R. Scott. *Government Financial Support for Civil Aircraft Research, Technology, and Development in Four European Countries and the United States*. Washington, D.C.: NASA, 1980.

Cohen, Wesley M., and David C. Mowery. "Firm Heterogeneity and R&D Investment: An Agenda for Research." In *Strategic Management of R&D: Interdisciplinary Perspectives*. Edited by Barry Bozeman, Michael Crow, and Albert Link. Lexington, Mass.: D.C. Heath, 1984.

Constant, Edward W. *The Origins of the Turbojet Revolution*. Baltimore, Md.: Johns Hopkins University Press, 1981.

Contractor, Farak J. "Licensing Versus Foreign Direct Investment in U.S. Corporate Strategy: An Analysis of Aggregate U.S. Data." In *International Technology Transfer*. Edited by C. Frischtak and N. Rosenberg. New York: Praeger, 1985.

Crane, Daniel M. "Joint Research and Development Ventures and the Antitrust Laws." *Harvard Journal on Legislation* 21 (1984): 405–58.

Crane, Keith, and Antoine Gilliot. "The Role of Western Multinational Corporations in Technology Exports: The Aircraft Industries in Brazil and Poland." Unpublished manuscript, The Rand Corporation, 1985.

Demisch, W.H., C.C. Demisch, and T.L. Concert. *The Jetliner Business*. New York: First Boston Corporation, 1984.

Dorfer, Ingemar. *System 37 Viggen: Arms, Technology, and the Domestication of Glory*. Oslo: Universitetsforlaget, 1973.

Douglas, George W., and James C. Miller. *Economic Regulation of Domestic Air Transport*. Washington, D.C.: Brookings Institution, 1974.

Dunning, John H. *International Production and the Multinational Enterprise*. London: George Allen and Unwin, 1981.

———, and John A. Cantwell. "The Changing Role of Multinational Enterprises in the International Creation, Transfer and Diffusion of Technology." Paper presented at the International Conference on the Diffusion of Innovations, Venice, Italy, March 1986.

"Dutch, Swedes Use Innovative Financing." *Aviation Week and Space Technology*, September 6, 1982, 171–73.

"Eastern Lease, New Sales Bolster Airbus Prospects." *Aviation Week and Space Technology*, June 6, 1977, 234–41.

Eckelmann, Robert L., and Lester A. Davis. *Japanese Industrial Policies and the Development of High Technology Industries: Computers and Aircraft.* Report prepared for the Office of Trade and Investment Analysis, International Trade Administration, U.S. Department of Commerce, Washington, D.C.: U.S. Government Printing Office, 1983.

Economic Planning Agency (Japan). *Japan in the Year 2000.* Translated by *The Japan Times.* Tokyo: *The Japan Times*, 1983.

"Europeans Ready Production Tooling." *Aviation Week and Space Technology*, May 2, 1977, 94–101.

"Fairchild Withdrawing from 340 Aircraft Project." *Aviation Week and Space Technology*, October 21, 1985, 23.

Feazel, Michael. "Large Engine Design Costs Dictate Consortium Efforts." *Aviation Week and Space Technology*, June 18, 1984, 108–09.

Feldman, Elliot J. *Concorde and Dissent.* Cambridge: Harvard University Press, 1985.

"Fiat Seeks Italian Government R&D for Civil Engines," *Flight International*, October 24. 1981, 1275.

Fink, Donald E. "Collaborative Transport Effort Weighed." *Aviation Week and Space Technology*, November 29, 1976, 12–13.

_____. "Economics Key to New Mercure Design." *Aviation Week and Space Technology*, February 7, 1977, 46–51.

_____. "Pratt, Rolls Launch New Turbofan." *Aviation Week and Space Technology*, November 7, 1983, 28–29.

"France Searching for Solutions to Continued Aerospatiale Losses." *Aviation Week and Space Technology*, April 19, 1976, 24–25.

Franko, Lawrence G. *Joint Venture Survival in Multinational Companies.* New York: Praeger, 1971.

Fraumeni, Barbara M., and Dale W. Jorgenson. "The Role of Capital in U.S. Economic Growth, 1948–76." In *Capital, Efficiency and Growth.* Edited by G.M. von Furstenberg. Cambridge, Mass.: Ballinger Publishing Co., 1980.

"French Pick U.S. Firm." *Aviation Week and Space Technology*, August 6, 1976, 12.

Frenkel, Orits. "Flying High: A Case Study of Japanese Industrial Policy." *Journal of Policy Analysis and Management* 3 (1984): 406–20.

"Fuel Pressure on Airline Costs Powers Increased Boeing Domination." *Air Transport World*, March 1981, 20–29.

Gellman, Aaron J., and Jeffrey P. Price. *Technology Transfer and Other Public Policy Implications of Multi-National Arrangements for the Production of Commercial Airframes.* Washington, D.C.: NASA, 1978.

Ginsburg, Douglas J. *Antitrust, Uncertainty, and Innovation.* Washington, D.C.: National Research Council, 1980.

Grieco, Joseph M. *Between Dependency and Autonomy: India's Experience with the International Computer Industry.* Berkeley: University of California Press, 1984.

Grossman, Gene M., and Carl Shapiro. "Normative Issues Raised by International Trade in Technology Services." Working paper, Fishman-Davidson Center for the Study of the Service Sector, Wharton School, University of Pennsylvania, 1985.

Grossman, Gene M., and J. David Richardson. "Strategic Trade Policy: A Survey of Issues and Early Analysis." *Special Papers in International Economics* #15. International Finance Section, Department of Economics, Princeton University, 1985.

Hadley, Eleanor M. "The Secret of Japan's Success." *Challenge* 26 (1983): 4–10.

Hall, G.R., and R.E. Johnson. "Transfers of United States Aerospace Technology to Japan." In *The Technology Factor in International Trade*, edited by R. Vernon. New York: Columbia University Press for the National Bureau of Economic Research, 1970.

Harrigan, Kathryn R. "Joint Ventures and Competitive Strategy." Working paper. New York: Columbia University Graduate School of Business, 1984.

_____. *Strategies for Joint Ventures.* Lexington, Mass.: D.C. Heath, 1985.

_____. *Managing for Joint Venture Success.* Lexington, Mass.: D.C. Heath, 1986.

Hayward, Keith. *Government and British Civil Aerospace.* Manchester: University of Manchester Press, 1983.

Henderson, David. "Two British Errors: Their Probable Size and Some Possible Lessons." *Oxford Economic Papers* 29 (1977).

Hirsch, Seev. "An International Trade and Investment Theory of the Firm." *Oxford Economic Papers* 28 (1976): 258–69.

Hirshleifer, Jack. "The Private and Social Value of Information and the Reward to Innovation." *American Economic Review* 61 (1971): 561–74.

Hladik, Karen J. *International Joint Ventures.* Lexington, Mass.: D.C. Heath, 1985.

Hochmuth, Milton S. "Aerospace." In *Big Business and the State.* Edited by R.S. Vernon. Cambridge, Mass.: Harvard University Press, 1974.

_____. *Organizing the Transnational: The Experience with Transnational Enterprise in Advanced Technology.* Cambridge, Mass.: Harvard University Press, 1974.

Hudson, Rexford A. "The Brazilian Way to Technological Independence: Foreign Joint Ventures and the Aircraft Industry." *Inter-American Economic Affairs* 37 (1983): 23–43.

Hymer, Steven H. *The International Operations of National Firms: A Study of Direct Foreign Investment.* Cambridge, Mass.: M.I.T. Press, 1969.

"Industry Observer." *Aviation Week and Space Technology*, September 21, 1981, 15.

"Japan Pushing Industry to Design New Engines." *Aviation Week and Space Technology*, June 28, 1982, 207–13.

"Japanese Doubts Rising Over F-15, P-3C." *Aviation Week and Space Technology*, June 6, 1977, 201–07.

"Japan's New Jet Fighter Will Be Homemade." *Business Week*, November 17, 1986, 82.

"A Jet Engine Creates an Unlikely Alliance." *Business Week*, September 13, 1982, 47.

Johnson, Chalmers. *MITI and the Japanese Miracle.* Stanford, Calif.: Stanford University Press, 1982.

"Joint U.S., Foreign Efforts Pushed." *Aviation Week and Space Technology*, February 2, 1976, 24–25.

Jones, Kent. "The Economic Implications of Restricting Trade in High-Technology Goods." Paper presented at the National Science Foundation Workshop on the Economic Implications of Restrictions to Trade in High-Technology Goods. Washington, D.C., October 3, 1984.

Jordan, William A. *Airline Regulation in America.* Baltimore, Md.: Johns Hopkins University Press, 1970.

Keeler, Theodore E. "Airline Regulation and Market Performance." *Bell Journal of Economics* 3 (1972): 399–424.

Kendrick, John W. *Productivity Trends in the United States.* Princeton, N.J.: Princeton University Press, 1961.

_____ . *Postwar Productivity Trends in the United States, 1948-69.* New York: Columbia University Press, 1973.

Kindleberger, Charles P. *American Business Abroad: Six Lectures on Direct Investment.* New Haven, Conn.: Yale University Press, 1969.

Krugman, Paul R. "Import Protection as Export Promotion: International Competition in the Presence of Oligopoly and Economies of Scale." In *Monopolistic Competition and International Trade.* Edited by H. Kierzkowski. Oxford: Oxford University Press, 1984.

_____ . "The U.S. Response to Foreign Industrial Targeting." *Brookings Papers on Economic Activity* (1984): 74–121.

Lenorovitz, Jeffrey M. "Snecma, General Electric Consider Joint Development of Unducted Fan." *Aviation Week and Space Technology*, February 25, 1985, 41–43.

_____ . "Snecma Takes Share of GE Unducted Fan, Talks with Rolls on Smaller Engine." *Aviation Week and Space Technology*, May 27, 1985, 20.

_____ . "Airbus Industrie Considering Production Line Rate Increases." *Aviation Week and Space Technology*, July 29, 1985, 29.

Lenz, R.C., J.A. Machnic, and A.W. Elkins. *The Influence of Aeronautical R&D Expenditures Upon the Productivity of Air Transportation.* Dayton, Oh.: University of Dayton Research Institute, 1981.

Lorell, Mark A. *Multinational Development of Large Aircraft: The European Experience.* Santa Monica, Calif.: The Rand Corporation, 1980.

Lynn, Leonard H. *How Japan Innovates: A Comparison with the U.S. in the Case of Oxygen Steelmaking.* Boulder, Colo.: Westview Press, 1982.

Magaziner, Ira C., and Thomas M. Hout. *Japanese Industrial Policy.* Policy Paper No. 15, Institute of International Affairs. Berkeley, Calif.: University of California Institute of International Affairs, 1980.

Mansfield, Edwin. "Technology and Technological Change." In *Economic Analysis and the Multinational Enterprise*, edited by J.H. Dunning. London: Allen & Unwin, 1974.

_____, Anthony Romeo, and Samuel Wagner. "Foreign Trade and U.S. Research and Development." *Review of Economics and Statistics* 61 (February 1979): 49–57.

_____, and Anthony Romeo. "Technology Transfer to Overseas Subsidiaries of U.S.-Based Firms." *Quarterly Journal of Economics* 95 (December 1980): 737–50.

McCulloch, Rachel. "International Competition in High-Technology Industries: The Consequences of Alternative Trade Regimes for Aircraft." Paper presented at the National Science Foundation Workshop on the Economic Implications of Restrictions to Trade in High-Technology Goods. Washington, D.C., October 3, 1984.

"McDonnell Douglas/Fokker Cancel 150-Seat Aircraft." *Aviation Week and Space Technology*, February 15, 1982, 34.

Miller, Ronald, and David Sawers. *The Technical Development of Modern Aviation.* London: Routledge and Kegan Paul, 1968.

Ministry of International Trade and Industry, Industrial Structure Council. *The Vision of MITI Policies in the 1980s.* Tokyo: Industrial Bank of Japan, 1980.

Monteverde, Kirk, and David J. Teece. "Supplier Switching Costs and Vertical Integration in the Automobile Industry." *Bell Journal of Economics* 13 (Spring 1982): 206–13.

Mowery, David C. "The Relationship between the Contractual and Intrafirm Forms of Industrial Research in American Manufacturing, 1900–1940." *Explorations in Economic History* 20 (1983): 351–74.

_____. "Economic Theory and Government Technology Policy." *Policy Sciences* 16 (1983): 27–43.

_____. "Firm Structure, Government Policy, and the Organization of Industrial Research: Great Britain and the United States, 1900–1950." *Business History Review* 58 (1984): 504–31.

_____. "Federal Funding of R&D in Transportation: The Case of Aviation." Paper presented at the National Academy of Sciences Symposium on the Impact of Federal R&D Funding, Washington, D.C., November 21–22, 1985.

_____, and Nathan Rosenberg. "The Commercial Aircraft Industry." In *Government and Technical Progress: A Cross-Industry Analysis*, edited by R.R. Nelson. New York: Pergamon Press, 1982.

_____. "Government Policy, Market Structure, and Industrial Development: The Japanese and U.S. Commercial Aircraft Industries, 1945–85." U.S.-Northeast Asia Forum on International Policy Occasional Paper. Stanford, Calif.: Stanford University Institute for Strategic and International Studies, 1984.

_____. "Competition and Cooperation: The U.S. and Japanese Commercial Aircraft Industries." *California Management Review* 27, no. 4 (1985): 70–82.

Moxon, Richard W., Thomas W. Roehl, and J. Frederick Truitt. *Emerging Sources of Foreign Competition in the Commercial Aircraft Manufacturing Industry*. Washington, D.C.: U.S. Department of Transportation, 1985.

"MTU–German Funding for PW2037 Participation." *Military Technology*, June 1982, 81.

National Academy of Engineering. *The Competitive Status of the U.S. Civil Aircraft Manufacturing Industry*. Washington, D.C.: National Academy Press, 1985.

National Academy of Sciences, Committee on the Machine Tool Industry. *The Machine Tool Industry and the Defense Industrial Base*. Washington, D.C.: National Academy Press, 1983.

National Academy of Sciences, Committee on the Role of the Manufacturing Technology Program in the Defense Industrial Base. *The Role of the Department of Defense in Supporting Manufacturing Technology Development*. Washington, D.C.: National Academy Press, 1986.

National Research Council. *Industrial Research Laboratories of the U.S., 1940*. Washington, D.C.: National Research Council, 1940.

_____. *Industrial Research Laboratories of the U.S., 1946*. Washington, D.C.: National Research Council, 1946.

_____. Committee on NASA Scientific and Technological Program Reviews. *Aeronautics Research and Technology: A Review of Proposed Reductions in the FY1983 NASA Program*. Washington, D.C.: National Research Council, 1982.

_____. *International Competition in Advanced Technology: Decisions for America*. Washington, D.C.: National Research Council, 1983.

National Science Board. *University-Industry Research Relationships*. Washington, D.C.: National Science Foundation, 1983.

_____. *Science Indicators—1985*. Washington, D.C.: National Science Foundation, 1985.

Nelkin, Dorothy, and Richard R. Nelson. "University-Industry Alliances." Paper presented at the Conference on New Alliances and Partnerships in American Science and Engineering, National Academy of Sciences, Washington, D.C., December 5, 1985.

Nelson, Richard R. "Government Stimulus of Technological Progress: Lessons from American History." In *Government and Technical Progress: A Cross-Industry Analysis*, edited by R.R. Nelson. New York: Pergamon Press, 1982.

_____. "Assessing Private Enterprise: An Exegesis of Tangled Doctrine." *Bell Journal of Economics* 12 (1981): 93–111.

_____, and Sidney G. Winter. *A Behavioral Theory of Economic Change.* Cambridge, Mass.: Harvard University Press, 1982.

"New Efforts Task Japanese Firms." *Aviation Week and Space Technology,* October 2, 1978, 31-33.

Newhouse, John. *The Sporty Game.* New York: Knopf, 1983.

"News Digest." *Aviation Week and Space Technology,* February 24, 1986, 31.

North, David M. "Beech Weighs Mitsubishi Purchase as Entry to Corporate Jet Market." *Aviation Week and Space Technology,* September 9, 1985, 24–25.

Office of Science and Technology Policy. *Aeronautical Research and Technology Policy,* vol. 2, *Final Report.* Washington, D.C.: Executive Office of the President, 1982.

Okimoto, Daniel I. *Pioneer and Pursuer: The Role of the State in the Evolution of the Japanese and American Semiconductor Industries.* Stanford, Calif.: Northeast Asia–United States Forum on International Policy, 1983.

O'Lone, Richard G. "Boeing Cools on Cooperative Programs." *Aviation Week and Space Technology,* June 6, 1977, 218-19.

_____. "United's Purchase Launches 767." *Aviation Week and Space Technology,* July 24, 1978, 14–16.

_____. "New Efforts Task Japanese Firms." *Aviation Week and Space Technology,* October 2, 1978.

_____. "Boeing Facing New Set of Challenges." *Aviation Week and Space Technology,* November 12, 1978, 43-55.

_____. "Japan Setting Higher Aerospace Goals." *Aviation Week and Space Technology,* November 21, 1983, 16-18.

_____. "Strong Commuter Market Leads Boeing to Acquire de Havilland." *Aviation Week and Space Technology,* December 9, 1985, 28-29.

Olsson, Ulf. *The Creation of a Modern Arms Industry: Sweden, 1939-1974.* Gothenburg: Institute of Economic History, Gothenburg University, 1977.

Ordover, Janus A., and Robert D. Willig. "Antitrust for High-Technology Industries: Assessing Research Joint Ventures and Mergers." *Journal of Law and Economics* 28 (1985): 311-33.

Parker, Elbert C. "Foreign Transfer of Technology: A Case Study of the GE/ SNECMA 10-Ton Engine Venture." Professional Study #5378. Montgomery, Alabama: Air War College, 1974.

"Parley Defines British Role in Airbus." *Aviation Week and Space Technology,* October 30, 1978, 16.

Peck, Merton J., and Akira Goto. "Technology and Economic Growth: The Case of Japan." *Research Policy* 10 (1981): 222-43.

Penrose, Edith. *The Theory of the Growth of the Firm.* Oxford: Blackwell, 1959.

Phillips, Almarin W. *Technology and Market Structure.* Lexington, Mass.: D.C. Heath, 1971.

Pierce, John P.L. "The Global Airplane." Paper presented at the National Aeronautic Association meeting, Washington, D.C., May 14, 1986.

Piore, Michael J., and Charles F. Sabel. *The Second Industrial Divide.* New York: Basic Books, 1984.

Piper, W. Stephen. "The Agreement on Trade in Civil Aircraft." Written statement printed in Subcommittee on International Trade, U.S. Senate Committee on Finance, *Hearings on S. 1376*, 96th Congress, 1st session, 1979.

_____ . "Unique Sectoral Agreement Establishes Free Trade Framework." *Journal of World Trade Law* 12 (1980): 221–53.

Rae, John. *Climb to Greatness.* Cambridge, Mass.: M.I.T. Press, 1968.

Rapoport, Alan. "A Macro Comparison of Civil Aviation and Civil Space R&D Projects among Major Industrial Countries during the 1970s." Paper prepared for the Division of Policy Research and Analysis, National Science Foundation, 1982.

Reddy, Judith V. "The IR&D Program of the Department of Defense." Peace Studies Program Occasional Paper #6, Ithaca, N.Y.: Cornell University, 1976.

Reed, Arthur. "Airbus takes Aim on the Future with Its New A300–600 Design." *Air Transport World.* February 1981, 27–30.

_____ . "British, Germans Ponder Their A320 Participation." *Air Transport World.* September 1981, 37–40.

_____ . "Fokker Moving Ahead with New P&W-Powered F27." *Air Transport World*, August 1983, 19–25.

_____ . "Fokker Moves Ahead on New Twinjet, Turboprop Programs." *Air Transport World*, January 1984, 47–49.

_____ . "Airbus A320 Launched with British Loan to BAe." *Air Transport World*, April 1984, 17–18.

_____ . "Airbus Talks about A320, Future Projects." *Air Transport World*, May 1984, 33–37.

Reich, Robert B. "A Faustian Bargain with the Japanese." *New York Times*, April 6, 1986, p. 2, section 3.

_____ , and Eric D. Mankin. "Joint Ventures with Japan Give Away Our Future." *Harvard Business Review* (March/April 1986).

Rich, Michael, William Stanley, John Birkler, and Michael Hess. *Multinational Coproduction of Military Aerospace Systems.* Santa Monica, Calif.: Rand Corporation, 1981.

Roland, Alex. *Model Research: The National Advisory Committee for Aeronautics, 1915–58.* Washington, D.C.: U.S. Government Printing Office, 1985.

"Rolls Confident of Major JT10D Task." *Aviation Week and Space Technology,* September 6, 1976, 109.

"Rolls-Royce Leaves JT10D Turbofan Development Program." *Aviation Week and Space Technology*, May 16, 1977, 17.

Ropelewski, Robert. "Mercure 200 Pact Sparks Uproar." *Aviation Week and Space Technology*, August 23, 1976, 12–13.

_____. "Europe Debates New Transport Designs." *Aviation Week and Space Technology*, November 7, 1977, 222–28.

_____. "Airbus to Develop Two A310 Versions." *Aviation Week and Space Technology*, September 4, 1978, 109–16.

Rosenberg, Nathan, Alexander Thompson, and Steven Belsley. *Technological Change and Productivity Growth in the Air Transport Industry.* NASA Technical Memorandum 78505. Springfield, Virginia: National Aeronautics and Space Administration, 1978.

Rugman, Alan M. *Inside the Multinationals: The Economics of Internal Markets.* New York: Columbia University Press, 1981.

Sarathy, Ravi. "High-Technology Exports from Newly Industrializing Countries: The Brazilian Commuter Aircraft Industry." *California Management Review* 27 (Winter 1985): 60–84.

Shifrin, Carole A. "Boeing Launches Long-Haul 747-400 with Northwest Order." *Aviation Week and Space Technology*, October 28, 1985, 33–34.

Shinohara, Miyohei. *Industrial Growth, Trade, and Dynamic Patterns in the Japanese Economy.* Tokyo: University of Tokyo Press, 1982.

"Short Brothers, Saab-Scania Join Boeing 7J7 Program." *Aviation Week and Space Technology*, March 31, 1986, 32–33.

"Small Firms Cooperate for U.S. Market." *Aviation Week and Space Technology*, September 3, 1984, 87–92.

Society of Japanese Aerospace Companies. *Aerospace Industry in Japan 1983–84.* Tokyo: SJAC, 1983.

Steiner, John E. "How Decisions are Made." AIAA Wright Brothers Lectureship in Aeronautics, Seattle, Washington, 1982.

Stobaugh, Robert B. "The Neotechnology Account of International Trade: The Case of Petrochemicals." In *The Product Life Cycle and International Trade*, edited by L.T. Wells. Boston: Harvard Business School, 1972.

Stocking, George W., and Myron Watkins. *Cartels in Action.* New York: Twentieth Century Fund, 1946.

Stuckey, John S. *Vertical Integration and Joint Ventures in the Aluminum Industry.* Cambridge: Harvard University Press, 1983.

Teece, David J. *The Multinational Corporation and the Resource Cost of International Technology Transfer.* Cambridge, Mass.: Ballinger Publishing Co., 1976.

_____. "Towards an Economic Theory of the Multiproduct Firm." *Journal of Economic Behavior and Organization* 3 (1982): 39–63.

_____. "Technology Transfer and R&D Activities of Multinational Firms: Some Theory and Evidence." In *Research in International Business and Finance,* vol. 2, edited by R.G. Hawkins and A.J. Prasad. Greenwich, Conn.: JAI Press, 1981.

_____. "Capturing Value from Technological Innovation: Integration, Strategic Partnering, and Licensing Decisions." Paper presented at the International Conference on Diffusion of Innovations, Venice, Italy, March 1986.

Teplensky, Jill D. "Technical Exchanges Between the U.S. and Japan in the Pharmaceuticals Industry." Working paper, Graduate School of Industrial Administration, Carnegie-Mellon University, 1985.

Terleckyj, Nestor. "The Time Pattern of the Effects of Industrial R&D on Productivity Growth." Paper presented at the Conference on Interindustry Differences in Productivity Growth, American Enterprise Institute, Washington, D.C., October 11–12, 1984.

U.S. Civil Aeronautics Board. *Aircraft Operating Cost and Performance Report*, vols. I–XVII. Washington, D.C.: U.S. Government Printing Office, 1966–1984.

U.S. Congress, House Committee on Ways and Means. Subcommittee on Trade. *United States-Japan Trade Report.* 96th Congress, 2d session, 1980.

U.S. Congress, Senate Committee on Aeronautical and Space Sciences. *Policy Planning for Aeronautical Research and Development: Staff Report.* Washington, D.C.: U.S. Government Printing Office, 1966.

U.S. Department of Commerce, Panel on Invention and Innovation. *Technological Innovation: Its Environment and Management.* Washington, D.C.: U.S. Government Printing Office, 1967.

U.S. Department of Commerce, Bureau of Industrial Economics. *1982 U.S. Industrial Outlook.* Washington, D.C.: U.S. Government Printing Office, 1982.

U.S. Department of Commerce, Bureau of Industrial Economics. *1983 U.S. Industrial Outlook.* Washington, D.C.: U.S. Government Printing Office, 1983.

U.S. Department of Commerce, Bureau of International Commerce. *Japan: The Government-Business Relationship.* Washington, D.C.: U.S. Government Printing Office, 1972.

U.S. Department of Commerce, International Trade Administration. *An Assessment of U.S. Competitiveness in High Technology Industries.* Washington, D.C.: U.S. Government Printing Office, 1983.

U.S. Department of Commerce, International Trade Administration. *A Competitive Assessment of the U.S. Civil Aircraft Industry.* Washington, D.C.: U.S. Government Printing Office, 1984.

"U.S.-European Trade Talks Focus on Subsidy Issues." *Aviation Week and Space Technology*, March 31, 1986, 36.

U.S. General Accounting Office. *Lower Airline Costs Per Passenger Are Possible and Could Result in Lower Fares.* Washington, D.C.: U.S. Government Printing Office, 1977.

U.S. General Accounting Office. *U.S. Military Co-production Agreements Assist Japan in Developing Its Civil Aircraft Industry.* Washington, D.C.: U.S. Government Printing Office, 1982.

U.S. General Accounting Office. *Trade Offsets in Foreign Military Sales.* Washington, D.C.: U.S. Government Printing Office, 1984.

U.S. International Trade Commission. *Certain Commuter Aircraft from Brazil*. Publication #1291, Washington, D.C.: U.S. International Trade Commission, 1982.

"U.S. Military Continues Push for NATO Armaments Cooperation." *Aviation Week and Space Technology*, June 3, 1985, 240–43.

U.S. Office of Management and Budget. *Impact of Offsets in Defense-Related Exports*. Washington, D.C.: Office of Management and Budget, 1985.

U.S. Senate Committee on Aeronautical and Space Sciences. *Policy Planning for Aeronautical Research and Development: A Staff Report*. Washington, D.C.: U.S. Government Printing Office, 1966.

Vernon, Raymond S. *Sovereignty at Bay*. New York: Basic Books, 1971.

_____ . "International Investment and International Trade in the Product Cycle." *Quarterly Journal of Economics* 80 (1966): 190–207.

_____ . "The Product Cycle Hypothesis in a New International Environment." *Oxford Bulletin of Economics and Statistics* 41 (1979): 255–67.

_____ . "Coping with Technological Change: U.S. Problems and Prospects." Paper presented at the National Academy of Engineering Symposium on World Technologies and National Sovereignty, Washington, D.C., February 1986.

"Veto Issue Stalls A310 Talks." *Aviation Week and Space Technology*, October 9, 1978, 26.

Von Hippel, Eric. "The Dominant Role of Users in the Scientific Instrument Innovation Process." *Research Policy* 5 (1976): 212–39.

_____ . "Transferring Process Equipment Innovations from User-Innovators to Equipment Manufacturing Firms." *Research Management* 8 (1977): 13–22.

Wilkins, Mira. *The Emergence of Multinational Enterprise: American Business Abroad from the Colonial Era to 1914*. Cambridge, Mass.: Harvard University Press, 1970.

_____ . *The Maturing of Multinational Enterprise: American Business Abroad from 1914 to 1970*. Cambridge, Mass.: Harvard University Press, 1974.

Williamson, Oliver E. *Markets and Hierarchies*. New York: Free Press, 1975.

Yoder, Stephen Kreider. "Japan is Abandoning Its Dream of Developing Airplanes Alone." *Wall Street Journal*, February 7, 1986, 34.

Yoshino, Michael. "Global Competition in a Salient High-Technology Industry: The Case of Commercial Aircraft." Paper presented at the Harvard Business School 75th Anniversary Colloquium, 1984.

INDEX

A300 (Airbus), 59 n. 9, 63 n. 41, 129,
132, 146 n. 26, 147 n. 37; development costs, 135; engine, 81; marketing, 105 n. 55; sales, 76, 135; U.S.
components, 51; wing design, 69
A300B (Airbus), 131, 132, 136–137
A-300B4 (Airbus), 139–140
A300-B10 (Airbus), 69–70; see also
A310
A300-600 (Airbus), 59 n. 11, 133,
134, 135; engine, 36, 134, 137,
147 n. 31, 164
A310 (Airbus), 59 ns. 9 and 10,
63 n. 41, 97–98, 101 n. 15, 133,
134, 136, 146 n. 26, 147 n. 37;
design, 137; engine, 8, 123, 134,
147 n. 31, 148 n. 38, 164; sales,
135, 137
A320 (Airbus), 59 n. 11, 73, 97–98,
134, 146 n. 28; design, 137; engine,
82, 83, 90, 92; sales, 135
A330 (Airbus), 134
A340 (Airbus), 134
Aeritalia, 97; and Boeing 767, 68,
98–99 n. 2, 100–101 n. 14; and
McDonnell-Douglas, 102 n. 31
Aermacchi, 116, 117, 120
Aerospatiale, 32; and Airbus, 129,
130, 132–133, 136; and Boeing,
69–70, 92; and Concorde, 137–138;

see also McDonnell Douglas
Dassault-Brequet-Aerospatiale
Agreement on Trade in Civil Aircraft,
17, 51–52, 158, 163
Airbus Industrie, 3, 59 n. 11, 60 n. 13,
128–129, 150; and Aerospatiale,
129, 130, 132–133, 136; and Boeing, 69–70, 92; and British Aerospace, 129–130, 131, 134, 146
n. 26; design, 131–132, 139–140;
and France, 128–133, 136, 137,
139, 148 n. 37, 169 n. 9; and
government support, 108, 128–139;
management, 152, 153; marketing,
105 n. 55, 137; political strength,
100–101 n. 15; product support,
33–34, 155; production rate, 147
n. 35, 155; and Rolls Royce, 129–
131, 134, 136–137; sales, 135, 137;
and SNECMA, 129, 130; and specialization, 155; subsidies, 147
ns. 33 and 34, 164; technology
transfer, 137–138, 152–157; and
United Kingdom, 128–131, 133,
134, 135, 136–137, 139, 141 ns.
26–29; U.S. components, 63 n. 41,
129, 164–165; and West Germany,
28 n. 32, 128–129, 130, 135–136,
137, 139, 146 n. 28; see also under
A300 through A340 aircraft

185

Airframes, 39–40; and engine type, 37–38, 73; number of manufacturers, 1, 39
Albrecht, Thomas, 101 n. 21
Alchian, Armen, 12
Allied, 36
Allison, 23 n. 1
Aluminum lithium alloys, 33
AMX fighter, 116, 117
Antitrust policy, 17–18, 21, 44, 94, 159–161
Apollo space program, 49
Arrow, Kenneth, 8, 12, 25–26 n. 20
Atomic Energy Commission, 40, 42
Automobile industry, 5, 162–163, 164
Aviation Week and Space Technology, 65–66 n. 55
Avionics, 32

B-1 bomber, 80
BAC 111, 59 n. 8
BAe. *See* British Aerospace
Bandeirante (Embraer), 115, 116, 117, 118, 120; marketing, 145; U.S. components, 51
Becker, Gary, 27–28 n. 26
Beech Aircraft, 87, 144 n. 13
Belgium, 65 n. 51, 65–66 n. 55
Benn, Anthony Wedgewood, 148 n. 20
Beteille, Roger H., 147 n. 36
Black box assembly of components, 53, 81, 82
Bluestone, Barry, 37
Boeing, 21, 23 n. 1; bonding techniques, 88; and British Aerospace, 69, 99 n. 7, 100 n. 13, 134; and De Havilland, 59–60 n. 11; development costs, 44–45, 75; employment, 122, 164–165; financial difficulties, 39–40; and France, 99–100 n. 8, 102 n. 32; and General Electric, 72–73; and Japan Commercial Aircraft, 11–12, 67–74, 98–99 n. 2, 100 n. 10, 153; management, 152; market dominance, 39; and Pratt & Whitney, 36; production volume, 35, 39, 135, 147 n. 35; and Rolls Royce, 129–130; and Saab-Scania, 73, 125, 146 n. 24; *see also individual aircraft under immediately following entries*

Boeing 7J7, 2, 11–12, 68, 72–74, 84, 101 n. 17, 112, 113, 151; and Saab-Scania, 73, 125, 146 n. 24
Boeing 707: development costs, 44–45, 48; development time, 59 n. 8; production volume, 35, 39, 135; and Saab-Scania, 125, 126
Boeing 727, 32, 33, 35, 39
Boeing 737, 68, 105 n. 55; and Japan, 110; production volume, 35
Boeing 737-300, 36, 81–82, 92
Boeing 747, 105 n. 55; development costs, 34; 39–40; engine, 36, 38, 60 n. 18, 82, 136–137; and Japan, 110; profit, 38; subcontracting, 35, 68
Boeing 757, 68–70, 92, 97–98, 134, 146 n. 26; costs, 100 n. 9; engine, 36, 90–91, 104 n. 49, 137; export financing, 164
Boeing 767, 2, 11–12, 67–74, 97–98, 154; costs, 100 n. 9; design, 32; development costs, 34; engine, 36, 123; and Japan, 110, 112, 113, 141; subcontracting, 35; technology transfer, 70–71, 73
Boeing 777, 99 n. 4
Bouilliouhn, E.H., 99 n. 2
Brasilia commuter aircraft (Embraer), 115, 116, 119
Brazil, 51, 114–120, 139, 140; domestic market, 114, 118–119; engines, 119–120; exports, 119; industrial development, 115–116; and Italy, 116; offsets, 117; and Piper Aircraft, 19, 116, 117–118, 120; technology transfer, 114–115, 116–118; *see also* Embraer
Breguet, 23; *see also* McDonnell Douglas Dassault-Breguet-Aerospatiale
Bristol, 23 n. 1
British Aerospace (BAe), 28 n. 32, 32, 60 n. 13, 86, 146; and Airbus, 129–130, 131, 134, 146 n. 26; and Boeing, 69, 99 n. 7, 100 n. 13, 134; and Saab-Scania, 86, 127
British Aircraft Corporation, 59 n. 8, 86, 131; and Concorde, 137–138; *see also* BAC 111
British Airways, 146 n. 26
Brodley, Joseph, 12, 27 n. 24

Brown, Postmaster General, 62 n. 29
Bush, Vannevar, 61 n. 23
Bypass ratio, 60 n. 17

C-5A, 39, 44, 49, 80
California interstate carriers, 46
Cantwell, John A., 28 n. 29
Capital infusions, 156
CASA, 86, 131
Catch-up government policies,
    107–108, 113–114, 115–120, 139;
    and joint ventures, 140, 155–156
Cavaille, Marcel, 99–100 n. 8
Caves, Richard E., 9–10, 24–25 n. 15,
    26 n. 20, 26–27 n. 23
Celma, 120
Centers of generic technology, 61
    n. 23
Centro Technico Aerospecial (CTA),
    115
Cessna, 87
CF6 turbofan engine, 49, 136–137
CF6-50 engine, 81, 130
CF6-80 engine, 37, 38, 81, 123–124,
    160, 164
CFM International, 37, 80–85, 92–93,
    96, 150; capital infusions, 156; and
    France, 102–103 n. 34, 165–166;
    management, 152, 154; procure-
    ment, 148 n. 42, and specialization,
    155; see also CFM56 engine
CFM56 engine 12, 37, 76, 77, 80–85,
    91, 93, 94, 130; and French govern-
    ment support, 102–103 n. 35, 133;
    management, 82–83, 153; and
    Mercure 100, 101 n. 26; and tech-
    nology transfer, 94, 102 n. 34,
    165–166
CFM56-3 engine, 92
CFM56-5 engine, 105 n. 53
Chemical industry, 23 n. 7, 161
Chinook helicopters, 142 n. 3
Civil Aeronautics Board, 45–47, 57
COGENT, 61 n. 23
Commerce Department Panel on
    Invention and Innovation, 25 n. 17
"Commonline" negotiations, 165
Commuter aircraft, 86, 113, 119, 140
Competitiveness and technology trans-
    fer, 149–152, 155–156, 157–167
Components trade, 51–52, 151–152;
    automobiles, 157–159; and military,

158–159; and technology transfer,
    141
Composite materials, 33, 73, 88, 117,
    150, 167–168 n. 2
Computer-aided design and manu-
    facturing, 18, 32, 100 n. 11
Concorde, 137–138, 148 n. 40
Consolidated Vultee, 39
Construcciones Aeronauticas, SA, 86
Convair, 23 n. 1, 39
Coproduction agreements, 3, 52–55,
    56, 166
Costs, 12–13; and commonality of
    parts, 100 n. 9; distribution, 25
    n. 17; maintenance, 34; manufactur-
    ing start-up, 23 n. 17; marketing,
    25 n. 17, 145 n. 18; operating, 48,
    58 n. 2; reduction, 35–36; and regu-
    lations, 46–47, 62 n. 32; research
    and development, 25 n. 17; and
    standardization of engine and air-
    frame, 59 n. 10; withdrawal, 156;
    see also Development costs
Crane, Keith, 117
Crookell, H., 9–10, 26 n. 20
Cross-licensing, 10, 44
CV-880, 39
CV-990

Dash 8 (De Havilland), 119
Dassault-Breguet, 76; see also McDon-
    nell Douglas-Dassault-Breguet-
    Aerospatiale
David, Paul, 27–28 n. 26
DC-3, 34
DC-8, 33, 34, 45, 75, 101 n. 23;
    engine, 81
DC-9/MD-80, 75, 76; engine, 36;
    and Japan, 110; production volume,
    35; stretch capacity, 78
DC-10, 39, 48, 75, 76; engine, 36;
    and Japan, 110
Defense considerations, 21, 159;
    see also Military aircraft
De Havilland, 23 n. 1, 88, 119; and
    Boeing, 59–60 n. 11
Delta, 102 n. 29
Demand, international, 15–16, 50–52
Demand uncertainty, 19, 48, 57
Demsetz, Harold, 12
Denmark, 65 n. 51
Deregulation, 19, 46–48, 86

Design process, 32–36, 120, 150; and A310, 137; and A320, 137; and Airbus, 131–132, 138–140; and Boeing 727, 32, 33; and Boeing 767, 32; costs, 25 n. 17, 32; development of capability, 140–141; feedback from customer, 22, 97–98; and market, 77–78; modification, 33

Development costs, 32–36, 42, 44–45, 75, 101 n. 27, 135, 138; growth, 48, 150, 167 n. 1; and military, 165–166

DHC-8, 88

Diamond 300, 112, 144 n. 13

Directed procurement, 17, 21, 51, 160, 162

Domestic markets: Brazil, 114, 118–119; Japan, 110–111, 112, 118; government support, 108, 129

Dorfer, Ingemar, 145 n. 19

Douglas Aircraft Corp., 23 n. 1, 39, 74–75; development costs, 45; losses, 101 n. 22; see also DC-3; DC-8; DC-9; DC-10; and McDonnell Douglas

Draken fighter, 122, 146 n. 23

Dunning, John, 4, 23 n. 6, 28 n. 29

Eastern Airlines, 133

Egyptian Air Force, 116

Electra (Lockheed), 34

Electronics, 4, 5, 32, 134

Embodied research intensity, 58 n. 4

Embraer, 3, 88, 115–120, 141; licensing agreements, 144–145 n. 17; marketing, 145 n. 18

Employment, 164–165, 167; and Boeing, 122, 164–165; see also Work force stability

Engineering, 77–78; costs, 25 n. 17

Engines, 73, 80–85, 90–96, 119–120, 127–128; and A300, 81; and A310, 8, 123, 134, 147 n. 31, 148 n. 38, 164; and A320, 82, 83, 90, 92; and airframes, 37–38, 73; and Boeing 747, 36, 38, 60 n. 18, 82, 136–137, 164; and Boeing 757, 36, 90–91, 104 n. 49, 137; and Boeing 767, 36, 123; and Brazil, 119–120; and C-5A, 44, 49, 80; and DC-8, 81; and DC-9, 36; and DC-10, 36; exports, 51; industry structure, 36–39; and

KC-135, 81, 132; manufacturers, 1; market structure, 36–37; and military, 80; scale economies, 38; spare parts, 38, 66 n. 56, 84; see also General Electric; Pratt & Whitney; Rolls Royce

Entry barriers, 34, 56

ESPRIT, 135

EUREKA, 135

"Europlane," 86

Exports and aircraft industry, 31, 36, 51, 158–159

Export finance agencies, 164

F-5 fighter, 117, 142 n. 3

F-15 fighter and Japan, 64 ns. 46 and 48, 109, 142 ns. 3 and 4

F-16 fighter, 54, 65 n. 51, 65–66 n. 55

F-27 (Fokker), 77

F-28 (Fokker), 77

F-86 fighter, 109

F-100 (Fokker), 102 n. 30

F101 engine, 80, 81

F-404 fighter, 84, 124

Fairchild. See Saab-Fairchild, 340

Fairchild Industries, 88–89

Fairchild-Republic Aviation, 87

Fanblade fabrication, 93

Federal Aviation Administration, 40, 42, 119

Feedback of information from customers, 9, 22, 56, 97–98

Fiat Aviazone, 90–94, 96, 97, 127

Fighter aircraft, 53, 74, 84; see also F-5 through F-404 fighters

Fixed costs, 35, 38

FJR710 engine, 91–92

Fokker, 131; see also McDonnell Douglas-Fokker

Fokker/VFW 614, 102 n. 33

Foreign investment, 3, 13–14; advantages, 6–7; automobiles, 162–163; risks and costs, 10–11; United States, 14–15

France, 23 n. 1; and Airbus, 128–133, 136, 137, 139, 148 n. 37, 169 n. 9; and Boeing, 99–100 n. 8, 102 n. 32; and CFM, 102–103 n. 34, 165–166; development time, 59 n. 8; funding, 83, 102–103 n. 35; see also Mercure 200

Fuji Heavy Industries, 68, 110

Garret Corporation, 124
General Accounting Office, 46
General Agreement on Trade and
Tariffs (GATT), 17, 51, 162
General Dynamics, 23 n. 1, 39, 65
n. 51, 65–66 n. 55
General Electric, 21, 23 n. 1, 36–37,
127, 153; and Airbus, 130; and
Boeing, 72–73; market share, 37;
military engines, 36; and Rolls
Royce, 37, 88, 92, 93, 160; and
Volvo, 123–124
General Electric-SNECMA, 2, 37,
75–76, 80–85; technology transfer,
102 n. 34, 151
General Motors. *See* Allison
General Motors-Toyota Agreement, 17
Gilliot, Antoine, 117
Governments, 107–141; divestiture
of publicly owned companies, 28
n. 32; and domestic markets, 35–36,
108, 129; funding, 93–94, 107,
126; influence for innovation,
45–47; and multinationals, 28–29
n. 33; offset demands, 16–17, 107,
150, 160; procurement policies, 17,
21, 51, 160, 162; research and development, 40–42, 43–44, 62 n. 28,
107, 163–164; subsidies, 51, 63
n. 43, 147 ns. 33 and 34; 162–163,
164
Gripen fighter (Sweden), 122, 124,
125, 127, 145–146 n. 23

Harrigan, Kathryn, 4
Harvard Multinational Enterprise
Project, 3–4
Hawker Siddeley, 69, 131
Hayward, Keith, 99 n. 7, 103 n. 36
Higginbottom, Samuel L., 104 n. 52
High-bypass engine, 36, 42, 44, 90–92,
160
Hirch, Seev, 5
Hladik, Karen, 3 4–5, 23 n. 7
Hochmuth, Milton S., 35
Honduran air force, 116
Hymer, Steven, 6–7, 24 n. 12

Import substitution policies, 140
India, 144–145 n. 17
Indian Airways, 105 n. 55

Industrial Modernization Incentive
Program (IMP), 168 n. 4
Information transfer costs, 18
International Aero Engines (IAE), 37,
90–96, 97, 141, 148 n. 42, 168 n. 7;
see also V2500 engine
International Trade Administration,
58, 145 n. 18
Ishikawajima-Harima Heavy Industries,
65 n. 49, 68, 90, 111, 142 n. 3
Italy, 28 n. 32, 70, 116; *see also*
Aerospatiale; Fiat Aviazone

Jaguar fighter, 54
Japan, 108–114, 167–168 n. 2; airlines, 28 n. 32; and Boeing, 70–74,
99 n. 5, 100 ns. 10 and 14, 109,
110, 112, 113, 150, 151, 153;
competitiveness with United States,
2, 109, 141 n. 1; costs, 142 n. 4;
electronics, 47; engine, 90–96,
104 n. 46, 109, 142 n. 3; domestic
market, 110–111, 112, 118; and
F-15 fighter, 64 ns. 46 and 48, 109,
142 ns. 3 and 4; government funding, 70, 72, 93–94, 110, 111–114;
history of aircraft industry, 109–
110; independent development
capacity, 105 n. 54; industrial policy,
63 n. 34, 68, 109, 112, 114, 143–
144 n. 11, 144 n. 15; licensing,
112; marketing, 110; military
coproduction, 55, 56, 64–65
ns. 45–49; MITI, 56–57, 68, 72, 94,
99 n. 3, 143–144 ns. 10 and 11;
product support, 110; research and
development, 111; technology transfer, 70–71, 73, 78, 141; and V2500
engine, 73, 90, 109, 110, 112, 113,
160–161
Japan Aero Engine Corporation
(JAEC), 3, 73, 90, 96, 110; and
Rolls Royce, 91–92, 93, 160–161
Japan Aircraft Development Corporation (JADC), 72, 73, 101 n. 17, 110,
151
Japan Commercial Aircraft Corporation, 3, 71, 72, 110; and Boeing,
11–12, 62–74, 98–99 n. 2, 110
n. 10, 153
Japan Commercial Transport Development Corporation (JCTDC), 70, 110

Japan Defense Agency, 113
Japan Electronic Computer Corpora-
    tion, 143 n. 9
Japan National Aeronautics
    Laboratory
Joint ventures, defined, 3–6
Jones, Kent, 28 n. 31
Jordan, William A., 46
JT8 engine, 36
JT8D engine, 37, 77, 124, 145 n. 22
JT9 engine, 36
JT9D engine, 37, 38, 60 n. 18, 82, 130
JT10D, 76, 90–91, 94, 98, 156;
    technology transfer, 102 n. 34, 165

Kawasaki Heavy Industries, 68, 90,
    99 n. 3, 110, 111, 142 n. 3
KC-10, 48
KC-135, 44–45, 48, 133
Keeler, Theodore E., 46
Keen, J.M.S., 104 n. 49, 105 n. 54
Keep-up government policies, 107–
    108, 121–128, 129, 139, 155
Keith, Kenneth, 103 n. 26
Killing, J.P., 9–10, 26 n. 20
Kindleberger, Charles P., 28–29 n. 33
Korean War, 109
Krugman, Paul R., 36, 47

L-1011, 39, 75; engine, 36, 40, 131,
    136–137
Lathiere, Bernard, 105 n. 55
Learning effects, 20, 35–36, 38, 60
    n. 16
Libya embargo, 63 n. 41
Licensing of international aircraft,
    19–20
Licensing of technology, 7–10, 11–12,
    56, 61–62 n. 26; and Embraer,
    144–145 n. 17; inefficiencies, 26–27
    n. 23; and Japan, 64–65 n. 23;
    markets for, 7; and military aircraft,
    3, 53–55; and patents, 8, 9, 44;
    see also Technology transfer
Lifespan of aircraft design, 33
Local content legislation, 158,
    164–165
Lockheed, 23 n. 1, 36, 39, 57, 88

M45H engine, 102 n. 33
McCulloch, Rachel, 35

McDonnell Douglas, 21, 39, 74–79,
    92; and China, 19, 102 n. 31; man-
    agement, 152, 153; and Saab-Scania,
    102 n. 31, 125, 126, 146 n. 24;
    see also McDonnell Douglas
    Dassault-Breguet-Aerospatiale
McDonnell Douglas Dassault-Breguet-
    Aerospatiale, 2–3, 74, 75–77, 79
McDonnell Douglas-Fokker, 2, 74,
    77–79, 80
Maintenance costs, 34
Management of joint ventures, 13,
    21–23, 137–138, 152–157; and
    Airbus, 152, 153; and CFM56
    engine, 82–83; equality of strengths,
    153–154; and MDF100, 78–79; and
    military coproduction, 54; and Saab-
    Fairchild, 87, 89–90, 137, 152; and
    technology transfer, 155; and V2500
    engine, 91, 95, 97
Mansfield, Edwin, 9, 26 n. 22
Manufacturers' Aircraft Association,
    61–62 n. 26
Manufacturing start-up costs, 25 n. 17
Manufacturing Technology (Man
    Tech) project, 168 n. 4
Market Access, 16, 17, 69, 71–72,
    100–101 n. 5, 153; and local con-
    tent, 158, 164–165
Marketing, 20, 86, 103 n. 42, 150;
    and A300, 105 n. 55; and Airbus,
    105 n. 55, 137; and Bandeirante,
    145; costs, 25 n. 17, 145 n. 18;
    and Embraer, 145 n. 18; as entry
    barrier, 34; and Japan, 110; scale
    economies, 18
Marriage, economics of, 27–28 n. 26
Martin, 39
Materials development, 32, 33, 117;
    see also Composite materials
Mature technologies, 9, 10
MBB, 86
MD-11, 39
MD-80, 39, 86, 102 n. 31
MD-82, 102 n. 31
MD-89, 90, 92
MDF-100, 74, 77–79, 83, 98, 102
    n. 30, 154, 156; engine, 101–102
    n. 28; and technology transfer, 78,
    79
Mercure 100, 76 101 n. 26

Mercure 200, 2–3, 74, 75–77, 79, 83, 133; development costs, 101 n. 27; management, 153
Mergers, 12–13
Messerschmitt-Boelkow-Blohm, 86
Metro, 87
Microelectronics and Computer Technology Corporation, 4
Military aircraft, 40, 129, 151–152; coproduction agreements, 52–55, 56, 166; divergence of technology for civilian aircraft, 48–50, 61 n. 22; and Japan, 55, 56, 64–65 ns. 45–49; jet engine development, 36; licensing, 3, 53–55; market, 154–155; research and development, 31–32, 40–42, 43, 44–45, 48–50, 61 n. 22, 158–159; and Sweden, 121–122, 125, 145 n. 20
Mitsubishi Heavy Industries, 68, 90, 99 n. 3, 109, 111, 112, 144 n. 13
Motivation for joint ventures, 14–18
Moxon, Richard W., 117, 145 n. 18
MTU, 90–95, 96, 97, 123, 127
MU-2, 112
Mutual Defense Assistance Agreement, 109
Multinational corporations, 18, 28 n. 29

National Academy of Engineering, 48–49
National Academy of Sciences, 158, 168 n. 4
National Advisory Committee on Aeronautics (NACA), 40, 42, 43–44, 45, 49
National Aeronautics and Space Administration (NASA), 40–42, 43–44, 45, 47–48, 49–50, 57, 63 n. 38, 135, 158–159, 163–164
National Cooperative Research Act, 18
National Science Board, 24 n. 8
National Security Council, 85
National Steel, 17
Netherlands, 65 n. 51, 65–66 n. 55, 169 n. 9; and Airbus, 131; airlines, 28 n. 32
Nippon Aircraft Manufacturing Company (NAMC), 110, 111
Nippon Kokan Steel, 17

Nixon, Richard M., 81
Northrup, 117, 120
Northwest Orient Airlines, 59 n. 10
Norway, 65 n. 51
Nuclear propulsion, 42

Office of Science and Technology, 58 n. 4
Offsets, 16–17, 107, 150, 160; and Brazil, 117; and military coproduction, 54, 55, 65 n. 51, 160, 168 n. 6
Offshore procurement of components, 52
Okimoto, Daniel I., 144 n. 11
Operating costs, 48, 58 n. 2
Ordover, James A., 168–169 n. 9
Organization for Economic Cooperation and Development, 63 n. 43, 165

P-3C patrol aircraft, 142 n. 3
Paper industry, 23 n. 7
Partner choice, 154
Patent protection, 8, 9, 44
People's Republic of China, 19, 102 n. 3
Petrochemical industry, 26 n. 22
Pickerell, David, 3, 102 n. 34
Piper Aircraft, 19, 87, 116, 117–118, 120
Pompidou, Georges, 81
Pratt & Whitney, 23 n. 1, 36–37, 80, 127; and Airbus, 130; market share, 37; and Rolls Royce, 37, 76, 90–96, 98, 160–161, 168–169 n. 7; and SNECMA, 80–81; specialization, 155; and technology transfer, 102 n. 34, 104 n. 52
Pricing, 35
Product cycles, 10, 14–15, 26 n. 22
Product support, 9, 33–34, 86, 87, 119, 150; and Airbus, 33–34, 133; and design feedback, 56; and engines, 38, 93, 94; and management, 22, 97, 103 n. 42; and Sweden, 145–146 n. 23
Production volume, 35, 56, 154–155; and Airbus, 147 n. 35, 155; and Boeing, 35, 39, 71, 135; and DC-9, 35; and engines, 38
Productivity, 31
Public policy issues, 20–21, 157–167

PW2037 engine, 37, 91, 92, 93, 160
PW4000 engine, 37, 38, 92, 160;
    equity, 104 ns. 47–48

Rand Corporation, 159
Rae, John, 34
RB207 engine, 130, 131, 146 n. 27
RB211 engine, 38, 131
RB211-524 engine, 134, 136, 137
RB211-535 engine, 37, 91, 93, 104
    n. 49, 136, 160, 164
Reagan administration, 65 n. 50
Regulatory policies, 45–46; costs,
    46–47, 62 n. 32; see also
    Deregulation
Reich, Robert B., 73, 101 n. 20
Research and development, 31–36, 56,
    140–141, 150, 163–164; costs, 25
    n. 17; electronics, 4, 32; expendi-
    tures, 40–43, 166, 169 n. 9; and
    GNP ratio, 28 n. 31; government
    support, 40–42, 43–44, 62 n. 28,
    107, 163–164; and Japan, 111; joint
    ventures, 4, 14; and military, 31–32,
    40–42, 43, 44–45, 48–50, 61 n. 22,
    158–159; and Sweden, 126
Reverse engineering, 8
Risks, 11, 12, 19, 48, 49, 57; and
    subcontracting, 35, 99 n. 2, 157–158
RJ500 engine, 91, 92, 95, 104 n. 46,
    142 n. 7, 161, 168 n. 7
RM8 engine, 145 n. 22
RM12 engine, 124, 127
Robotics, 5, 9
Rolls Royce, 23 n. 1, 37, 83–84, 103
    n. 36; and Airbus, 129–131, 134,
    136–137; bankruptcy, 36, 39, 40;
    and Boeing, 129–130; and General
    Electric, 37, 88, 92, 160; and Pratt
    & Whitney, 37, 76, 90–96, 98,
    160–161, 168–169 n. 7; specializa-
    tion, 155; and Sweden, 123; and
    technology transfer, 104 n. 52;
    testing facilities, 142 n. 7

Saab-Fairchild 340, 3, 85–90, 119,
    125, 126–127, 154; management,
    87, 89–90, 137, 152
Saab-Scania Aircraft, 3, 89, 121–123,
    124–128, 140; automobiles, 145
    n. 21; and Boeing 7J7, 73, 125,

146 n. 24; and McDonnell Douglas,
    102 n. 31, 125, 126, 146 n. 24;
    specialization, 155; see also Saab-
    Fairchild 340
Sales in Aircraft industry, 31, 76,
    135, 137
Saunders Roe, 23 n. 1
Scale economies, 27 n. 24, 56; and
    engines, 38; and marketing, 18;
    and military coproduction agree-
    ments, 54
Second-tier suppliers, 21, 51, 141,
    157; see also Components trade
Semiconductor Research Corporation,
    4
Shin Meiwa Industries, 110
Shinohara, Myohei, 143 n. 9
Short Brothers, 73, 116
Showa Aircraft, 110
Siddeley, 23 n. 1
Skilled labor and capital ratio, 28
    n. 31
SNECMA, 123, 127, 155, 156; and
    Airbus, 129, 130; see also General
    Electric-SNECMA
Societe Nationale d'Etude et de Con-
    struction de Moteurs d'Aviation.
    See SNECMA
South Korea, 111–112
Spain, 86, 131
Spare parts, 40; and engines, 38, 66
    n. 56, 84; international market,
    51–52; inventories, 34
Specialization, 22, 138–139, 140, 155
Standards, 10
Steel industry, 5, 11
Steiner, John, 32
Stevenson-Wydler Act, 61 n. 23
Stone, clay and glass industry, 23 n. 7
Strategic Defense Initiative, 166
Stretching of airframe, 33, 59 n. 9, 78
Subcontracting, 34–35, 151; and
    Boeing, 68–70, 98–99 ns. 1 and 2;
    and Japan, 110; and risk sharing,
    35, 99 n. 2, 157–158
Sud-Est Aviation, 23 n. 1
Supersonic transport (SST), 39, 40,
    150–151
Svenska Aeroplan Aktiebolaget.
    See Saab-Scania
Swarttouw, Frans, 102 n. 28

Swearingen Aircraft, 87
Sweden, 85–86, 121–128, 139;
    employment, 122–123; engines, 121;
    government funding, 126; industry
    development, 121–125; military
    aircraft, 121–122, 125, 145 n. 20;
    product support, 145–146 n. 23;
    research and development, 126;
    see also Saab-Scania
Swedish Aeronautical Research Insti-
    tute, 126
Swedish Industry Fund, 87
Swedish Royal Institute of Technol-
    ogy, 126

T-33 trainer, 109
Taiwan, 111
Technological spillover: and Airbus,
    138; and military aircraft develop-
    ment, 19, 48–50, 61 n. 22, 81
Technology Modernization (Tech
    Mod) program, 158
Technology transfer, 1 5–6, 96–97,
    141; and Airbus, 136; and Boeing
    767, 70–71, 73; and Brazil, 114–
    115, 116–118, 120; CFM, 94, 102
    n. 34, 165–166; and competitive-
    ness, 149–152, 155–156, 157–167;
    embodied, 120; and entry to com-
    mercial aircraft market, 107, 108,
    151–152, 155–156; government
    control, 84–85, 157, 165–166; and
    Japan, 70–71, 73, 78, 141; and
    licensing, 7–10, 20; and manage-
    ment, 22, 155; and Pratt & Whitney,
    102 n. 34, 104 n. 52; as public good,
    25–26 n. 20; and public policy
    issues, 20–21, 157–167; and speciali-
    zation, 138–139, 155; and U.S.
    Department of Defense controls,
    80, 82, 84, 102 n. 34, 152, 165–
    166; and V2500 engine, 82, 94–96,
    104 n. 52, 153, 165
Teece, David, 25 n. 18
Telecommunications industry, 8–9,
    134
Ten-ton engine, 81–85
TF39 engine, 49, 80
Thermal coatings, 124
Tooling requirements, 65 n. 54
Tornado fighters, 54

Toyota and General Motors, 17
Trade restrictions, 158–159, 161–165
Tucano military trainers, 115, 117

Unducted fan (UDF) engines, 73, 84,
    103 ns. 37 and 38, 150
United Airlines, 102 n. 28
United Kingdom, 23 n. 1, 169 n. 9;
    air force, 116; and Airbus, 128–
    131, 133, 134, 135, 136–137, 139,
    146 ns. 26–29, 148 ns. 37 and 38;
    and Boeing, 69; and Concorde, 137–
    138, development time, 59 n. 8;
    divestitures of public firms, 28 n. 32;
    and Japan, 104 n. 46
United Nations Center on Trans-
    national Corporations, 23 n. 6
United States: antitrust law, 17–18,
    21, 94, 159–161; commercial air-
    craft sales, 16; competitiveness,
    effects of joint ventures on, 149–
    152, 155–156, 157–167; develop-
    ment time, 59 n. 8; domestic
    demand, 50; employment in aircraft
    industry, 164–165; foreign markets,
    14–15, 16; joint venture growth,
    2, 4–5; market penetration by for-
    eign firms, 16, 17; military aid, 129;
    and offsets, 160
U.S. Department of Defense, 49;
    procurement policies, 159, 166, 168
    n. 4; research and development, 135;
    technology transfer controls, 80, 82,
    84, 91, 94, 102 n. 34, 152, 165–166
U.S. Department of Justice. *See* Anti-
    trust policy
U.S. Department of State, 85
U.S. Export-Import Bank, 164
United Technologies, 21
University-industry research, 4, 24
    n. 8, 150
User-active innovation, 9, 10

V2500 engine, 2, 37, 90–96, 104
    n. 49, 134, 155, 160–161; develop-
    ment costs, 34; development time,
    104–105 n. 53; and Japan, 73, 90,
    109, 110, 112, 113, 160–161; man-
    agement, 91, 95, 97; and technology
    transfer, 82, 94–96, 104 n. 52, 153,
    165

Vernon, Raymond, 14–15, 28–29
    n. 33
Vickers, 23 n. 1
Viggen fighter (Sweden), 122, 125,
    145 n. 22, 146 n. 23
Volvo Flygmotor, 3, 97, 121, 122–
    124, 125–128, 145 n. 22; and
    General Electric, 123–124; speciali-
    zation, 140, 155
Von Hippel, Eric, 9

Wallenberg interests, 121
Wasp engine (P&W), 44
West Germany, 169 n. 9; Airbus,
    28 n. 32, 128–129, 130, 135–136,
    137, 139, 146 n. 28

Westinghouse, 23 n. 1, 36
Wide-body passenger jets, 39–40, 42
Williamson, Oliver, 12, 25 n. 16
Willig, Robert D., 168–169 n. 7
Wing design, 59 n. 9, 88–89, 100
    n. 13, 148 n. 37; and Mercure 200,
    76–77, 101 n. 27
Withdrawal costs, 156
Work force stability, 54, 65 n. 53, 97,
    147 n. 35, 155

Xavante fighter (Brazil), 116, 117
Xingu (Brazil), 116, 119

Yoder, Stephen Kreider, 144 n. 15
YS-11 transport, 110, 112, 118

ABOUT THE AUTHOR

David C. Mowery is associate professor of economics and social sciences in the Social and Decision Sciences Department of Carnegie-Mellon University. During 1987, Dr. Mowery is serving as the study director for the Panel on Technology and Employment, sponsored by the National Academy of Sciences, the National Academy of Engineering, and the Institute of Medicine. He has published a number of papers on the economics and management of technological change, has served as a consultant to several corporations and government agencies, and has testified before Congress on science and industrial policy issues. He was a member of the National Academy of Engineering's Panel on the Competitive Status of the U.S. Civil Aviation Manufacturing Industry, which issued its report in 1985. Dr. Mowery received his Ph.D. in economics from Stanford University.